GENERAL SEMANTICS

AND CONTEMPORARY THOMISM

General Semantics
and Contemporary Thomism

MARGARET GORMAN, R.S.C.J.
Newton College of the Sacred Heart

Introduction by
S. I. Hayakawa

UNIVERSITY OF NEBRASKA PRESS · Lincoln · 1962

Originally published by The Catholic University of America Press as *The Educational Implications of the Theory of Meaning and Symbolism of General Semantics,* from which edition this Bison Book is prepared.

INTRODUCTION

To one who has just begun to make his acquaintance with the literature of general semantics, Mother Gorman's book will prove an invaluable guide. From her first chapter giving a historical sketch of the sources of the main ideas to her final chapter surveying the ways in which they have influenced education in America, the book is a mine of useful information. Mother Gorman is not a general semanticist. Her reservations about what she regards as the profound philosophical errors of general semantics naturally keep her from aligning herself with this school of thought. But she is an unusually interested bystander and a diligent scholar. Hence she has made an extremely thorough search of the literature, with the result that in many ways she knows a lot more about general semantics than many who call themselves semanticists.

Mother Gorman's book is an extremely rewarding experience, too, to the reader who is already well acquainted with general semantics, for here are presented familiar ideas in an unfamiliar context. Mother Gorman explains many of the ideas of general semantics in a vocabulary that general semanticists have either neglected to learn or have consciously rejected. Alfred Korzybski (1879-1950), Polish-American philosopher and educator who founded general semantics, used to declare that if you change its vocabulary, you destroy it. He may have been right—I am not going to argue the matter pro or con here. But the task Mother Gorman has set for herself is neither to destroy general semantics nor to espouse it. It is to explain and clarify it from the point of view of her own Catholic philosophy, and within that framework to place it and pass judgment on what in general semantics is acceptable and what is unacceptable.

Some Catholic philosophers and educators (and Mother Gorman quotes occasionally from them), realizing that *some* of general semantics is unacceptable to them as Catholics, have scornfully rejected *all* of it. Mother Gorman is not one of these. Above all things, she is fair-minded. In evaluating general semantics, she herself practices general semantics, listening carefully to all that the general semanticists have to say before drawing her own inferences and making her own conclusions. I myself profoundly believe that the purposes of discussion and debate should be neither self-expression nor victory (since victory does not convert the defeated, in any case), but self-insight and clarification. I am sure that Mother Gorman understands her own Catholic philosophy better, as well as general semantics, as a result of her labors; and I am sure she has clarified some of the central isues—perhaps *the* central issues—about which Thomists and general semanticists must necessarily differ.

Of these differences between Thomism and general semantics, two stand out as especially significant in Mother Gorman's eyes— and in mine. The first may be illustrated by the following passage from this book: "Words signify concepts which, in turn, signify 'events' or 'entities' or 'relations' in the world. This double signification and two-step removal from reality on the part of the symbols which make up language is not clearly pointed out by the general semanticist. The ladder of abstraction does not account for words as being separate from human knowledge."

Mother Gorman is right. The ladder of abstraction does not show words as being separate from human knowledge, because communicable knowledge (as distinct from "intuitions," "feelings," "hunches") is in words (and sometimes in other symbols), either spoken to others or to one's self. Her three-stage account of the relationship of words to concepts to reality is reduced by the general semanticist to two stages: words and reality, maps and territories.

Why is this so? General semanticists (or at least those who have explicitly written on this subject) reduce the three levels to two because they regard the term "concept" as one that can be dispensed with. A word is not simply a sound. If it has no meaning (or, as is often said, if it "conveys no concept"), it isn't a word. Hence the word "word" covers, in the view of general semanticists, *both* what Mother Gorman calls "word" *and* what she calls the corresponding "concept." The existence of "concepts" cannot be physically shown. All we can show is words which are said to "stand for concepts." Hence general semanticists, like descriptive linguists generally, when they are being meticulous in their language, avoid the term "concept." They do not say *dog* and *chien* "represent the same concept." They say, rather, that in contexts where some people say *dog*, other people say *chien*.

The other major difference between Thomists and general semanticists, again accurately pinpointed by Mother Gorman, centers on the doctrine of substance. The assertion that the world is always changing—that all is process—ultimately entails, Mother Gorman says, the denial of substance. In this, she is certainly correct. But her own position, which is also that of Thomistic philosophy, is that without substance the world cannot be made intelligible. An apple changes from potential apple to green apple to ripe apple to rotten apple. If it can be said that "the apple changes." there must be an essential "apple" that undergoes change. "Substance" is that essence. Substance, Mother Gorman says, is "a metaphysical reality arrived at by the intellect (not by the senses) in its penetration into reality. It is a dynamic principle of identity, activity and organization." In short, substance is that upon which identity rests; without substance, there can be no identity. Agreed, says the general semanticist; we deny *both* substance *and* identity.

So there you have it. I am not going to argue against Mother Gorman here. After all, this is *her* book, and the reader's job now is to discover why she believes that the denial of substance is an extremely serious philosophical error, ultimately likely to be corrosive of values and therefore dangerous as an educational influence. The reader will learn also from her book, however, that she believes other parts of general semantics to be of great value to education: in sensitizing students to the pitfalls and ambiguities of language; in improving critical reading and thinking by alerting students to the differences between, for example, referential and effective uses of language, between one level of abstraction and another; in encouraging students to relate words to experience; in bringing about a keener awareness of language as an instrument of cummunication.

Mother Margaret Gorman, head of the Department of Psychology at the Newton College of the Sacred Heart in Newton, Massachusetts, is a member of a teaching order, the Society of the Sacred Heart, founded in France in 1800 and represented by over thirty schools and colleges in the United States. She was born in Kingston, N.Y., in 1919, received her bachelor's degree in English at Trinity College, Washington, D.C., her master's degree in philosophy at Fordham University. The present volume, prepared originally as a doctoral dissertation in educational psychology at the Catholic University of America, was written under the guidance of Professor Robert Nordberg. Dr. Nordberg received his doctorate from the University of Denver, where he studied general semantics under the guidance of Professor Elwood Murray. Dr. Murray studied general semantics under Alfred Korzybski, and also often lectured at seminars conducted by Korzybski. The present volume reflects credit not only on the author, but also on her teacher, her teacher's teacher, and her teacher's teacher's teacher. Thus does the process of time-binding keep on rollin' along.

S. I. HAYAKAWA

San Francisco State College

PREFACE

A mere glance at periodical indices will reveal how prevalent is the concern with the problem of words, their meaning, and their effects on reader and listener. This interest has been sparked by two trends:

    a. *in philosophy,* the growth of logical positivism. Once Locke and Hume denied universals and modern philosophy was condemned to nominalism in theory, "semantics reaches deliberately for a nominalism in practice."[1]
    b. *in society,* the growth of mass communication media such as television and radio, and the corresponding growth of the dangers of propaganda and false advertising.

This increasing interest in language study, both as one of the chief means of communication and as a factor in forming man's view of his world, has inspired many books in fields such as philosophy, psychology, social psychology, education, linguistics and anthropology. Gradually, certain ideas are becoming crystallized and certain definite trends can be noted:

    1. there is a growing conviction that, while our language undoubtedly expresses our outlook upon the world about us, that outlook is itself affected, to a very great degree, by the language habits we adopt in discussing the world.[2]
    2. the conviction that "the structure of our language unfortunately has not changed in any major respect since ancient times when human knowledge of the world was pretty primitive. . . . This time lag applies to all languages except that of mathematics."[3]

---

[1] Vincent Edward Smith, *Idea Men of Today* (Milwaukee: Bruce Publishing Company, 1950), p. 134.

[2] Norman T. Newton, *An Approach to Design* (Cambridge, Mass.: Addison-Wesley Press, Inc., 1951), p. 15. See also Benjamin Lee Whorf, *Four Articles on Metalinguistics* (Washington, D. C.: Foreign Service Institute, 1949).

[3] Newton, p. 27.

3. the conviction that much of the tension, unrest and lack of mental health today is due to failures in communication which, in turn, are due to the inability of current language systems to express adequately the insights of science.

4. the efforts made to overcome this failure in communication and to prevent further failures take the form of

    a. more courses in communication in colleges and secondary schools;

    b. greater emphasis in college and high school textbooks on the meanings of words and on the necessity for distinguishing various uses of words;

    c. greater emphasis on critical thinking and on "how to" detect the errors in propaganda, biased reports, etc.

One of the more recent and controversial schools of thought concerned with these trends is the school of general semantics, founded by the late Count Alfred Korzybski in 1933. Other noted writers in the field are C. K. Ogden, I. A. Richards, and Charles Morris.[4, 5] As Max Black says:

> Ever since men began to reflect critically upon the quality of their thinking they have been conscious of the imperfections of their language. . . .
>
> Yet the results remain disappointing; and never before has so much attention been given to the criticism and reform of symbolism. The popular name for such studies in the science of meaning is semantics—a discipline to which Peirce, Mead, Karl Buhler, C. K. Ogden, I. A. Richards, Bertrand Russell, Wittgenstein and Carnap, among others, have made noteworthy contributions. None of these writers, however, has had so much popular influence as Count Alfred Korzybski.[6]

---

[4] Charles K. Ogden and Ivor Armstrong Richards, *The Meaning of Meaning* (10th ed.; New York: Harcourt, Brace and Co., 1949).

[5] Charles William Morris, *Signs, Language and Behavior* (New York: Prentice-Hall, Inc., 1946).

[6] Max Black, *Language and Philosophy; Studies in Method* (Ithaca: Cornell Univ. Press, 1949), p. 223.

The present study essays an evaluation of the educational aspects of the theories of symbolism and meaning proposed by the general semanticists in order that educators may use some of their ideas and, at the same time, be on guard against some of the dangers which would follow from an unrestricted adaptation of their principles. Since general semantics is primarily a movement based on modern scientific or "non-Aristotelian" ways of thought, much of what is evaluated here can be applied to the scientific, non-Aristotelian movement as it affects education.[8] After considerable discussion, it was decided that this study should be of a critical nature in order to provide an orientation for empirical studies which might follow. Inasmuch as the entire system of general semantics is an elaboration of a few basic premises, both metaphysical and psychological, it was felt that an adequate evaluation could be made only at the level implied by these premises.[9]

The plan of the study is as follows: Chapter I will discuss the meaning of general semantics and its relation to the various branches of the study of language and to epistemology; its origin and its historical development, as well as current criticisms of the movement both here and abroad. Chapter II will present the theories of general semantics which form the basis for its efforts

---

[7] John A. Carroll points out that it is difficult to find any "rigorous evaluation of general semantics in all its aspects. Jeannette Anderson's (1943) tirade is too charged with emotion to be taken seriously. Dunham (1947) expresses doubts as to whether a knowledge of semantic principles can really help one avoid falling into errors of thought and interpretation. Kenneth Burke (1948) and Max Black (1949) find themselves disturbed about the epistemological foundations of general semantics." See Carroll's chapter on "Education" (*A Study of Language* [Cambridge, Mass.: Harvard University Press, 1938]). See also P. Hallie's article, "Criticism of General Semantics," *College English*, XIV, 1952, p. 17: "A doctrine that is now so influential must no longer be ignored."

[8] Max Black thinks it important to note that Korzybski's theories have important consequences for a number of controversial and perplexing problems in the philosophy and methodology of science (*Language and Philosophy*, p. 225). It may be pointed out that the evils and errors evaluated are due to scientism and not to science. Scientism is an exaggerated attitude of mind which claims that science can answer all questions on all levels.

[9] *Ibid.*, p. xviii. "On Korzybski's showing the program of general semantics depends on the validity of its theoretical foundations."

to reform the language habits of men.[10] Chapter III will compare
these theories with those of Thomistic philosophy and evaluate
them. Chapter IV will present the educational implications of
general semantics on all three levels of education—primary, secondary and higher education. Finally, in Chapter V, the findings
will be summarized and suggestions will be given for the modifica-
tions of its principles in order better to profit from some of the
practical contributions made by general semantics.

The system of general semantics, as presented here, is a
synthesis of the works of Alfred Korzybski and of those who have
adopted his principles and have had the greatest influence in the
educational world, namely, Samuel I. Hayakawa, Irving J. Lee,
Anatol Rapoport and Wendell Johnson. It was deemed wise to
present this particular synthesis since general semantics is making
its impact on the education world in this form. The popularizations
by Hayakawa, Lee, and Johnson have had the largest influence;
the articles of Rapoport have represented and described general
semantics in more scholarly journals and books. While the works
of Korzybski are listed in many bibliographies and are recommended for teachers as reference reading, his ideas are being
diffused largely through the presentations of these four men and
through the articles in *Etc.,* the publication of the International
Society of General Semantics.

The discussion of the principles of general semantics will be in
the light of Thomistic principles. This, too, will be drawn from
the ideas of St. Thomas himself and of those contemporary writers

---

[10] These basic theories must, of necessity include Korzybski's ideas on the
nature of the world, of man, of man's knowledge and of the process of
symbolism, both as Korzybski presented them and as modified or expanded
and popularized by his followers. As Doob points out in his *Social Psychology* (New York: Henry Holt and Co., 1952), pp. 117-118:

"Again and again he [Korzybski] emphasizes that if language is only a
map which symbolizes the territory it represents, the nature of that territory
must be understood. For this reason, the world as it is—for Korzybski, this
means as it is known or conceptualized by modern science—must be first
apprehended. Only thereafter can the accuracy of the symbols which stand
for that world be represented. The nature of the human organism must also
be fully explored both physiologically and psychologically, since symbols
are employed by people and employed most imperfectly. Korzybski, it is
apparent, analyzes only one function of language—its use in communication."

who interpret and apply his principles to the very problems raised by the general semanticists. The chief writers consulted were: Reginald Garrigou-Lagrange, Robert Brennan, Fernand Van Steenberghen, Frederick Wilhelmsen, Joseph Pieper, and Jacques Maritain and John Oesterle, for the psychological and epistemological aspects; and for other aspects, Regis Jolivet, Vincent E. Smith and some studies on substance published at the Catholic University of America. When, therefore, reference is made in the body of this work to Thomism and the Thomists, the terms are used in this synthetic sense to represent the thought of St. Thomas in relation to contemporary problems as expressed by him and some contemporary scholars of his work. It in no sense implies that there are definitive Thomistic answers to these problems, but, rather, that these are the insights given by St. Thomas and Thomistic scholars of today. As one of these has said: "Truth cannot be exhausted by any (human) knowledge; it remains therefore always open to new formulations."[11] It is the new formulation of Truth, not any new truth, that we are seeking.

The writer takes this occasion to express her appreciation to Dr. Robert Nordberg, who directed this dissertation, for his unfailing help and encouragement. She also thanks the Right Reverend Monsignor John K. Ryan, Right Reverend Monsignor Francis J. Houlahan, Reverend Bernard T. Rattigan and Dr. James Craig LaDrière for valuable suggestions and constructive criticisms. For the courteous assistance of the staffs of the Library of Congress and of the Mullen Library at Catholic University, especially of Miss Marcella Dorsey, the writer is sincerely grateful.

The following publishers have kindly permitted the reproduction of diagrams: Harcourt, Brace and Company, the abstraction ladder, from *Language in Thought and Action* by S. I. Hayakawa; Harper and Brothers, the process of communication, from *People in Quandaries* by Wendell Johnson; the Ronald Press Company, the process of abstracting, from "The Role of Language in the Perceptual Processes" by Alfred Korzybski in *Perception—An Approach to Personality,* edited by Robert R. Blake and Glenn V. Ramsey, Copyright 1951.

---

[11] Joseph Pieper, *The Silence of St. Thomas,* trans. John Murray and Daniel O'Connor (New York: Pantheon Books, Inc., 1957), p. 103. See also pp. 84-85.

TABLE OF CONTENTS

CHAPTER 1

Background of General Semantics

DEFINITION OF TERMS AND HISTORICAL SKETCH

There are many definitions of general semantics given by its founder, by its followers, and by its critics.[1] The *Dictionary of Linguistics* says:

> General Semantics: a philosophy of language meaning first propounded by Alfred Korzybski whose work is being continued at present by Samuel I. Hayakawa.[2]

Korzybski himself used as one definition the following:

> General Semantics is not any 'philosophy' or 'psychology' or 'logic' in the ordinary sense. It is a new extensional discipline which explains and trains us how to use our nervous system most efficiently.[3]

Even this definition presupposes understanding of the term "extensional" which, in Korzybski's system, has a special meaning. This term, when defined by general semanticists, in turn involves other terms which must be defined. It, therefore, appears wise to let the special terminology of general semantics become clear as the theories are explained, rather than to list and define the terms here. It also seems advisable to clarify the term 'general semantics' by showing its historical and theoretical relation to other

---

[1] See Appendix I for some definitions of general semantics, arranged in chronological order.

[2] Mario Pei and Frank Gaynor, *A Dictionary of Linguistics* (New York: Philosophical Library, 1954), p. 81.

[3] Alfred Korzybski, *Science and Sanity*: An Introduction to Non-Aristotelian Systems and General Semantics (2nd ed., Lakeville, Conn.: Non-Aristotelian Library Publishing Co., 1950), pp. xi and xxv.

1

disciplines concerned with the study of language. We begin, then, with the history of the word "semantics," as traced by Allen Walker Read.[4]

So far as is now known, the adjective "semantick" first appeared in English in the seventeenth century in John Spencer's second edition of *A Discourse Concerning Prodigies*: wherein the Vanity of Presages by them is Reprehended and their True and Proper Ends Asserted and Vindicated. (2nd ed., London, 1665.)[5] From the context, "Semantick Philosophy" must have referred to the prediction of the future on the basis of signs, or to the study of the different kinds of divinations as they were then called. It is assumed that Spencer borrowed the word from the Greek and Latin classics.

Michael Bréal, the French linguist, was the first to establish the active usage of the word *semantics* in linguistics, applying it to the laws which govern the changes of meanings.[6] Mrs. Henry Cust used the word for the first time in English when she translated Bréal's work. From that time on, the word was used frequently in the *Athenaeum*. Although it became more generally accepted than the term *semasiology*, it kept the narrow meaning of a mere etymological science up to 1920.

Bronislaw Malinowski was among the first to widen the meaning of *semantics* when he perceived the need for a thorough study of the relation between form and meaning. He was one of the first, also, to state relationships among semantics, psychology,

---

[4] Allen Walker Read, "An Account of the Word 'Semantics,'" *Word*, IV (August 1948), pp. 78-97. Much of the matter on the next few pages is only indirectly connected with the subject of this paper. But because the term "general semantics" and the movement are so new, a brief clarification of the word "semantics" and of the other sciences of language was inserted here in order to show more clearly just what general semantics is and what it is not. The Polish logicians referred to on page 3 are discussed in Read's article.

[5] Read, *Word*, IV (August, 1948), p. 79.

[6] "Comme cette étude . . . merite d'avoir son nom, nous l'appellérons la SEMANTIQUE (du verbe σημαινω) c'est à dire, la science des significations," in *Les Lois Intellectuelles du Language;* fragment de sémantique, Annuaire de l'Association pour l'encouragement des études grecques en France, XVII, 132-142 (1883) as quoted in Read, *Word*, IV (August, 1948), p. 79.

anthropology and philosophy, and the need for more theoretical considerations underlying the science of language.[7]

Although C. K. Ogden and I. A. Richards did not use the word *semantics* themselves, but *science of symbolism,* the former word does appear in *The Meaning of Meaning* in a paraphrase on page 2.[8]

According to Bloomfield, the task of telling what meanings are attached to the several phonetic forms is called *semantics* and it is ordinarily divided into two parts, grammar and lexicon.[9] But some of the stricter linguists exclude matters of meaning from the scope of linguistics—which, they say, is "concerned with linguistic symbols themselves," although they admit that language, as differentiated from noise, involves meaning.[10]

Semantics took on a more philosophical aspect with its adoption by some of the logical positivists. The first to do so were the Polish logicians and mathematicians led by Lesniewski, Lukasiewicz, Kolarbinski, Adjukiewicz, Chwistek, and Tarski. Chwistek was the first of the group to use the word "semantics." He did so in 1922, although the philosophical world first heard of the Polish school of semantics only in 1935 at the *Congrés International de Philosophie Scientifique* in Paris. At this time, Chwistek claimed that semantics would and could avoid metaphysics, but he was severely criticized for his sweeping claims, which were later retracted.

At this congress, also, Charles Morris presented his "semeiotic," which, at that time, contained the word "existential" instead of the word "semantic."[11] In his latter publications he clarified the division of semeiotic into:

1. *semantics* or the problem of the relations between the sign vehicle or the meaning and the object or designatum.

[7] Bronislaw Malinowski, "The Problem of Meaning in Primitive Languages," in C. K. Ogden and I. A. Richards, *The Meaning of Meaning* (2nd ed., New York: Harcourt, Brace and Co., 1927), pp. 296-336.

[8] C. K. Ogden and I. A. Richards, *The Meaning of Meaning,* p. 2

[9] Leonard Bloomfield, *Language* (New York: Henry Holt and Co., 1933), p. 138.

[10] Bernard Bloch and George L. Trager, *Outline of Linguistic Analysis* (Baltimore: Linguistic Society of America, Waverly Press, 1942), p. 6.

[11] Charles Morris, *Foundation of the Theory of Signs* (Chicago: International Encyclopedia of Unified Science I, No. 2, 1938).

2. *syntactics* or the relations of signs to each other.
3. *pragmatics* or the relation between sign producers and interpreters, a science evolving from psychology, ethnology and sociology.[12]

Rudolph Carnap developed and adopted Morris's division of semeiotic and Tarski's ideas of semantic rules. A group of self-named "logical empiricists" (Otto Neurath, Niels Bohr, Bertrand Russell, John Dewey, Rudolph Carnap, and Charles Morris) started the publication of the *International Encyclopedia of Unified Sciences* in 1938. This was a series of studies based on the conviction that an adequate theory of signs would be the base for the unification of all knowledge. This would be achieved not by a relating of the knowledge of each field but by relating the language of speculative sciences to each other, and of scientific language to the languages of other areas of human activity.

Pragmatism also influenced semantics through the works of C. S. Peirce, John Dewey, and George H. Mead, especially in its idea that the meaning of a word or symbol lies exclusively in its effects on human behavior and not in any transcendental realm of ideas.[13]

According to Read, the popularization of the word "semantics" is due to the works of Alfred Korzybski,"[14] but it can be noted that the whole general trend of thought was favorable to some sort of analysis of signs and symbols. In the first draft of his major work in 1928, Korzybski did not use the words "semantics," "general semantics," or "semantic reaction." His thought was less influenced by the linguistic semantics of Bréal and popular writers on the glamor of word study, than it was by the logical positivists and the Polish School and, even more so, by the current "scientific" attack on Aristotelian thought and metaphysics. This connection will be shown in the next section of this chapter. But, as Read points out, Korzybski had kept in touch with the Polish mathematicians. He attended the Congrés des Mathé-

---

[12] Charles Morris, *Signs, Language and Behavior* (New York: Prentice-Hall, Inc., 1946).

[13] S. I. Hayakawa, "What Is Semantics?" *Etc.*, IX, 4 (Summer, 1952), pp. 221-237.

[14] Read, *Word,* IV (August, 1948), p. 88.

maticiens des Pays Slavs in Warsaw in 1927. At New Orleans
in a paper given before the American Mathematical Society in
1931, Korzybski spoke of "the restricted semantic school represented by Chwistek and his pupils and announced his own use
of the term 'general semantics' and the results of his research :
the discovery of a general semantic mechanism underlying human
behavior, many new interrelations and formulations culminating
in a non-Aristotelianism system." This occasion may well be called
the beginning of general semantics as a formal system.[15]

Korzybski himself disclaims any connection with the linguistic
aspects of semantics.

> My work was developed entirely independently of
> 'semantics,' 'significs,' 'semeiotic,' 'semasiology,' etc.,
> although I know today and respect the works of the
> corresponding investigators in those fields, who explicitly
> state they do not deal with a general theory of values.
> Those works do not touch my field, and as my work
> progressed it has become obvious that a theory of 'mean-
> ing' is impossible and "significs,' etc., are unworkable.
> Had I not become acquainted with those accomplish-
> ments shortly before publication of this book, I would
> have labelled my work by another name, but the system
> would have remained fundamentally unaltered. The
> original manuscript did not contain the word 'semantics'
> or "semantic" but when I had to select some terms, from
> a time-binding point of view and in consideration of the
> efforts of others, I introduced the term '*General* Seman-
> tics' for the *modus operandi* of this first non-aristotelian
> system. This seemed appropriate for historical continuity.
> A theory of evaluation appeared to follow naturally in
> an evolutionary sense from 1) 'meaning' to 2) 'signif-
> icance' to 3) '*evaluation.*' *General* Semantics turned out
> to be an empirical natural science of non-elementalistic
> evaluation, which takes into account the living indi-
> vidual, not divorcing him from his reactions altogether,
> nor from his neuro-linguistic and neuro-semantic environ-
> ments, but allocating him in a *plenum* of some values,
> no matter what.[16]

It may be well to distinguish general semantics further by show-

---

[15] Korzybski, *Science and Sanity* (3rd ed., 1949), p. 748.
[16] *Ibid.,* p. viii.

ing briefly the meanings of the synonyms for *semantics* and also
by giving a summary of the matter considered by each of the
sciences of language in order to show how general semantics is
distinguished from each of them.

The most important of these synonyms are:

1. *semasiology,* used in Germany by a professor of Latin at the
University of Halle, Christian Karl Reisig who died in 1829. It
was first recorded in the OED in 1877 and by 1945 was so commonly used in America that H. L. Mencken could say:

> Semantics is a new name for semasiology, the study of
> the meaning of words.[17]

Hayakawa claimed that it was originally used to mean, in philology,
the historical study of the changes in the meanings of words.[18]

2. *significs*—coined by Lady Welby in 1911 and including
semantics. It was Lady Welby who first stressed the practical
importance of significs in education. She defined significs as: "the
study of the relation between words and things, later extended
to the study of relations between language, thought, and behavior,
that is how action is influenced by words spoken to others or to
self."[19] According to Hayakawa, *The Meaning of Meaning* of
Ogden and Richards is a "brilliant continuation of the significs
of Lady Welby."[20]

3. *Semeiotic*—"the study of laws and conditions under which
signs and symbols including words may be said to be meaningful[21]
or the "science of signs."[22] It was first incorporated in the philosophical system of Charles S. Peirce, who had taken a frag-
mentary hint from Locke. In an unidentified fragment written
about 1897, but not published until 1932, Peirce said:

> Logic in its general sense is as I believe I have shown

[17] H. L. Mencken, *The American Language*: Supplement I (New York: Alfred A. Knopf, 1945), p. 102, note.

[18] S. I. Hayakawa, *Etc.,* IX, 4 (Summer, 1952), p. 223.

[19] Viola Welby, "Significs," *Encyclopedia Britannica,* 11th ed., Vol. XXV, 79, 1911.

[20] Hayakawa, *Etc.,* IX, 4 (Summer, 1952), p. 223.

[21] *Ibid.,* p. 227.

[22] Charles Morris, *Signs, Language and Behavior*.

only another name for semeiotic (σπμειωτχη) the quasi-necessary or formal doctrine of signs.[23]

Peirce influenced much of present day thinking in America by his work on signs. He defined a sign as something which represents or signifies an object to some interpretant.

4. *Semiology*—a term coined by Ferdinand de Saussure,[24] refers to an analytical study of the function of words in everyday social life, a part of social psychology. Linguistics would only be a part of this general science which he proposed to establish. His work greatly influenced linguistic thinking and directed it towards lines later taken up by Benjamin Lee Whorf and Korzybski.

The various sciences of language are:

1. *Lexicography*—the making of dictionaries.
2. *Grammar*—originally purely descriptive of current forms, now containing prescriptive codes of correct usage.
3. *Etymology*—studies the true meaning of words through the investigation of their origins.
4. *Philology*—the study of language as a means of understanding the culture of a particular society.
5. *Linguistics*—the examination of a particular language in itself. Its sounds, forms and functional patterns are the ultimate objectives of this science.
6. *Comparative Linguistics*—study of the genetic connections between various languages of presumed common origin.
7. *Semeiotic*—doctrine of signs and the three sciences of Charles Morris:

   Syntactics: study of the relation of signs to one another (linguistics).

   Semantics: study of the relation of signs to the objects they signify (philosophy-epistemology).

   Pragmatics: study the relations between signs and the users of signs.

---

[23] Charles S. Peirce, *Collected Papers of Charles Sanders Peirce* (Cambridge, Mass.: Harvard Univ. Press, 1932), 2.134 No. 227.

[24] Ferdinand de Saussure, *Cours de Linguistique Generale* (Lausanne 1916), p. 34.

Thus it is evident that there is a triadic relation between linguistics, philosophy and psychology such that psychology holds the key to some of the central problems of meaning. A theory of signs, as defined by Peirce, recognizes that a sign has no meaning unless there is an organism which has an interpretant, unless there is some psychological process by which the organism is aware of what the sign represents.[25], [26] Philosophy discusses just how the sign represents the object. In fact, the relation of language to philosophy arouses the age-old question of the individuality of things and the generality of language, and the related question of universals, which was one of the major questions of the middle ages and has been coherently or vaguely present in every period of philosophical thought. It may be well here to review very briefly some of the points in the controversy over universals in order to see how Korzybski and his followers may be grouped with the neo-nominalists.

Plato is credited with the useful distinction between generalized concepts embodied in language and the numerous specific instances to which these concepts (and words corresponding to them) apply. He, however, placed these ideas in a world more real than the specific instances which were only shadows of them.[27]

The medieval realists stated that, while universals did not exist in themselves, they are real, but only in the intellect, although they have objective correlatives in individual things.[28] The nominalists who opposed the medieval realists maintained that all general things (reason, justice, etc.), were mere verbal utterances, manmade names which were helpful in classifying phenomena, but ultimately misleading.

Locke denied the existence, in any sense, of universals; Hume said that all general ideas are nothing but particular ideas annexed

---

[25] John Carroll, *The Study of Language*, p. 136.

[26] For a concise summary of the relation of general semantics to the contemporary disciplines of linguistics, anthropology, counseling, mathematical physics and biology, and cybernetics see S. I. Hayakawa, "Semantics," *Etc.*, IX, 4 (Summer, 1952), pp. 221-237.

[27] This is generally conceded to be the interpretation of the famous cave image in the *Republic* although some people are not convinced that this is what Plato really meant.

[28] Sum. Theo., Ia, q. 13, resp. 9.

to certain terms to give more extensive significance. The idea, in
turn, was a faded sense impression, according to Hume. Kant
denied the ability of the human mind to reach the essence of
things in order to form universals. Since the grasp of noumena
was denied to man, he established categories into which all reality
must fit, as it were, a kind of procrustean bed made by man.
Whitehead and Russell continued the nominalist trend as they
considered a definition as a mere manipulation of words:

> A definition is, strictly speaking, no part of the subject
> in which it occurs. For a definition is concerned wholly
> with the symbols not with what they symbolize. More-
> over it is not true or false, being the expression of a
> volition, not of a proposition.[29]

Neo-nominalism is more thorough-going than its antecedents and
denies, besides the reality of universals, the reality of individuals
also. In its more extreme forms, it denies reality to all except the
flux of sensations. It thus becomes a panfictionism, according to
which to name a thing at all is to turn it into a fiction. There are
at least three schools of neo-nominalism—those of Russell, of
Bergson and of Whitehead. The first pulverizes the universe into
nouns and makes us talk no longer about tables, things, etc., but
about strings of events and relations. Whitehead, too, would have
science redesign language to eliminate the terms of subject,
predicate, substance and quality, particular and universal, for
present day language does not, he said, reflect reality.[30]

Korzybski is well in the line of thought of such neo-nominalists.
This is evidenced not only by the whole trend of his thought, but
more directly by his many quotations from Whitehead and Russell
in *Science and Sanity* and by his own explicit acknowledgment of
his indebtedness to these men as expressed in the foreword to
Science and Sanity.

From this brief survey it can be seen that there are three
branches of semantics at present—the linguistic or scientific branch,

---

[29] Bertrand Russell and Alfred North Whitehead, *Principia Mathematico*
(Cambridge, London: University Press, 1910).

[30] Wilbur H. Urban, *Language and Reality* (New York: The Macmillan
Co., 1939), pp. 741-747.

the philosophical or logical branch and the branch of general semantics. Korzybski disavows any connection with the first but acknowledges connections with the second. The next section will trace more fully the intellectual heritage of Korzybski and the general semantics movement.

In *Science and the Goals of Man,* Anatol Rapoport gives the intellectual heritage of the non-Aristotelian movement. He claims that it consists of three main currents: the materialist current, the semantic current and the neuro-linguistic current.[31]

1. *The Materialist Current*: Aristotle is cited as the first contributor to this current since he sought natural causes "and clearly stated the principle of cause and effect to be residing in the interaction of material things."[32] Both Rapoport and Korzybski defended Aristotle in this point even though they are upholding a non-Aristotelian system. The non-Aristotelian does not attack Aristotle but simply maintains that his methods are outmoded in view of the discoveries and methods of modern science.

> The beginning of experimental science during the Renaissance is often considered as a revolt against "Aristotelian" (purely speculative) science of the Middle Ages. But Aristotle himself was less Aristotelian than the scholastics who venerated him. Although he performed practically no controlled experiments, he made some remarkably accurate observations, especially in biology.[33]

And Korzybski says:

> To avoid misunderstandings, I wish to acknowledge explicitly my profound admiration for the extraordinary

---

[31] Anatol Rapoport, *Science and the Goals of Man*: a Study in Semantic Orientation (New York: Harper and Brothers, 1950), pp. 161-165. Anatol Rapoport is the associate editor of *Etc.*, the official organ for the International Society for General Semantics. He says in *Science and the Goals of Man*, p. 162: "The resemblance our non-Aristotelian system bears to various thinkers from William of Occam to Alfred Korzybski are not coincidental. They are clear evidences of paternity."
[32] A. Rapoport, *Science and the Goals of Man,* p. 162.
[33] *Ibid.,* p. 162.

genius of Aristotle, particularly in consideration of the period in which he lived. . . . From what we know about Aristotle, there is little doubt that, if alive, he would not tolerate such twistings and artificial immobility of the system usually ascribed to him.[34]

Rapoport then goes on to describe the advance of materialism brought on by William of Occam who preferred to base his idea of reality on individuals alone and to eliminate the need for universals. Bacon and Locke, the English empiricists who held that all knowledge is derived from experience, and the French Encyclopedists, were also contributors to the materialistic current. Rapoport credits the dialectical materialists with giving rise to the notion of nature as being in a state of flux, when they transformed Hegel's dialectic of thought and made it apply to nature, also.

With the flux notion, the immutable "objects," "qualities," "categories," "species," etc., of Aristotelian metaphysics lost their "eternal" reality.[35]

The modern non-Aristotelian regards modern physics as best able to describe reality—a reality composed of events, interactions, of matter-energy in spacetime. "Spirit," "Will," "Providence" are discarded as meaningless or as explainable as mere configurations of events. Thus, by their own avowal, and by their own theoretical basis as will be seen later, the modern non-Aristotelians of the general semantics movement are materialists.

2. *The semantic current* consists of many groups. Those interested in logic and in the theory of meaning include Lady Viola Welby, Bertrand Russell, C. K. Ogden and I. A. Richards, and others. In Austria, the theory of relativity was first formulated by Ernst Mach (1838-1916). Mach held that physical laws are simply economies of thought, constructs of the mind, for it is simpler to treat the world of objects as a construct than to complicate knowledge by setting things into a status apart from the mind.

---

[34] Korzybski, *Science and Sanity,* p. lxvi.
[35] Rapoport, *Science and the Goals of Man,* p. 164.

The theory of relativity is a striking application of the theory of meaning based on operational definition. It is not correct to say that the theory of relativity introduced modern semantics into philosophy since operationism was already evident in the writings of Mach and Poincaré before Einstein's formulation in 1905. It is, however, a manifestation of increasing semantic awareness in science as seen also in the works of Peano, Whitehead and Russell. Two other thoughts came from the physicists—the new criterion of truth based on predictability: "the truth value of an assertion is measured by how much you are able to predict on the basis of it."[36] The other concept was that of the operational definition first formulated by P. W. Bridgeman: "In general, we mean by a concept nothing more than a set of operations; the concept is synonymous with the corresponding set of operations."[37] The physicists both influenced and were influenced by the logical positivists. In his logic Russell owes much to Mach. Mach also influenced Einstein, whose work can be considered as the non-Newtonian pillar in the non-Euclidean, non-Newtonian, non-Aristotelian orientation.[38] Frank said of Einstein, "The theory of relativity was a reform not in metaphysics but in semantics."[39] This statement is highly debatable, of course, but indicates a tendency to confuse levels of knowledge, quite prevalent today.

Mach also influenced the famous "Vienna Circle" of logical positivists consisting chiefly of Rudolf Carnap (now at Chicago), Ludwig Wittgenstein (now at Cambridge) and Otto Neurath (deceased). It was Wittgenstein who asserted that the problems of

---

[36] Rapoport, *Science and the Goals of Man,* p. 161.

[37] P. W. Bridgeman, *The Logic of Modern Physics* (New York: The Macmillan Co., 1932).

[38] Anatol Rapoport, "Dialectical Materialism and General Semantics," *Etc.,* V, 1948, pp. 81-104.

[39] ———, *Science and the Goals of Man,* p. 171. Strictly speaking, Einstein at first was looking for *objective measurements.* His "relativity" then meant only that events in separate places cannot be judged to be "simultaneous." The extent to which Einstein dabbled with the more dubious aspects of operationism in his more theoretical writings leaves him open to the criticism of reductionism which can be applied to the pragmatist-operationist error in general. It is the error in the proposition that the concept is *nothing but* the consequences.

philosophy are those of language alone.[40] The Polish logicians (Tarski, Chwistek, etc.) also applied the operational theory to a critique of traditional philosophy and to traditional Aristotelian logic. The dismissal of traditional philosophy as meaningless jargon was expressed by A. J. Ayer in addition to Wittgenstein. Today Carnap and Charles Morris feel that semantics can answer questions that the older philosophies sought to solve through ideas or sense images. Thus, this union of science and epistemology has given rise to the theory that the meaning of a statement *is* the somewhat arbitrary empiriological rule for verifying it or the empirical operations by which it is tested.[41]

The semantic current, then, has been marked by the union of science and epistemology and has contributed, among other ideas, the operational definition, the criterion of predictability as a yardstick of truth, and the ideas of "relativity" and of flux, to characterize the reality to be expressed by language.

3. *The neuro-linguistic current*: finds its chief exponent in Alfred Korzybski who examines meaning "psycho-logically" more than "logically." The very term "non-Aristotelian" is due to Korzybski. In fact the discipline of general semantics is often referred to as a non-Aristotelian system or methodology. As Korzybski says:

> It is called "non-aristotelian" because, although it includes the still prevailing aristotelian system as a special case, it is a wider, more general formulation to fit the world and 'human nature' as we know it today, rather than as Aristotle knew it c 350 B. C. The aristotelian assumptions influenced the euclidean system and both underlie the later newtonian system. The first non-aristotelian system takes into account newly discovered complexities in all fields and parallels and is interdependent methodologically with the new non-euclidean and non-newtonian developments in mathematics and mathematical physics which made possible even the release of nuclear energy.[42]

---

[40] Ludwig Wittgenstein, *Tractatus Logico-Philosophicus* (New York: Harcourt, Brace and Co., Inc., 1922).

———, *Philosophical Investigations* (New York: The Macmillan Co., 1953).

[41] Vincent E. Smith, *Idea Men,* p. 135.

[42] Alfred Korzybski: "General Semantics," *American Peoples Encyclopedia,* X (1949), 359.

There is a sharp division of opinion over the actual relationship between the academic semantics described above and general semantics, with protests coming from both sides when efforts are made to show the connecting ideas in both fields. Rapoport claims that the four basic principles of the academic semanticists have counterparts in the general semantics system.[43] These four basic principles are: 1) Russell's propositional function; 2) Russell's theory of types; 3) the operational definition; 4) predictive value as the criterion of truth, first formulated by Mach and more clearly stated by Bridgman and Carnap.

Korzybski's principle of self-reflexiveness corresponds to the theory of types as he himself admits.[44] His stress on extensionalism has its counterpart in the operational definition and in the criterion of truth as predictability which his followers Rapoport and Hayakawa stress even more. Both of these principles demand reference to actually experienced events in the present or in the future. The general semanticists stress "non-allness" and "non-identity" which are connected with the propositional function. Korzybski's attacks on the subject-predicate language, his scorn of either-or judgments and his praise of the language of science and of science itself are similar to the attacks of the modern logician on Aristotelian logic and to his efforts to construct a multi-valued logic and a symbolic logic which would have the manipulatory ease of mathematics.

While Rapoport admits and even points out that Korzybski's principles have a close relationship with semantic principles and that his whole system is an outgrowth of the semantic current, he maintains that general semantics goes much further. It is, in fact, "as far removed from semantics as semantics is from logic and as logic is from grammar." For,

1. grammar deals with word-to-word relations, not with relations to facts or with relations to other sentences.

---

[43] Anatol Rapoport, "What Is Semantics?" *Etc.*, X, 1 (Autumn, 1952), 12-24.

[44] Korzybski, "General Semantics," p. 400 and in, "The Role of Language in the Perceptual Processes," *Perception: An Approach to Personality,* ed. Robert R. Blake, Glen V. Ramsey, et al. (New York: The Ronald Press Co., 1951), p. 190.

2. logic deals with the relation between assertions or sentences but words and assertions need not have any relation to the world of fact. Logic seeks only consistency, not correspondence to real facts.
3. in semantics, words and assertions have meaning only if related relationally. Validity and truth are defined and demanded. The truth demanded is, of course, based on the criterion of predictability.
4. general semantics deals with all of the above—with words, as does grammar; with assertions, as does logic; with referents in nature, as does semantics; and also with the effects of these words and assertions on human behavior.[45]

Rapoport concludes that general semantics deals with all that the other three disciplines consider plus the "chain that goes from fact to nervous system, to language, to nervous system, to action." It is this chain, going from fact to the nervous system, *only,* and back again, that is considered by the general semanticists and which will be the chief object of consideration in this study.

Thus it is evident that the question of Korzybski's originality or erudition or dilettantism is not so important here as the fact that he was influenced by the scientists, logicians and psychologists of the twentieth century and his ideas are definitely related to the current of logical empiricism which is still strong in America today. A common element of materialist theory unites the strands we have been considering. For the development of his theory he utilized the entire conceptual apparatus of semantics (operational philosophy) developed in Europe, from the positivism of Mach to the logical empiricism of the Vienna Circle as well as the generalization of logic made or attempted by Whitehead, Russell, and the Polish School. General semantics can thus be viewed as a theory or science of man founded in the ideas flowing out of the characteristic twentieth century philosophy of science.[46] This philosophy is not, as will be argued later, really compatible with the spirit of experimental science. It is necessary to make this point at

---

[45] Anatol Rapoport, "What Is Semantics," *Etc.,* X, 1 (Autumn, 1952). p. 22.
[46] Rapoport, *Etc.,* X, 1 (Autumn, 1952), pp. 23-24.

the moment to avoid leaving the impression that a rejection of the underlying philosophy of general semantics would involve a wholesale rejection of the method, results and authentic philosophy of science.

HISTORY OF THE DEVELOPMENT OF THE GENERAL SEMANTICS MOVEMENT ITSELF

Since the publication of *Science and Sanity* in 1933 and the establishment of the Institute of General Semantics in 1938, a number of writers in various disciplines have acknowledged their debt to Korzybski. This section will trace briefly the growth of the movement as it can be found in the various issues of the two publications, *Etc.* and the *General Semantics Bulletin.*

Irving J. Lee, in 1952,[47] reviewed the accomplishments of general semantics from 1933 up until that time. They may be summarized thus:

1. 1933—The first book, *Science and Sanity* was published.

2. 1935—The first congress on general semantics was held at Ellensburg, Washington.[48] There have been two other congresses since then, in 1941 and 1949, both taking place at Denver, Colorado.[49, 50] A fourth congress is planned for 1958 in connection with the twenty-fifth anniversary of the publication of *Science and Sanity.*[51]

3. 1938—The first popularization was *The Tyranny of Words,* by Stuart Chase.[52]

---

[47] Irving J. Lee, "General Semantics, 1952," *Etc.,* IX, 2 (Winter, 1952), 103-118.

[48] Hansell Baugh (ed.), *General Semantics*: papers from the first American Congress for General Semantics (New York: Arrow Editions, 1938).

[49] M. Kendig, *Papers from the Second Congress on General Semantics* (Chicago: Institute of General Semantics, 1943).

[50] M. Kendig (ed.), *Papers from the Third American Congress on General Semantics* (Chicago: Institute of General Semantics, 1949).

[51] From Paper sent out by Institute of General Semantics, Lakeville, Conn., 1957.

[52] Stuart Chase, *The Tyranny of Words* (New York: Harcourt Brace and Co., 1938).

side by side with the accomplishments, Lee also listed some
lacunae, chief among which were:

1. The fact that no department or professorship in general
semantics had been established in any college or university. (We
wonder if this has been "remedied," since Sandro Zolette is described as Professor of General Semantics on the cover of his
books.)[60]

2. There had been no full-dress autobiography or case study of
the use and effect of general semantics on a subject.

3. There had been no validated pencil-and-paper test drawn
up or other reliable objective means to be used for diagnostic or
prognostic purposes. (This, too, had been remedied. Thomas Weiss
constructed an experimental study to measure adjustment and maladjustment, based on general semantics principles. He spoke of a
study done in March, 1952 by Dr. Henry Peters, Chief Clinical
Psychologist at the Veterans Administration Hospital, Little
Rock, Arkansas. Both tests, those of Weiss and of Peters, tried to
measure the relation of individual language behavior to social adjustment by pencil-and-paper means.)[61]

4. There was, in 1952, no course of study with lesson plans
and assignments for elementary or high school classes, although
Minteer and Moore had begun to produce just this. (This will be
discussed in chapter IV.)

Perhaps the widest influence has been exercised by the publication *Etc.* which has found its way into sixty-seven countries.
Many of the libraries subscribing, it is true, belong to U. S. Information centers; nevertheless, the influence is international.
The International Society for General Semantics, of which *Etc.*
is the organ, has members in twenty-two countries as well as
in practically every state in the United States. This society is
affiliated also with the Japanese Language Society in Tokyo, the
Institute for the Science of Thought, also in Tokyo, the International Society for Significs, Amsterdam, Netherlands, and the

---

[60] Sandro Zolette, *Basic Principles of General Semantics with Exercises
and Discussions* (Philadelphia: Drexel Institute of Technology, 1955).

[61] Thomas Michael Weiss, *An Experimental Study Applying non-
Aristotelian Principles in the Measurement of Adjustment and Maladjustment* (Ann Arbor, Mich.: University of Michigan Microfilms, 1954).

4. 1939—The first outline course was print
by Wendell Johnson.[53]

5. 1940-1941—The first textbooks were printed
Hayakawa and Irving J. Lee. (*Language in A*
guage Habits in Human Affairs.)[54, 55]

6. 1943—the first journal was published—*Etc.*[5

7. 1949—the second journal, the *General Sema*
was begun.[57]

By 1952, there were two organizations with four th
ing members, two journals, a "must" reading list of
basic bibliography of three hundred items, articles in t
clopedias,[58] courses listed in the catalogues of some t
colleges and universities with about one hundred teache
porating its principles in other courses.[59]

Lee lists several fields and writers in those fields in
which the formulations of general semantics have played
The chief fields of interest in this study are those of comm
tion, including reading and the teaching of English, tho
counseling and of teaching. The influence of general semanti
these fields from the educational point of view will be consid
in chapter IV.

---

[53] Wendell Johnson, *Language and Speech Hygiene*: an application of ge
eral semantics (Chicago: Institute of General Semantics, 1939), Genera
Semantics Monograph No. 1).

[54] S. I. Hayakawa, *Language in Action* (New York: Harcourt, Brace,
1941).

[55] Irving J. Lee, *Language Habits in Human Affairs* (New York: Harper
and Bros., 1941).

[56] *Etc.: A Review of General Semantics.* Official Organ of the International Society for the encouragement of scientific research and theoretical
inquiry into Non-Aristotelian Systems and General Semantics. An international quarterly concerned with the role of language and other symbols in
human behavior and human affairs.

[57] The *General Semantics Bulletin* is the official publication of the Institute
of General Semantics since 1949—a functional medium of intercommunica-
tion for students, workers and the Institute (M. Kendig, founder and editor).

[58] *The American Peoples Encyclopedia,* 1949; *Americana,* XVI (1953),
530; Encyclopedia Britannica, *Ten Eventful Years.*

[59] Irving J. Lee, "General Semantics, 1952," *Etc.,* IX (Winter, 1952), pp.
104-105.

Asociacion Argentina de Epistemologia, Buenos Aires, Argentina. The articles for and against general semantics are also not confined to articles in American periodicals. Nor are these articles limited to the fields of psychology, communication and education as both Weiss and Lee have indicated.[62, 63] Perhaps the chief writers are those listed by Rapoport:

> Stuart Chase in social science
> S. I. Hayakawa in linguistics, literature and social criticism
> I. J. Lee in speech
> Wendell Johnson in psychology and speech pathology
> Vogt in ecology
> Frohman in psychiatry
> Russell Meyers in neurology
> Francis P. Chisholm in general semantics, etc.[64]

The evaluations of general semantics both here and abroad range from unquestioning acceptance, even adulation, to virulent denunciation. Since this study is concerned primarily with the educational aspects of meaning and symbolism in the movement, only the major criticisms by writers in those fields not covered by Lee[65] and Maloney[66] will be reported.

Kenneth Burke notes that Korzybski is psychologically acute and says:

> whatever may be the shortcomings of Korzybski's semantics as a way into the analysis of linguistic forms, anyone would be cheating himself who failed to recognize the importance of Korzybski's concern with the abstractive process inherent in even the most concrete of words.[67]

Burke considers general semantics to be a truncated study of dia-

---

[62] I. J. Lee, *Etc.*, IX, 2 (Winter, 1952), pp. 103-118.
[63] Weiss, *An Experimental Study*, pp. 26-30.
[64] Rapoport, *Science and the Goals of Man*, p. 166.
[65] Lee, *Etc.*, IX, 2 (Winter, 1952).
[66] Martin Maloney, "How to Avoid an Idea," *Etc.*, XIII (1950). pp. 214-224.
[67] Kenneth Burke, *A Grammar of Motives* (New York: Prentice-Hall, Inc., 1945), p. 239.

lectics because it does not recognize its own dialectical nature. It is essentially "scientist" and nominalist,[68] *devoted to the systematic elimination of the notion of substance.*[69] He points out that while Korzybski condemns a two-valued orientation, he bases his whole system on the two-valued opposition between aristotelianism and non-aristotelianism.[70] Finally, he condemns the famous structural differential (praised by some) as reductive rather than representative of the process of getting meanings.[71]

Four years later, Max Black concentrated his criticism on the theoretical rather than the practical aspects of general semantics. He showed in a closely-reasoned paper that the attack on Aristotle was due to *a profound lack of understanding of what is asserted in Aristotelian logic.* For Korzybski insists on regarding logic as empirical when it has been held as non-empirical almost without exception by logicians and philosophers.[72] After pointing out the difficulties and confusions in the theory of abstraction proposed by the system, Black says that very little remains "except some hypothetical neurology fortified with dogmatic metaphysics."[73] Korzybski was not an expert on neurology. Finally, though he regards "the theoretical foundations of general semantics as logically incoherent and in need of thoroughgoing revision," he adds, "this does not necessarily imply a finally adverse judgment on the merits of general semantics." He advocates a thorough housecleaning of the foundations of the system.[74]

John Carroll made a survey in 1953 of the field of language study in all disciplines, linguistics in particular. Like Rapoport, he recognizes that one of the chief problems of semantics is that

---

[68] *Ibid.,* p. 247.

[69] *Ibid.,* p. 251.

[70] *Ibid.,* p. 440.

[71] *Ibid.,* p. 511.

[72] Max Black, *Language and Philosophy,* p. 233. Black's other criticisms include the following: (1) that Aristotle pointed out non-reversibility of propositions, thus avoiding " 'is' of identity" erroneously ascribed to him (p. 230) ; (2) Korzybski *nowhere* quotes Aristotle to justify the latter's alleged acceptance of this "is" (p. 299) ; and (3) Korzybski's notion of abstracting as leaving out some details is erroneous (p. 234).

[73] *Ibid.,* p. 245.

[74] *Ibid.,* p. 246.

of meaning, but he points out the dangers of the popularizing
nature of the twentieth century movements. He regards general
semantics as an educational enterprise rather than as a scientific
discipline. Carroll also remarked that its aim is to make one
adopt a scientific orientation towards a world of events which are
in continual process. He claims that certain semantic movements,
especially that of general semantics, preach a watered-down scientism.[75] He decries the cultism of its early days but admits that
"the pages of *Etc.* have shown evidence of a desire on the part of
its sponsors to rectify the careless, vague and inexact statements
made in the early days of the movement."[76] While welcomed by
speech educators, pathologists and remedial reading experts, general semantics had been ignored by most psychologists, linguists,
anthropologists and philosophers, who dislike the air of cultism
and recognize that it is not an investigative discipline in the true
sense of the word. In fact, general semanticists do not claim such
status, as Chisholm said in his address as retiring president of
the Society of General Semantics: "the object of the society lies
in training the nervous systems of as many people as possible to
act in terms of the order empirically known to be healthy."[77]

Like Black, Carroll gives a favorable prognosis as to the success of general semantics in achieving its objectives, provided it
can carry through the house-cleaning of its premises and will
cease to claim that it has the answer to almost any psychological
or social problem. There is a definite place in education for semantics. This fact is being recognized by more and more educators, as chapter IV will indicate. Carroll feels that some of the
instructional devices and techniques, even the structural differential (condemned by Burke),[78] appear to be of considerable promise
in pointing out to children the nature of a symbol and of an
abstraction.[79]

Thus, inconsistent theoretical foundations and cultism are the
chief weaknesses, according to these critics whose remarks may

[75] Carroll, *The Study of Language,* p. 163.
[76] *Ibid.,* p. 165.
[77] *Ibid.,* p. 167.
[78] Supra, p. 20.
[79] Carroll, *The Study of Language,* p. 168.

be considered to be representative of the criticisms in America after 1947.

The answer of the general semanticists is probably best stated by Anatol Rapoport.[80] In 1952, he spoke of the rift between the academic and general semanticists in which the academicians continue to associate semantics with a theory of signs and symbolic logic, referring to their science as an *ology,* while the extreme Korzybskites speak of non-verbal levels, semantic reactions, etc., and consider their movement as an *ics*—a technique of psychotherapy. He admits that the accusations of cultism have some foundation. The United States has a large floating population of truth-seekers who, as he says, lack the capacity for strenuous intellectual effort. And the very nature of the seminars of the Institute of General Semantics, emphasizing problems of human relations, "attracted considerable numbers of people without sufficient background to understand the philosophical implications of Korzybski's ideas. . . . and helped to spread the cult."[81]

Rapoport also admits that the annoyance of scientists is due to Korzybski's careless use of terms (regrettable in an expert in communication) and to his statements made without empirical evidence, especially those with reference to colloidal chemistry and neurophysiology. Scientists are further annoyed in that Korzybski persisted in disavowing his intellectual debts and continued to use the extreme terminology so annoying to academicians, often coining new words for no apparent reason. Rapoport then goes on to list what he considered to be the significant contributions made by Korzybski—a list which is again open to controversy, and the proof of which, strictly speaking, falls outside the scope of this study:

1. He pointed a way toward the establishment of an empirical science of man.
2. He is the precursor of an intellectual revolution which is just now beginning and which promises to rival that of the Renaissance.
3. There is evidence that his vision of an empirical

---

[80] Rapoport, *Etc.,* X, 1 (Autumn, 1952), pp. 12-24.

[81] *Ibid.,* p. 16. Requirements for admission to these seminars are described in the announcements as "flexible."

science of man formulated in structural language similar
to that of mathematical physics is already beginning to be
realized in the directions of automation technology or the
cybernetics of Norbert Weiner, the hybrid science of
mathematical biology developing under Nicholas Rashevsky at the University of Chicago.[82]

Elsewhere he pointed to the more practical influence of Korzybski which is of more concern here.

The value of Korzybski's contributions must be sought
elsewhere—in the work he has inspired among students
and practitioners of communication, in the classrooms of
grade schools, where a teacher is applying the elementary
extensional devices (pointing out the differences between
talk and what is talked about) and thereby introducing
the children to a philosophic orientation so totally lacking
in traditional American education. . . . In short, Korzybski's contribution to semantics should not be judged
as a theoretical contribution, but as the contribution of
a visionary dedicated to make the principles of semantics
serve those of emotional and social hygiene.[83, 84]

Europeans are not so strong either in the criticism or in their
praise of general semantics. Practically all admit the educational
value or therapeutic value of the movement but none discuss fully
the problem under consideration here—i.e., the problem of meaning as presented by the general semanticists: how can the same
word mean different things to a different person and why does
this cause failures and conflicts in communication?[85] Only Ull-

---

[82] *Ibid.*, pp. 23-24.

[83] Anatol Rapoport, "Semantics: The Problem of Meaning," *American
Philosophy,* ed. Ralph Winn (New York: Philosophical Library, 1955),
pp. 64-83.

[84] For the most recent criticisms of general semantics and the answers,
see Joshua A. Fishman's review of *Language, Meaning and Maturity* in
Etc., XIII (Spring, 1956), pp. 225-232 and the answer by Martin S. James,
"Why Am I Always the Bridesmaid?" *Etc.,* XIV (Autumn, 1956), pp.
47-50.

[85] France was the first to discuss Korzybski in Gaston Bachelard's, *La
Philosophie du Non*: Essai d'une philosophie du nouvel esprit scientifique
(Paris: Presses Universitaire de France, 1940), pp. 105-134. Bachelard is

man of England considers the problem of meaning at any length, but he thinks that the general semanticists, with their practical aims, do not have to take a stand for or against metaphysics, for or against the existence of universals.[86] He does admit, however, that they have their roots in contemporary philosophy and affinities with Russell, Whitehead, and the various currents of logical positivism. He describes the three branches of semantics as the philological branch of Bréal, the philosophical branch of Carnap and Morris (in its present form too abstruse to be understood by

---

professor of the History and Philosophy of Sciences at La Sorbonne and Honorary Trustee of the Institute of General Semantics appointed by Korzybski at the time of its foundation.

A German anthropologist discussed the movement as a more accurately formulated problem of universals. Cf. Herman Wein, "Towards Philosophical Anthropology?" *Etc.,* XI, 1 (Autumn, 1953), pp. 21-27.

Around the same time in Brussels, Mario Lins, a member of the Brazilian Institute of Philosophy, summarized the bases and contributions of general semantics published in: "The Supports of the New General Semantics," *Proceedings of the Eleventh International Congress of Philosophy,* Brussels, Aug. 20-26, 1953, V (North Holland Publishing Co., 1954), pp. 115-120.

Francesco Barone of the University of Turin feels that the therapeutic aspects of general semantics have far greater possibilities than the theoretical aspects as he writes in an article entitled, "La Semantica Generale," in *Archivio di Filosofica*: Semantico No. 3 (Fratelli Bocca Editori, 1955), pp. 407-418.

Two Soviet criticisms castigate semantics as a "subjective-idealist movement in bourgeois philosophy . . . a modernized scholastic nominalism and a limited expression of logical positivism—a pitiful attempt of the reactionary ideologists of class struggle to counterpoise to the workers' yearning for the overthrow of capitalism, a semantic scholasticism and a reform of language as a magical means for overcoming all difficulties and all the evils in life." They recommend the work of J. V. Stalin, "Marxism and Questions of Linguistics." Cf. B. Bykhovsky, "The Morass of Modern Philosophy," *Etc.,* VI, 1 (Autumn, 1948), pp. 1-15, tr. by Anatol Rapoport from *The Bolshevik*: A Theoretical Political Journal, XXIV (Moscow, Aug. 30, 1947) ; and "Semantic Philosophy" in *The Short Philosophical Dictionary,* ed. Rosenthal and Yudin (Moscow: State Publishing House for Political Literature, 1951) in "A Soviet Account of Semantics," tr. Fenton Jameson, *Language, Meaning and Maturity* (New York: Harper and Bros., 1954), pp. 347-349.

[86] Stephen Ullman, *Words and Their Use* (London: Frederick Muller, 1951), p. 97.

any but a small group of initiates), and general semantics, which
has two branches—that of C. K. Ogden and I. A. Richards, and
that of Korzybski and his followers.[87] Like all critics of semantics, he finds assessment of the whole movement very difficult. But
like them, too, he has little doubt that general semantics responds
to a real need with a substantial contribution.[88] After warning
against the danger of mistaking genuine problems for linguistic
ones and vice versa, he counsels for a combination of all three
types of semantics in a science of meaning. Philosophical semantics would prove the framework of analysis and symbolization;
linguistics would provide the empirical evidence; general semantics would complete and interpret this evidence in the light of
everyday experience. Again, those chiefly profiting from this new
science would be educators, translators, writers, scientists, and
even the general public.[89]

Thus, European and American critics comment on somewhat
the same aspects of general semantics:

1. its philosophical origins in nominalism, logical positivism
and contemporary science and its theoretical weaknesses.

2. the exaggeration of its therapeutic value by some of its proponents amounting almost to a cultism which has resulted in

3. the alienation of scientists, psychologists and academic or
philosophical semanticists.

4. the recognition of its educational value and of the need for
some training in language behavior such as the general semanticists propose, provided the theoretical foundations are "cleaned
up."

The educational value lies in its efforts to prevent confusion
over word meanings. It is the purpose of this study to see if its
practical value can be secured without incurring the dangers inevitable from its confused epistemological and ontological foundations as pointed out by so many competent critics.

---

[87] *Ibid.*, p. 8.
[88] *Ibid.*, p. 105.
[89] *Ibid.*, pp. 95-108.

SUMMARY OF BACKGROUND OF GENERAL SEMANTICS

1. The movement began in 1933 with the publication of *Science and Sanity* by Alfred Korzybski.

2. Korzybski disclaims any connection with the linguistic branch of semantics.

3. But it does claim to have been influenced by the Polish mathematical logicians, and later by the Vienna Circle of the logical positivists.

4. It is opposed to Aristotelianism and claims to set up a new non-Aristotelian science in closer correspondence with the scientific knowledge of the world.

5. It claims to be not a philosophy, a psychology or a logic, but a new discipline which explains how to use our nervous systems in speaking and listening; how to react to words; how to guard against the inadequacies and confusions of words.

6. It was first popularized by Chase, who included the ideas of Ogden and Richards.

7. The books most influential in educational circles are:

Hayakawa, *Language in Thought and Action*

Johnson, *People in Quandaries*

Lee, *Language Habits in Public Affairs*

which are used in many colleges today (see chapter IV on educational implications).

8. Through *Etc.* and the International Society of General Semantics, the movement has spread its information and theories to libraries over the world. This magazine contains articles showing the application of general semantics principles in other fields as well as articles by non-general semanticists with similar ideas.

9. *The General Semantics Bulletin* and the Institute of General Semantics in Lakeville, Connecticut, under the direction of M. Kendig may be considered to be the direct heirs of Korzybski's ideas. The Institute publishes all of Korzybski's works and conducts seminars to train people intensively in non-Aristotelian orientation.

10. There have been many critics of general semantics, some virulent in their treatment, some superficial; others, more thoughtful and measured, question the epistemological basis for Korzybski's theories of meaning and of language.

11. Because of these doubts of the critics, and because of its growing influence in education, it has been deemed advisable to make a thorough study of its theory of meaning, symbolism and communication, including its most basic premises in order to see if the practical value recognized by most critics is lessened or need be harmed by the confusion in its theoretical foundations.

CHAPTER II

THE COMMUNICATION ASPECT OF THE PROBLEM OF MEANING AS CONSIDERED BY THE GENERAL SEMANTICISTS

The general semanticists are primarily interested in the effect of language on behavior. They are concerned with a problem met frequently in every day experience: why and how the same words mean different things to different peoples, so that confusion and inadequate communication frequently result. The examination of their insights into this problem (which, in an age of mass communication, has become acute) will be according to the following plan. In this chapter, at first, an overall survey of their chief ideas and insights into this problem will be given. Then, each of the main ideas will be developed more fully by references to and quotations from the works of the general semanticists themselves.[1] This will be reportorial presentation and interpretation of their theories. In the next chapter there will be a discussion of the weaknesses and strengths of these theories.

The theory of meaning as presented by the general semanticists may be summed up as follows:

1. Meanings are individual and different for each person[2] because of:

> a. for one thing, the way man obtains meanings, i.e., by abstraction and the analysis of semantic reactions.[3] Each man has his own nervous system and his own past experiences.
> b. the nature of the world man knows—a world of individual events in continual process, and therefore different at each instant.
>
> Therefore meanings are a composite of the man who reacts and the world to which he reacts.[4]

---

[1] The general semanticists whose works will be discussed are A. Korzybski, A. Rapoport, I. Lee, W. Johnson.

[2] Korzybski, *Science and Sanity*, p. 23.

[3] *Ibid.*, p. 24.

[4] *Ibid.*, p. 23.

2. Language expresses this meaning, so personal to each man. It must correspond as closely as possible to the structure of the world man wishes to symbolize in his language.[5]

3. Originally language merely reflected man's semantic reactions to the world about him—or *his* meaning of the world, his *weltanschauung*. Once formulated, language can and does impose its metaphysics, or the metaphysics which formed it, upon subsequent generations of men.[6]

4. Therefore, not only do meanings change with individual men, but also with the knowledge of reality that each age has. Each age has its own view of the universe, its own meanings, usually formulated by either philosophers or, today, by scientists. As science changes its view of the universe, the meaning of the universe for the men of that age should change and their language should also change to correspond to the new meaning of the universe now held by men. If not, tension results because of the lack of correspondence between language and reality.[7]

5. Three of the great sources of conflict over confusions of meanings are evident from the ideas just stated:

a. Language today is the subject-predicate language structure according to the Aristotelian model of a universe of substance-quality, time and space, body and mind dualism. But science presents to man a universe of events in process with no individual substances that are static—only interrelated events. Language and reality, as science sees it today, do not correspond in structure.[8]

b. People, today, are unaware not only of the fact that the world is not static while their language so represents it, but also that their knowledge and expression of that reality is a selective process and never wholly represents reality. They react as if their meanings and expressions of that meaning were identical with reality.[9]

---

[5] *Ibid.*, pp. 11, 751, 24.

[6] Alfred Korzybski, "The Brotherhood of Doctrines," *Etc.*, I (August, 1943), p. 52; also, *Science and Sanity*, p. 89, and Wendell Johnson, *Peoples in Quandaries*, p. 19.

[7] Rapoport, *Science and the Goals of Men*, p. 91.

[8] Korzybski, *Science and Sanity*, p. 45; W. Johnson, *People*, p. 6 and p. 32, p. 18.

[9] Korzybski, *Perception*, p. 191.

6. Basically, a triple remedy is proposed:

    a. eliminate the Aristotelian absolutistic language by correcting the Aristotelian view of the world.[10]
    b. Make people more conscious of the abstractive or selective process of their knowledge so that their symbolic reactions will be more controlled and more in accord with reality.
    c. attempt to mathematize language in order to get it to correspond more closely to the reality science presents to man.[11]

The ideas then which will be developed more fully, as the general semanticists present them, are:

1. A brief statement of the nature of the "Aristotelian language" and of the substance-quality view of the universe which it expresses; the inevitable consequences of such a language which, according to the general semanticists, occur in society.

2. Presentation of the "scientific" view of the world of events in process to which language must correspond in order to express as accurately as possible the meanings of the events of the universe to each man.

3. Presentation of the general semantic theory of abstraction and semantic reaction, or, in other words, the process by which man secures or constructs (it is not quite clear which is meant) meanings of this world in process. This would also involve a brief statement on Korzybski's idea of man as a time-binding class of life.

4. Presentation of Korzybski's proposals to improve man's grasp and expression of meaning:

    a. by operational definitions instead of intensional ones.
    b. by introduction of mathematical devices to indicate the relational nature of the universe.
    c. by classification of words as meaningless if the criterion of predictability does not apply—true, false and meaningless statements.
    d. by the elimination of metaphysics and all such meaningless jargon.

---

[10] Korzybski, *Science and Sanity*, pp. 761, 68, 69.
[11] *Ibid.*, p. 44.

5. Practical consequences and summary of these theories

    a. the denial of substances and of essences
    b. emphasis on operational definition
    c. the relativity of truth according to
        1) the knowledge of the contemporary age
        2) the past experiences of the speaker and listener.

It must be repeated that the presentation of the above ideas will be, it is hoped, an objective and an accurate presentation of what the general semanticists hold regarding this very important problem. The discussion and statement of agreement or disagreement with these insights will be given only in Chapter III.

THE ATTACK ON ARISTOTELIAN LANGUAGE AND THOUGHT

According to Korzybski, the main features of the Aristotelian language-structure are the subject-predicate habit, the habit of identity, two-valued orientations and elementalism.[12] In keeping with his theory that language is an outgrowth of man's view of the universe, he shows that this Aristotelian language is the result of the pre-scientific attitude when the observer, without scientific instruments, recognized what seemed to be stable objects with changing qualities inhering in or belonging to them.[13] A subject-predicate language best expresses this view in such sentences as, "The leaf is green," "The boy is strong," etc.[14] This tendency to regard objects as static resulted in another tendency to stress similarities and to ignore differences which soon resulted in the classification terms so common in Aristotelian language. Implicitly developed, also, was the belief that objects of a certain class were identical: "Man is an animal." The "is of identity,"[15] both in predication and in classification, was further emphasized by the

---

[12] Korzybski, *Perception*, p. 194.

[13] Johnson, *People in Quandaries*, p. 32.

[14] Korzybski, *Science and Sanity*, p. 89.

[15] Aristotle is alleged to have taught the "is of identity" on which such statements as "water is wet" and "Dewey is a philosopher" means that water is identical with wetness; and Dewey is identical with the character of being a philosopher. Aristotelians are further accused of identifying the word with the thing and reacting to the word "fire," for example, as if it *were* fire.

tendency to believe that objects were static, always the same. Eventually it led to the identification of the word with the object.

The two-valued orientation developed from the law of identity, because it is merely another expression of the law of the excluded middle. The law of identity says: Whatever is, is itself absolutely, and goes on to say that words are things. Symbols are equated with what they represent; the two sides of the semantic equation are equivalent.[16] There can be no middle ground—a thing either is, or is not. The rigidity, totalitarianism and authoritarianism of the Aristotelian orientation results.[17] A thing is either black or white, good or bad, true or false. We, then, have the law of contradiction: a thing cannot both be and not be at the same time so that a man cannot be good and bad at the same time.[18]

According to Korzybski and his followers, this rigidity of orientation was actually due, in large part, to the rulers and philosophers who perpetuated "the primitive and animalistic responses to reality" by imposing their own "infantilism" on our institutions, educational methods and doctrines and so produced leaders afflicted with their own "animalistic, non-scientific, primitive limitations." The philosophers guessed at a primitive structure of the world; their metaphysics is outmoded today.[19] Other writers, notably F. S. C. Northrop, make even more explicit this attack on

[16] Korzybski, *Science and Sanity*, p. 201.

[17] Johnson, *People in Quandaries*, pp. 83-87.

[18] *Ibid.*, p. 6.

[19] This attack on Aristotelian thinking is summed up by both Korzybski and Johnson. Cf. *Science and Sanity*, pp. xxv, 555-557, 92-93 and *People in Quandaries*, pp. 83-87. Rapoport further extends the criticism to St. Thomas Aquinas. While strictly not a part of the theory of meaning, still this attack has educational implications in that it represents both Aristotle and Aquinas in an unfavorable light and the student is prejudiced before examining the works of both. In so far as metaphysical terms and Aristotelian metaphysics are considered "meaningless, useless ghosts to the scientists," discussions of them have a place here. Rapoport says in *Science and the Goals of Man*, pp. 107-114 (apropos of such maxims as "Where there is motion, there is a mover," "A thing exists only because there is a sufficient reason for its existence," and "Causes always precede effects") : "These maxims, essential to philosophy and theology are meaningless noises in view of our present knowledge obtained by controlled experiment." For his criticism of St. Thomas, see the same work, pp. 202-203.

the non-scientific orientation, holding that the notion of substance in the order of existence and of essence in the order of knowledge and the dualism this entails are the grossest errors of this attitude of mind.

> Material substance by scientific definition is an entity of the relatedness which is automatically constructed mathematical space. By its scientific character it is such that it can only act in space. Mental substances are not in space. For them, space is the relatedness of entities within their internal private consciousness. Clearly a substance which can only act within space cannot contact a substance which is not in space. The theory of the interaction between mind and body conceived as mental and material substance becomes untenable. And the whole Aristotelian theory that sensed entities in sensed time and space are related to scientific objects in scientific space and time by two-termed relation of predication becomes untenable also.
>
> This is the heart of what Count Korzybski was maintaining quite correctly when he attacked Aristotelian thinking and the pseudo-problems which its implicit presence in our ordinary language creates for us.[20]

Thus a radical reform in language must be preceded by a reform in metaphysics and the "formulation of the present infinite-valued non-Aristotelian system becomes an imperative necessity."[21] With the new structural metaphysics, all of the older philosophies would be rejected except epistemology—which, in turn, would merge with a scientific "psychologics" based on "general semantics, structure, relations, multi-dimensional order and the quantum mechanics of a given date."[22] But the whole emphasis on reform of metaphysics is in view of the practical problem—the effect of meaning on human behavior.

> Once we eliminate identification, we must accept *structure* as the only possible content of "knowledge" and also

[20] F. S. C. Northrop, "Mathematical Physics and Korzybski's Semantics," Alfred Korzybski Memorial Lecture, *General Semantics Bulletin,* No. 16-17 (1955), p. 14. Korzybski also quotes Whitehead's attack on the medieval thinkers in his *Science and Sanity,* p. 367.

[21] Korzybski, *Science and Sanity,* p. 28.

[22] *Ibid.,* p. 139.

realize that no "knowledge" is ever free from some structural assumptions. . . . The real problem before mankind
presents itself in the selection of a structural metaphysics. If we accept primitive structural assumptions
and have to live under present conditions we must become a split personality which cannot adjust itself. [Be-
fore] we did not analyze the structure of language and its
role in our lives and *begin* with a structural linguistic
revision. Once this revision is accomplished and we build
a A(Non-Aristotelian) language, the semantic background is prepared for a natural acceptance of modern
structural metaphysics (science) of each date and the
older popularization become unnecessary. Such a procedure would help to integrate the individual while the
older methods only help to split him.[23]

It can be said, then, that *the principal criticism of Aristotelian
thought is by way of denial of the notion of substance, in the order
of existence, and of the notion of essence, its counterpart, in the
order of knowledge.* What matters here is not whether Korzybski
has misrepresented Aristotle, as many writers have indicated.[24]
What matters is that Korzybski and the general semanticists
demonstrated by their opposition to Aristotelian metaphysics and
language some of the chief premises in their theory of meaning:

1. meanings should correspond in a relational way to
man's view of reality.
2. language should correspond to this view and, when
it fails to do so, it affects the view of reality and hence
the meanings become falsified.
3. it is not clear whether the first reform should be in
metaphysics or in language. From the passage just
quoted, it would seem that science has presented man with
a new correct metaphysics to which language must be
made to correspond. By reforming the language of the
man of the street according to science's view of the universe, his meanings or view of the universe (i.e., the
view of the man in the street) would then be corrected.
"It becomes clear now—our language as a whole may be
regarded as a vast system of assumptions and potential

---

[23] *Ibid.*, pp. 483-484.
[24] Black, *Language*, p. 231.

doctrines with fixed logical boundaries. . . . With the mathematical clarification of a very few of such fundamental concepts, we may confidently expect that many of our difficulties will vanish, that the universe will become correspondingly intelligible and man correspondingly intelligent."[25]

THE GENERAL SEMANTICISTS' IDEA OF REALITY AS PROCESS

If the general semanticists reject Aristotle's world of static objects with properties and natures, and adopt or subscribe to a more modern metaphysics to which they wish to make our language conform, then, before examining the theory of language and meaning, we must see the nature of the reality of the general semanticists which their new language is to symbolize. According to them, the modern world consists of events and processes rather than of things or entities so that the *regularities* in the occurrence of events are the object of knowledge, and not the "nature" of things.[26]

In 1950, we must visualize the world in general as a submicroscopic dynamic electronic process and life in particular as an electro-colloidal process of still much higher complexity.[27]

It logically follows that, since the real universe consists of a vast collection of point-events, there is no sameness, no identity anywhere, and the principle of non-identity rather than of identity must be held.[28]

Yet while each thing is in process, it is acting upon and is being acted upon by the rest of the universe, inextricably connected with everything else and dependent upon everything else.[29] Therefore, the term "matter," which belongs to space and time, should be

---

[25] Korzybski, "Fate and Freedom" in Irving J. Lee, *The Language of Wisdom una Folly* (New York: Harper and Bros., 1949), p. 349.

[26] Rapoport, *Science and the Goals of Man,* p. 147.

[27] Korzybski, *Perception,* p. 190.

[28] Korzybski, *Science and Sanity,* p. 194; Johnson, *People in Quandaries,* pp. 23, 32, 36.

[29] Korzybski, *Science and Sanity,* p. 390.

abandoned. *Substance,* on the microscopic level, becomes *invariance of function* on the submicroscopic level. There is no need to postulate either a permanent substratum, or substance or essence since invariance of function is sufficient hypothesis.[30]

> The general sub-microscopic atomic and sub-atomic structure of all materials simply gives us the persistence of the microscopic characteristics as the relative invariance of function due to dynamic equilibrium and ultimately reflected and conditioned by this sub-microscopic structure of all materials. Under such actual structural conditions, terms like 'substance,' 'material' and 'function,' 'energy,' 'action' become interconnected—largely a problem of preference or necessity of selecting the level with which we want to deal.[31]

Korzybski then quotes Whitehead to show that the idea of matter is really a projection of the mind: "What is a mere procedure of mind in the translation of sense-awareness into discursive knowledge has been transmuted into a fundamental character of nature."[32] Whitehead blames this on the unquestioned acceptance of the Aristotelian logic which has led "to an ingrained tendency to postulate a substratum for whatever is disclosed to sense-awareness, namely to look below what we are aware of for the substance in the sense of the concrete being."[33]

But, while condemning this postulational origin of the notion of substance, Korzybski admits that *the idea or notion of the submicroscopic world in process is also an inferential notion.*[34] The senses are not able to register these processes without the help of extra-neural means and higher order abstractions (science). Whitehead defines an object as "the recognizable part of the

---

[30] *Ibid.,* pp. 382 and 163.

[31] *Ibid.,* p. 162.

[32] Alfred Korzybski, *Fate and Freedom* in Irving J. Lee, *The Language . . . ,* p. 166.

[33] *Ibid.,* p. 167.

[34] Korzybski, "The Role of Language, etc.," p. 194 and Zollette, *Basic Principles,* p. 27.

event"[35] so that what man calls objects, as such, are really what human beings recognize when stimulated by reality.

> Objects as such could be considered as relations between sub-microscopic events and the human nervous system . . . we find that an object represents an abstraction of a low order produced by the nervous system as the result of the sub-microscopic events acting as stimuli on the nervous system.[36]
>
> On the sub-microscopic levels, iron or anything else means only a persistence for a limited time of certain gross characteristics representing a process (structurally a four-dimensional notion involving time) which becomes a question of structure.[37]

Though we know the process world only through inference of modern scientists, these assumptions give us high predictability so that it is safe to act as if these events do exist and behave in this manner. Things behave as if the electro-magnetic energies do exist. Scientists do not assert their existence as non-controvertible, but as most satisfactory hypotheses. There is no identification of our knowledge about empirical reality with empirical reality. As a matter of fact, we live in three worlds,

1. the world of events (inferential data)
2. the world of objects (macroscopic and microscopic)
3. the world of symbols (names, labels, inferences, etc.)[38]

The process notion of reality is basic to the theory of the levels of abstraction. This theory of abstraction is one of the ideas of general semantics which has had the widest influence, as it is found not only in the pure general semantics textbooks of Lee, Hayakawa and Johnson, but also in many high school texts which do not adopt the whole of the general semantics system. (See Chapter IV.) It may be said, by way of summary, that the general semanticists describe reality in the following way: The world is in process, meanings are in process, and language must reflect this

---

[35] Quoted in *Science and Sanity*, p. 390.
[36] Korzybski, *Science and Sanity*, p. 20.
[37] *Ibid.*, p. 162.
[38] Zollette, *Basic Principles*, p. 27.

changing nature of both the world and the meanings. Language must represent the relational structure of the world; language, meanings and the world are relative. It may be noted here that the general semanticists have transferred a scientific hypothesis as to the nature of the sub-microscopic world into the structural metaphysics they wished to construct in order to replace the Aristotelian rigid metaphysics they themselves condemned because it was postulational. They have replaced one hypothesis by another.

MAN'S REACTION TO THE PROCESS WORLD—ABSTRACTION AND SEMANTIC REACTION

Before considering man's reaction to the process world or the way in which he secures meanings, which are to be symbolized in language, it is necessary to consider briefly the theory of man, the symbolizer, as presented by the general semanticists,—what he is and how he "thinks" in general. In brief, man is presented as a time-binding class of life; life is a kind of colloidal behavior; thinking is a response of the colloidal structure to the stimulus of electric currents.[39] Each one of these ideas can be explained in the light of their relation to the theory of meaning.

Man is a time-binding class of life. In point of time, this theory was first in the development of Korzybski's system.[40] He was led to this formulation when puzzling over the cataclysm of World War I. Seeing that the constructions of engineers do not collapse while those of economic, political and social systems sporadically collapse, he found the answer in the fact that engineers use a form of symbolization (mathematics) which was similar in structure to the facts they dealt with, while builders of social systems, etc., were using neurological symbols and language quite dissimilar in

---

[39] Korzybski, *Science and Sanity*, p. 119. "A colloid is a substance that when apparently dissolved in water or other liquid diffuses not at all or very slowly through a membrane and shows other properties as lack of pronounced effect on the freezing point or vapor pressure of the solvent," according to the 1957 Webster's Dictionary.

[40] Alfred Korzybski, *Manhood of Humanity*: The Science and Art of Human Engineering (2nd ed., Lakeville, Conn.: International Non-Aristotelian Library Publishing Co., 1950).

structure to the facts presented by science today. He concluded that a new science of man was necessary and began to investigate previous theories of man. He finally came to the conclusion that there are three classes of life: 1) chemistry-binders (plants), 2) the space-binders (animals), and 3) the time-binders (man). Man, as a time-binding class of life, differs essentially from animals in that, through language, he can span the ages and profit by the achievements of the past.

What is pertinent here is the fact that Korzybski treats the differences between animals and man on the basis of the fact that man has made hypotheses about the structure of the universe, has investigated the meaning of the universe, and animals have not.[41] Structurally, however, they seem to be similar.[42] Both are colloidal structures, both material;[43] in fact the only structural difference, according to Korzybski, is "a quarter of an inch of cortex."[44] Since the structures are similar, it follows that the actions and reactions of man and animal are also similar. In fact "thinking" is simply a higher form of conditioned or conditional reflex."[45]

---

[41] *Ibid.,* pp. 46-92.

[42] Korzybski, *Science and Sanity,* p. 395. He says: "It is undeniable that Fido does not know and cannot know that he abstracts because it takes science to know that we abstract and Fido has no science. . . . Science was made possible by the human nervous system and the invention of extra-neural means for investigation which the animals lack entirely. . . . Whoever claims that animals have science should, to say the least, show libraries and scientific laboratories and instruments produced by animals."

[43] *Ibid.,* p. 395—"Dogs abstract. . . . If his nervous system is similar to ours."

[44] Stuart Chase, *The Power of Words* (New York: Harcourt, Brace and Co., 1954), p. 150. Korzybski describes the difference more explicitly in *Science and Sanity,* p. 18: "For our purpose we may consider a rough structural difference between the nervous system of man and animal. Briefly, we can distinguish in the brain, two kinds of nervous fibres and the radiating fibres and the tangential correlations and association fibres. With the increase of complexities and modifiability of the behavior, we find an increased number and more complex interrelations of association fibres. The main difference for instance between the brain of a man and the brain of a higher ape is found not in the projection apparatus but in the association paths which are enormously enlarged, more numerous and more complex in man than in any animal."

[45] Korzybski, *Science and Sanity,* p. 470.

While the "conditional reflex" or semantic reaction of man to events will be considered more fully in connection with meaning, a few quotations here will indicate how this concept flows out of the understanding of the nature of man and of the general semantics theory of how man secures meanings.

> To emphasize the fact that human responses to "conditioned stimuli, though they are "conditioned" in the sense defined, are not automatic, but are instead "conditional" on a great many other psycho-physiological factors, such as the attitude of the individual, competing "thoughts" and his "will," it is helpful to take the suggestion of Korzybski and to speak of "conditional" instead of conditioned responses.[46] . . . To say that a sign has meaning for an individual in these days is thus simply a verbal short cut for the statement that the individual is conditioned to respond to or with the sign. A semantic reaction is the conditional response of a human being to or with verbal signs.[47]

Rapoport says just as directly, "For us the phenomenon of the conditioned reflex indicates what in all probability lies at the root of meaning. Meaning in its most basic form is the association of one experience with another."[48]

Korzybski compares the use of language to the reflexes acquired in driving a car:

> Fundamentally there is no structural difference between the use of language and the use of any other mechanical device. They all involve reflex action. . . . We all know what amazing unconscious reflex-adjustments a good driver of a car can make in case of unexpected danger.
> A similar semantic reflex-skill is required in handling our linguistic apparatus.[49]

[46] Thomas Clark Pollock, *The Nature of Literature* (Princeton: Princeton University Press, 1942), p. 36. He refers here to *Science and Sanity*, p. 328.

[47] Pollock, *The Nature*, p. 38. Cf. Korzybski, *Science and Sanity*, pp. 19-34, to which Pollock refers the reader.

[48] Rapoport, *Science and the Goals of Man*, p. 77. See also, Wendell Johnson, "The Spoken Word and the Great Unsaid," *Etc.* (Autumn, 1953), p. 29, and Rapoport, "Technological Models of the Nervous System," *Etc.*, XI, 4 (Summer, 1953), pp. 272-283.

[49] Korzybski, *Science and Sanity*, p. 470.

The conclusion of this consideration of man is, as Max Black says, "one of the most important and basic notions of general semantics—that of the nervous response made by an organism consisting of symbols and thus, since meanings are natural events of the nervous system of the organism, the study of meaning becomes a branch of physiology."[50]

THE PROCESS BY WHICH MAN GETS MEANINGS—ABSTRACTION

From the concept of man as a symbol-making and symbol-using, highly complex organism of electro-colloidal structure, interacting upon and being acted upon by a world in process, we turn to the nature of this reaction, which is called by the general semanticists, "abstraction." According to them, man's knowledge is the result of nervous abstraction.[51] It is a *"neural process of selecting certain characteristics and omitting many others."*[52] (Italics mine.) It is the means by which we can recognize the structure of the world as modern science tells it to us.[53] Korzybski chose this term because it implied most clearly his idea that the human organism, in reacting to the outside world, was incapable of reacting to *all* of that world. What we see or observe is necessarily a nervous response to the non-verbal reality we are looking at. "The world, as we see it, is a joint product of observer and observed."[54] Abstracting means leaving out, selecting, omitting.[55]

> We see that the term abstracting implies structurally and semantically the activities characteristic of the nervous system and so serves as an excellent functional physiological term.[56]

---

[50] Max Black, *Language,* p. 226.

[51] Korzybski, *Science and Sanity,* p. 254.

[52] Zollette, *Basic Principles,* p. 31. See also Wendell Johnson, *Language and Speech Hygiene* (Chicago: Institute of General Semantics, 1939), p. 14, and Korzybski, *Science and Sanity,* p. 384.

[53] Korzybski, *Science and Sanity,* p. 235.

[54] Zollette, *Basic Principles,* p. 18.

[55] Korzybski, *Science and Sanity,* p. 379. Cf. Rapoport, *Science and Goals,* p. 68.

[56] Korzybski, *Science and Sanity,* p. 166.

Human beings are not the only form of life that can abstract. All living beings abstract, for all react to external stimuli by a kind of leaving out. In fact, abstraction is due to the very structure of protoplasm. When a stone falls on our foot, the stone is not identical with the pain we feel as it touches our foot. "A bit of protoplasm is affected only partially and in a specific way by the stimulus."[57] Since, then, on no level of living protoplasm is there reaction identical with the stimulus either in kind or in quantity or degree, the term *abstraction,* which implies selection, is appropriate.

> In life we deal structurally only with non-allness and so the term abstracting in different orders seems to be structurally and uniquely appropriate for describing the effects of external stimuli on living protoplasm.[58]

Animals, as well as human beings, abstract. Their abstraction takes place in the thalamus and is only on the non-verbal level. Intelligence in the human being is just a more complex kind of abstraction and takes place in the cortex.[59]

> Intelligence of any kind is connected with the abstracting (non-allness) which is characteristic of all protoplasm response. Similarities are perceived only as differences become blurred, and therefore the process is one of abstracting.[60]

Korzybski admits that his usage of the term "abstracting" differs from the old usages.[61] The great difference lies in the fact that he has grouped together the reactions to external stimuli of all living protoplasm since these reactions all imply leaving out something of reality. On the non-verbal level, the senses never reproduce in their reactions the whole of the stimuli. It is thus consistent that the general semanticists call naming or labelling a kind of

---

[57] *Ibid.,* p. 165.

[58] Korzybski, *Science and Sanity,* p. 166.

[59] *Ibid.,* p. 290.

[60] *Ibid.,* p. 166.

[61] *Ibid.,* p. 580 and Joseph DuBois, *Explorations in Awareness* (New York: Harper and Bros., 1957), pp. 135-137.

abstraction, since the label obviously cannot describe the whole event.

> Abstracting is a mechanism by which an infinite variety of experiences can be mapped on short noises (words). The mapping is accomplished by selecting only a few characteristics of the experience.[62]

Not only does verbal abstraction include naming the object but also making inferences about it, since these inferences are also selective—that is, they emphasize some aspects of the event at the expense of leaving out others.

> The term [abstracting] implies a general activity not only of the nervous system as a whole but even of all living protoplasm. The characteristic activities of the nervous system such as summarizing, integrating, are also included by implication.[63]

Scattered throughout *Science and Sanity* there are descriptions of different levels of abstraction. In order to get a clearer idea of just what this process of abstraction is, as general semanticists see it, all of the descriptions will be summarized or quoted and the two chief diagrams of Korzybski and Hayakawa will be reproduced.

In the first part of *Science and Sanity*, Korzybski distinguishes two types of abstraction:

1. objective or physical abstractions which include our daily life notions. In this kind of abstraction, particulars are left out, and deductions can work only relatively, no matter how correctly they are made.

2. mathematical abstractions, at present, taken from pure mathematics in a restricted sense and later generalized. Mathematical abstractions leave all particulars in and therefore work absolutely if correctly made.[64]

---

[62] Rapoport, *Science and the Goals of Man*, p. 68.

[63] Korzybski, *Science and Sanity*, p. 166.

[64] Korzybski, *Science and Sanity*, pp. 67-68. In other pages he notes that mathematics has no physical content. (*Science and Sanity*, pp. 294, 302, 306.) This is hard to reconcile with the statement here that all particulars are left in.

Both of these types of abstractions are made by man alone, according to Korzybski.

Later on, he expands the levels of abstraction to include those made by all types of living protoplasm. At first he mentions three levels:

1. the submicroscopic level of science—the molecules, electrons of, for example, a pencil. These electrons, etc., are inferences of science.

2. the gross macroscopic daily experience level of rough objects. This is the "thing," the gross appearance, etc., that our senses abstract of the "event" we call, for example, pencil. This is neural abstracting performed directly by the nervous system.

3. the verbal level.[65]

A few pages later Korzybski refers to four levels:

1. the event or scientific object or submicroscopic physico-chemical processes.

2. the ordinary object manufactured from the event by our lower nervous systems.

3. the psychological picture, probably manufactured by the higher centers of the nervous system.[66]

4. the verbal definition of the term.[67]

The definitive number of the levels of abstraction is probably indicated by the description of the famous structural differential, a device to represent in three-dimensional form, the fact that our knowledge and our words about things leave out much that belongs in the actual "event." This structural differential refers

---

[65] *Ibid.*, 376. Sometimes Korzybski and his followers refer to a level between the submicroscopic and the macroscopic levels. This is the microscopic level where the details of the event are perceived by the aid of a microscope, telescope or other extra-neural aids created by science as an aid to our nervous system.

[66] This "psychological picture" level is absent from the diagrams of Johnson and Hayakawa which produce the ladder of abstraction. Cf. Johnson, *People in Quandaries*, p. 163, and Hayakawa, *Language in Thought and Action*, p. 169, and Lee, *Language Habits in Human Affairs*, p. 302.

[67] Korzybski, *Science and Sanity*, p. 384.

to at least five levels but indicates that *these levels can go on indefinitely* in man:

1. the "unspeakable" event, the scientific object (process) on the submicroscopic levels which constitute stimuli registered by our nervous systems as objects.

2. the external, objective, also unspeakable levels on which we see with our eyes and other senses.

3. the unspeakable psycho-logical pictures and semantic reactions.

4. verbal description of our facts-symbol reaction.

5. inferences followed by inferences about inferences, etc.[68]

The non-verbal or unspeakable abstractions made on macroscopic levels are called first order abstractions.[69] They are incomplete, personal, changeable and useful depending upon social agreement. Animals can perform these abstractions but can go no higher.[70]

Man can make higher-order abstractions which are called second-order facts or second-order abstractions. In this verbal level there are unlimited number of levels, beginning with description and going to inference, then inference about inference, etc. Science is a very high level of inference and yet, it must be noted that the very existence of the lowest level of all is a high-level scientific inference. Korzybski asserts this point, one which Black criticizes severely.[71]

Korzybski does not clearly distinguish between the first knowledge of the thing on man's level and the labelling of it. After describing the non-verbal levels of abstracting and showing that in daily life we abstract and according to the degree of intelligence and information, we summarize, he says this about the manner in which we arrive at the *"term" man*.

In the building of our language a similar neurological process becomes evident. If we were to see a series of

[68] *Ibid.*, p. 447.
[69] *Ibid.*, p. 445.
[70] *Ibid.*, p. 439.
[71] Korzybski, in *Perception*, p. 194 and Black, *Language*, p. 240.

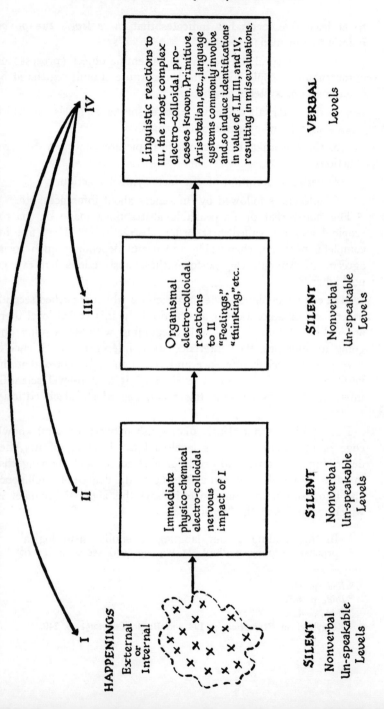

THE PROCESS OF ABSTRACTION FROM AN ELECTRO-COLLOIDAL NON-ARISTOTELIAN POINT OF VIEW.[77]

different individuals, whom we might call Smith, Brown, Jones, we could, by a process of abstracting the characteristics, segregate the individuals by sizes and colors. Then by concentration on one characteristic and disregarding the others, we could build classes or higher abstractions such as whites and blacks. . . . Abstracting again with the rejection of the color difference . . . we would finally reach the term 'man.' This procedure is general.[72]

The structural differential or a printed verbal diagram of it has appeared in the works of Hayakawa,[73] Johnson,[74] Lee,[75] and in modified form in the high school texts incorporating this idea of the levels of abstraction.[76] Korzybski also produced another diagram printed in his posthumous work, which reveals these levels and points out the dangers of confusing the different levels. The two diagrams will be reproduced on the following pages as a further clarification of this key notion of the general semantic movement.

As indicated in the foregoing diagram, Korzybski believes that Aristotelian languages have confused the levels of abstraction, especially the levels of III and IV. He quotes Whitehead as saying:

The fallacy of misplaced concreteness consists in neglecting the degree of abstracting involved when an actual entity is considered merely as far as it exemplifies certain categories of thought.[78]

Level IV in human life represents the "means for intercommunicating and transmitting from individual to individual and generation to generation the accumulated experiences of individuals and the race." He calls this human capacity the time-binding character-

---

[72] Korzybski, *Science and Sanity*, p. 377.
[73] Hayakawa, *Language in Thought and Action*, p. 169.
[74] Johnson, *People in Quandaries*, p. 163.
[75] Lee, *Language Habits in Human Affairs*, p. 202.
[76] See chapter IV, pp. 147-154.
[77] Korzybski, *Perception*, p. 173.
[78] Korzybski, *Science and Sanity*, p. 369.

istic.[79] These symbolic levels are the source of the differences between human reactions and the signal reactions of the lower forms
of life. If they are not properly verbalized and distinguished one
from another, confusion, chaos and faulty development result. The
remedy is *to train human beings to be conscious that they are
abstracting,* to be conscious of the different levels of abstraction
as well as of the fact that no reaction or response is identical with
the stimuli but always leaves something out. Thus we have the
two basic principles of the therapeutic aspect of general semantics:
Non-Identity and Non-Allness.

There is a slight difference in the use of these diagrams by the
various general semanticists. Korzybski stressed the dangers of
confusing verbal and non-verbal levels, of thinking that the word
is the thing, while his followers, especially Hayakawa, stress the
dangers of confusing the different levels of verbal abstractions
themselves, especially, the difference between description, or factual
report, and inference. The confusion on the verbal levels is also
stressed in the high school and college texts which have adopted
this idea in modified form. For educational purposes, too,
Hayakawa and others have incorporated some of the ideas of
Ogden and Richards concerning the difference between emotive
and informative language, persuasive and directive words.[81]

There is also a kind of ambivalence regarding the dangers and
the advantages of abstraction, at least in Korzybski's works. He
points out that abstraction takes one from reality because it leaves
out something of the event; the higher the order of abstraction,
the more of reality is left out. Science, however, is one of the
highest orders of abstraction, and, at the same time, the kind of
knowledge that Korzybski felt is needed in society today. He
realizes the necessity for abstracting from the absolute differences
present in every individual, in order to have knowledge of science.

> In our world of only absolute differences, without
> similarities, recognition and therefore intelligence would
> be impossible. In our work we start structurally close to
> nature (absolute individuals on objective levels), we make

---

[79] Korzybski, *Perception,* p. 175.

[81] S. I. Hayakawa, *Language in Action* (New York: Harcourt, Brace and
Co., 1941), p. 337.

ABSTRACTION LADDER [80]

Start reading from the bottom UP

VIII. "wealth"

VIII. The word "wealth" is at an extremely high level of abstraction, omitting *almost* all reference to the characteristics of Bessie.

VII. "asset"

VII. When Bessie is referred to as an "asset", still more of her characteristics are left out.

VI. "farm assets"

VI. When Bessie is included among "farm assets", reference is made only to what she has in common with all other salable items on the farm.

V. "livestock"

V. When Bessie is referred to as "livestock", only those characteristics she has in common with pigs, chickens, goats, etc., are referred to.

IV. "cow"

IV. The word "cow": stands for the characteristics we have abstracted as common to cow_1, cow_2, cow_3, ... cow_n. Characteristics peculiar to specific cows are left out.

III. "Bessie"

III. The word "Bessie" (cow_1): this is the *name* we give to the object of perception of level II. The name *is not* the object; it merely *stands for* the object and omits reference to many of the characteristics of the object.

II.

II. The cow we perceive: not the word, but the object of experience; that which our nervous system abstracts (selects) from the totality that constitutes the process-cow. Many of the characteristics of the process-cow are left out.

I. The cow known to science: ultimately consisting of atoms, electrons, etc., according to present-day scientific inference. Characteristics (represented by circles) are infinite at this level and ever-changing. This is the *process level*.

---

[80] Hayakawa, *Language in Thought and Action,* p. 169.

> differences fundamental, similarities appearing only at a
> later stage of higher abstractions.[82]

Science is the highest structural abstraction and the aim of education should be to put back into "the nervous circuits the beneficial
results of the highest abstraction." The minds of the children
must be trained to the higher order abstractions which look to the
past and the future and thus make minds more efficient.[83] It is,
then, not the *level* of abstraction that is causing the conflict and
error; it is the fact that people are not *aware* of the selective
nature of abstraction and of the various levels on which they are
abstracting.

Thus it is evident that this theory of abstraction applies to all
living organisms and describes the selective nature of the response
of organisms to stimuli. As a result, it is emphasized that the
reaction is never identical with nor equal to the stimulus. Man
alone can be aware of the different levels of orders of abstraction
and it is imperative that he do so in order to avoid the confusion
of levels which often characterize the reactions of primitive man
or of the infant. If there is continual identification—of levels of
abstraction, of words with objects, of descriptions with inferences,
disagreements and even maladjustment can and often result. Man
should be encouraged, however, to abstract on ever-higher and
higher levels since there is no limit to the number of levels he
can abstract upon, while animals can never reach the level of
science.

A more detailed examination of the general semantic theory of
the verbal levels of abstractions to see how they are symbolic of
the world in process and what meaning they convey must now
be made. In other words, the next topic is the theory of symbolism
and of meaning as presented by the general semanticists.

THE THEORY OF MEANING AND OF SYMBOLISM

The theory of meaning and of symbolism according to the general semantics system is a direct consequence of the premises

---

[82] Korzybski, *Science and Sanity*, p. 165, and p. 166. Similarity is structurally a manufactured article produced by the nervous system of the
observer.

[83] *Ibid.*, p. 483.

regarding the process world, man and abstraction which have just been presented. The chief idea in this theory may be termed the relative or relational character of meanings.[84] Meanings of things are relative for two reasons:

1. the world itself is only a structure of interrelated events. Therefore the only content of knowledge and of meaning is structural.[85]

2. meanings are the unique reactions of each individual nervous system—Each nervous system is unique; therefore, each reaction or meaning is unique, a composite of the affective, cognitive and abstractive activities of man.[86]

Korzybski claims that his whole non-Aristotelian system involves a new theory of meaning based on non-elementalistic semantics and considering "the neurological attitude toward meanings as the only structurally correct and useful one." This theory is an organic unity, according to Korzybski, since no matter which of the three basic principles concerning the nature of the world (that of order, non-identity or differentiation) we start with, we reach the same conclusions: rejection of the Aristotelian system of language and acceptance of the general semantic system of evaluation.[87]

If we start with the principle of order, that the world is an ordered structure, we recognize that the order concerns relations of objects, events, processes in a structure; this leads to the recognition of the differences between objects as well as their stratification. This, in turn, eliminates the tendency to identify objects and/or the levels of abstraction, or to think that we can know all of a process event. Thus, consciousness of abstracting and of the selective nature of human reactions to stimuli necessitates the acceptance of the theory of probability and of the infinite-valued general semantics instead of the either-or orientation of Aristotelianism.[88]

---

[84] Korzybski says in *Science and Sanity*, p. 751, "The only link between the non-verbal and verbal is in terms of relations. Relations are the sole content of human knowledge."

[85] Korzybski, *Science and Sanity*, p. 20 and p. 23.

[86] *Ibid.*, p. 23.

[87] *Ibid.*, pp. 751-760.

[88] *Ibid.*, p. 759.

Or we may start with the recognition of the scientific principle of non-identity—that is, that everything is constantly changing, that no two things are identical in all respects, and that no one thing is ever the same thing as itself. What is called structure is function taking place at a comparatively slow rate of change. Even symbolic expressions such as one is identical with one ($1 = 1$) do not represent sameness in all aspects. "Absolute sameness in all aspects would necessitate an identity of different nervous systems which produce and use these symbols, an identity of the different states of the nervous system of the person who wrote the above symbols, an identity of the surface, etc., of the different parts of the paper, in the distribution of the ink and what not. To demand such impossible conditions is of course absurd."[89] Acceptance of this principle of non-identity leads to a recognition that there is order among these non-identical things and in this process world, because things are ordered and related in a definite structure. Although our language and our knowledge cannot, because of its abstractive nature, include all about life facts, they can correspond to the structure of the relational world. But a subject-predicate language which considers objects as static and as having qualities in them, when they are really a result of the interaction of observer and observed, does not so correspond to the structure and the interrelatedness of the process world.[90]

> The meaning of meanings in a given case in a given individual at a given moment represent composite affective, psychological configurations of all relations pertaining to the case, colored by past experiences, state of health, mood of the moment and other contingencies. . . . From what has been said, we see that not only the structure of the world is such that it is made up of absolute individuals but that meanings in general and the mean-

---

[89] *Ibid.*, pp. 194-195. See below, pp. 129-130.

[90] Korzybski, *Science and Sanity*, p. 760. See also Wendell Johnson, *Your Most Enchanted Listener* (New York: Harper Bros., 1956), p. 150, in which he says: "That is why the subject-predicate form of sentence brings such trouble. It seems to make out that the speaker is talking solely about the world outside himself when he is talking about something going on inside himself. The grass is not green but his reaction to the grass is what he calls green."

ings of meanings in particular—the last representing probably the unspeakable first order effects—also share in common with ordinary objects the absolute individuality of the objective level.[91]

If man were conscious of the abstractive nature of our knowledge and of the relational character of the world, an either-or orientation would be rejected and the infinite-valued semantics would be adopted in which there were not only true and false statements but meaningless and indeterminate ones. Proper adjustment and evaluation, the aim of general semantics, would speedily follow.

In similar manner it can be shown that if we start with the principle of differentiation or stratification, we proceed to the principles of order, relation, structure, non-identification, non-allness, consciousness of abstracting and proper evaluation.[92]

Thus the relational character of man's knowledge, due to the relational character of the world and to the abstractive character of his reaction to the world, is consistent with the premises of general semantics. At this point, the twofold aspect of the problem of meaning must be discussed. Things have meanings and meanings are symbolized usually in words. Throughout the whole exposition of general semantics, there seems to be confusion over the two aspects. The problem of meaning seems to involve ideas and expressions of ideas or words (or definitions), and the distinction between the two often is not clear. For example, the three major principles of Korzybski: the map is not the territory, the map is not all of the territory and the map is self-reflexive, explicitly refer to words. And, as indicated in the ladder of abstraction,[93] there seems to be a gap between the reaction on the gross sense level and the labelling or naming of the object. This may be due to the fact that the semanticists are using the pragmatic theory that the meaning of a word lies exclusively in its practical effects on human behavior and not in any transcendental realm of ideas.[94] In fact, this confusion is evident in two statements. One of the more

---

[91] Korzybski, *Science and Sanity,* p. 23.

[92] *Ibid.,* p. 545.

[93] *Supra,* p. 49.

[94] *Supra,* p. 4.

recent books on general semantics says: "we regard our *knowl-edge* as a map . . . and we cannot know anything. We can only know our *ideas (maps)* about things."[95] While Korzybski says: "Any *map or language* must be similar in structure," etc.[96]

What corresponds to the traditional idea of the meaning of a thing as distinguished from the meaning of a word labelling that thing may be the general semanticist's so called "semantic re-action." This is the psychological aspect of meaning that he considers here. The epistemological aspect is considered in the dis-cussion of definitions, truth and meaningless words and state-ments. We will consider both aspects beginning with the "semantic reaction," i.e., how does man *get* the meaning, as distinguished from how he *expresses* the meaning.

Korzybski designates all psychophysiological reactions to stimuli involving meanings as semantic reactions.

> A semantic reaction can be described as the psycho-logical reaction of a given individual to words and lan-guage and other symbols and events in connection with their meanings and the psychological reactions which be-come meanings and relational configurations the moment the given individual begins to analyze them or someone else does it for him. It is of great importance to realize that the term semantic is non-elementalistic as it involves conjointly the emotional as well as the intellectual factors.[97]

And again, a semantic reaction is

> a psychological response to a stimulus in connection with meaning, this response being expressed by a number of such words as 'implies,' 'follows,' 'becomes,' 'evokes,' 'feels,' 'reacts,' 'evaluates,' and many others.[98]

When the reaction is undelayed, automatic, without consciousness

---

[95] Zollette, *Basic Principles,* p. 28 (italics ours).

[96] Korzybski, *Science and Sanity,* p. 11; also Hayakawa, *Language in Thought and Action,* pp. 31-32.

[97] Korzybski, *Science and Sanity,* p. 24.

[98] *Ibid.,* p. 26.

of the abstracting nature of our reaction to the stimulus, it is termed *signal reaction* and is similar to the reaction of animals to their signs. When, however, the response is delayed to give time to remember the levels of abstraction and to evaluate the symbol, it is termed a symbol *reaction*. This reaction, both symbol and signal, includes the reaction of the whole organism,—'body'- 'mind'- 'emotions.'[99] Every symbol too, not merely represents the external world but also represents the reaction of the observer to the observed. It is the *internal* affair, not the events outside the nervous system, that we transfer into words or other symbols, fictitious entities—privately filtered through our nervous system.[100] All of the work of getting or giving proper semantic reactions for human beings depends on the integrity of the cortex.

> in general, one of the most important functions of the cerebral cortex is that of reacting to innumerable stimuli of invariable significance which act as signals in animals and symbols in humans and give means of very subtle adjustment of the organism to the environment. In psychological terms, we speak of 'associations,' 'selection,' 'intelligence'; in mathematical terms of 'relations,' structure,' 'order'; in psycho-physiological terms of 'semantic reactions.'[101]

Whether or not this semantic reaction is the meaning of the process event, as distinct from the word which designates the meaning, is not clear. It is difficult to find out whether the general semanticists hold for two steps in symbolization or one—i.e., that the meaning of an event as known by a person, symbolizes the event; in turn, the meaning is symbolized by the word. Korzybski does not spend any words or time on stressing the fact that our *knowledge* is not identical with the event. His great emphasis is on the fact that the *word* is not identical with the event. His reform is more of the language than of the meanings as received by each man. Thus the inquiry of general semantics into the problem of meaning veers down the path of language and the

---

[99] *Ibid.,* pp. 24-26.
[100] Wendell Johnson, *Your Most Enchanted Listener,* p. 171.
[101] Korzybski, *Science and Sanity,* p. 333.

adequacy of language to transmit meanings of things. Meanings as *known* before they are *expressed* by human beings seem to have been by-passed.

The next consideration, then, will be of language as expressive of or symbolic of meaning. The three basic premises of the general semantics movement regarding this aspect of meaning are, as shown above:

1. words are not things—or the map is not the territory
2. words are not all the things—or the map is not all the territory
3. words are self-reflexive.

The inadequacy of language can be remedied by borrowing certain devices from mathematics, which Korzybski maintains is the ideal language. This conviction is based on the fact that everything in the world is an absolute unique individual and that similarities are the result of abstraction.[102] Now mathematics can represent uniqueness by numbers 1, 2, 3 and similarities by making these numbers subscripts to letters, e.g., x_1, x_2, x_3.[103] This language is similar to the world which is full of absolutely different individuals and to our nervous system which makes the higher abstractions or generalization essential in order to act humanly.

Korzybski suggests that certain devices should be used to clarify the present language. To indicate that things are not the same from hour to hour and year to year, he suggests subscripts of dates. "Smith$_{1940}$ is not Smith$_{1957}$." To avoid identification of the word with the thing he suggests using subscripts 1, 2, 3. American$_1$ is not the same as American$_2$ so that to say "Americans spend money lavishly" should be clarified to indicate what Americans and where and when. To avoid the tendency to think we have said all about a thing, and to cultivate the non-allness which consciousness of abstracting should bring about, he advocates using "etc." after most statements. His followers sometimes advocate such devices but more often advocate merely the *habit of mind* brought about by thinking that these devices were attached to the

---

[102] Korzybski, *Perception*, p. 190.
[103] Korzybski, *Science and Sanity*, p. 262.

words being read or heard or spoken. Such devices, however, are merely practical applications of the theory of meaning as applied to language.

A more pertinent aspect of this theory is the discussion over meaningless words. This involves discussion of the distinction between symbol and sign, and of the process by which words acquire meanings as well as that process by which man acquires the meanings of certain *words*.[104]

Wendell Johnson lists the steps by which communication occurs. His graphic representation of it shows its relation to the information theory and to cybernetics.[105]

But recently Allen Read advocated a more restricted use of the term "meaning." He offered the following conclusions:

> 1. the retaining of the word "meaning" for use in the abstract generalized application describing a necessary component of the data of language itself is justifiable.
> 2. Beyond this one application, however, the word "meaning" seems to cause havoc and confusion wherever it is used. It can hardly be used without implying structurally that a mentalistic entity corresponds to a form. Such mentalistic entities are beyond the reach of scientific investigation. Instead, we have to find some formulation that makes investigation possible.
> 3. in the study of the lexicon, there should be reemphasis on context and the function of symbols in personal and social situations. The listings of meanings in the dictionaries sets verbal patterns that create entities out of symbolical relationships.

------

[104] This whole problem is still under consideration by scientists. Osgood on page 681 in his *Method and Theory in Experimental Psychology* (New York: Oxford University Press, 1953) indicates the difficulty which may well lie at the base of the vagueness of the theory of the general semanticists concerning meaning: "What lies behind all this expelling of air through conformations of the vocal apparatus? What is lacking in this mechanical monstrosity? Meaning must be brought into the picture somehow, and here's the rub—*meaning has no accepted material correlate*. If we are to hold to our materialistic moorings, we must postulate material events for meaning and then investigate the theoretical consequences of this postulation." (Italics ours.)

[105] Wendell Johnson, *People in Quandaries*, p. 472.

GRAPHIC REPRESENTATION OF THE PROCESS OF COMMUNICATION
ACCORDING TO WENDELL JOHNSON

1. An event occurs

2. which stimulates Mr. A through eyes, ears, or other sensory organs, and the resulting

3. nervous impulses travel to Mr. A's brain, and from there to his muscles and glands, producing tensions, preverbal "feelings", etc.

4. which Mr. A then begins to translate into words, according to his accustomed verbal patterns, and out of all the words he "thinks of"

5. he "selects" or abstracts certain ones which he arranges in some fashion, and then

by means of sound waves

and light waves

Mr. A speaks to Mr. B

6. whose ears and eyes are stimulated by the sound waves and light waves, respectively, and the resulting

7. nervous impulses travel to Mr. B's brain, and from there to his muscles and glands, producing tensions, preverbal "feelings", etc.

8. which Mr. B then begins to translate into words according to *his* accustomed verbal patterns, and out of all the words *he* "thinks of"

9. he "selects" or abstracts certain ones which he arranges in some fashion, and then

Etc. Mr. B speaks, or acts, accordingly, thereby stimulating Mr. A—or somebody else—and so the process of communication goes on, and on —

4. in syntax, too, the term "structural meaning" has its dangers in appearing to establish entities. Greater reliance on words like relation and function serve to put analysis on a sounder basis.

5. In areas beyond linguistics, such phrases as "the meaning of life" or "the meaning of it all" have a hallowed dedicated ring about them. If they are to be transmuted into usable formulations, the terms evaluation and orientation represent a sounder approach.[106]

MEANING, SYMBOLISM, AND MEANINGLESSNESS

Meaning is inextricably bound up with symbolism according to Korzybski. For symbols are signs which stand for something. There are two kinds of existence—the physical existence, of which our senses become aware, and logical existence, defined by Poincaré as a statement free from self-contradiction. In order for a thought to be a thought, it must be free of self-contradiction. If it is self-contradictory, it has no logical existence. It is meaningless. Symbols too can be meaningless when they do not stand for anything. They are then meaningless signs. Now, according to the general semanticists, not all the so-called words we utter can be considered as symbols or as valid words. They are empty noises when they do not refer to anything so far as the external world is concerned. We must distinguish between words, that is true symbols which symbolize something, and noises which do not symbolize anything and therefore have no meaning. The foundations of many old philosophies contain meaningless noises since the noises did not stand for anything. Now disputes can be settled only if we use words (symbols for something). From the meaningless noises of the old philosophies many useless arguments arose.[107]

This idea that some noises which we consider words are in actuality mere noises because they either have no physical existence since they do not represent something in the external world, or have no logical existence, since they are self-contradictory, explains the emphasis of the general semanticists on the operational

---

[100] Allen Walker Read, "The Term Meaning in Linguistics," *Etc.*, XIII, 1 (Autumn, 1955), p. 45.

[107] Korzybski, *Science and Sanity*, p. 382.

and extensional definition as the basis for arriving at the true meaning of a word.[108] The whole section on definition is of great educational importance as will be shown in chapter IV. The practical applications will be indicated briefly here.

There are three types of definitions which are considered to be the most important: the intensional, the extensional and the operational definitions. General semantics deals with the last two. The intensional definitions, according to the general semanticists, are based on verbalizations, associations, with disregard for observation. They are couched in subject-predicate language which ignores relations, differences and the asymmetrical relation between observer and observed.[109] The so-called intensional definitions or concepts are far removed from reality and are only words about words; they are nominal or verbal, emphasizing connotations. They are really definitions by postulation, with no facts secured by empirical science. Man can fixate the essence of an entity by definition and by this process the realities which are fundamentally functional or behavioral facts of nature are reified into substantial, self-identical things.[110] (The intensional definition consisted of the qualities possessed by an object; since today science does not recognize qualities as possessed by objects, these definitions are meaningless.) These definitions, then, rarely indicate things in existence; frequently they are meaningless.

On the other hand, the extensional meaning consists of the objects to which the term may be applied. Extensional definitions are verbalized only after observation and investigation. The extensional method is the only method which is in accordance with the structure of the world and of our nervous system, and is, therefore, necessary for survival. In extensional definitions, denotation is emphasized; these are real definitions since they are definitions by inspection based on facts derived from empirical science.[111] However, since we refer our thoughts to the world of

---

[108] *Ibid.*, p. 173.
[109] *Ibid.*, p. 172.
[110] *Ibid.*, p. 176.
[111] *Ibid.*, p. 175.

concrete objects, words and symbols must denote as well as connote. We must be both intensional and extensional.[112]

Operational definitions are really certain types of extensional
definitions whereby we define a thing by telling what to do to
experience the thing defined, e.g., the definition of a cake is its
recipe. It was first described by P. W. Bridgman as it was used
in physics,[113] and has been elaborated on by the general semanticists. Anatol Rapoport claims that the consequences of the
operational definition as a criterion of meaning are at the root
of the semantic approach to the theory of knowledge and could
be said to constitute what he calls scientific semantics.[114] The
semanticist prefers the extensional definition, either operational
or by enumeration, since it succeeds most effectively in bridging
the gap between words and experience.

> Another great advantage in making definitions by ex-
> hibiting an example is that one cannot define fictions that
> way. Just try to define Jabberwocky or the First Cause
> by pointing to something to see how sticking to defini-
> tions by exhibiting an example protects you from be-
> lieving in ghosts.[115]

It also prevents sterility because failure to keep in mind that
meaning means the link between words and experience has been
at the root of the sterility of most traditional philosophies.[116]
Rapoport notes, however, that the search for meaningfulness is
the search for invariance amid change. Most systems of reality
have either never defined the invariances upon which their meaningfulness depends, or have defined them in terms not readily re-
portable. Stable invariants are reality. To determine the reality

---

[112] Oliver Reiser, "Non-Aristotelian Systems and General Semantics,"
Papers from the First American General Semantics Congress, ed. Hansell
Baugh (New York: Arrow Editions, 1938), p. 37.

[113] P. W. Bridgman, *The Logic of Modern Physics* (New York: The
Macmillan Co., 1932).

[114] Anatol Rapoport, "Semantics: The Problem of Meaning," *American
Philosophy,* p. 66.

[115] Rapoport, *Science and the Goals of Men,* p. 57.

[116] A. Rapoport, *Operational Philosophy* (New York: Harper and Bros.,
1953), p. 18.

of every term is done by giving an operational definition of it which will then connect it to commonly shared experiences. The meaningfulness of the term is measured by the extent to which the experience it represents has been or can be shared in experience.[117] In other words, to use the terminology of Ogden and Richards, words must have referents in experience in order to be meaningful.

While extensional definitions apply only to the here and now existent, intensional definitions are even more limited. They tell us nothing about things, are obtainable only by logical analysis, and are therefore only linguistic habits, statements about language, "what noises people make under certain conditions."[118] Definitions are formal truths, not factual truths.[119]

But not all words can or should be defined. All language systems and, of course, all mathematical systems, depend ultimately on a few undefined terms. All language can be considered as names for entities which, in reality, are relations between the entity and the human nervous system, or as names for all other types of relations. Now despite the fact that, in theory, Korzybski decries the use of definitions, he admits they are necessary. A man, John, cannot communicate to another man, Bill, exactly what he abstracts unless Bill knows the meaning of the symbol or word which John uses to symbolize this abstraction. The meaning must be given by a definition, the meaning of which in turn must be given by another definition. Soon a set of terms must be reached which could not be further defined because of lack of words. In all linguistic schemes the meaning of a word depends on the meaning of other words defining it and this relation ultimately depends on the "multi-ordinality of the undefined terms which at a given point cannot be elucidated further."[120]

There is no escape from the fact that we must start with undefined terms which express silent structural creeds or metaphysics. If we state our undefined terms explicitly

---

[117] *Ibid.*, p. 26.

[118] Hayakawa, *Language in Thought and Action*, p. 1.

[119] *Ibid.*, p. 171.

[120] Korzybski, *Science and Sanity*, p. 21.

we at least make our metaphysics conscious and public and so we facilitate criticism and cooperation. The modern undefined scientific terms such as "order" for instance, underlie the exact sciences and our wider world outlook. We must start with these undefined terms as well as the modern structural world outlook as given by science 1933. That settles the important semantic point of our structural metaphysics.[121]

Rapoport concludes that on the basis of the undefined terms, *structure, order* and *relations,* as well as on the idea of *predictability,* a positivist conception of the universe, including man, is formulated by the general semanticists.[122]

Not only are there undefined terms in the general semantics theory of meaning but there are what are termed, "multi-ordinal terms." These are words which have no meanings of themselves but only in context. In different contexts or on different levels of abstraction, they have different meanings, analogous meanings. Some of these words are: 'yes,' 'no,' 'true,' 'false,' 'existence,' 'is,' 'relation,' 'knowing,' etc. We must also be conscious of the different contextual meanings of multi-ordinal terms which seem to be symbolic of no one thing.

Thus it would seem that the meanings of words or other symbols are best given according to experienced objects or processes, by enumeration, description, and, in the case of multi-ordinal terms, by context. Yet even then, they involve the emotional as well as the intellectual factors and ultimately lead to undefined terms. Meanings are really semantic reactions analyzed or recognized, and, as such, they are psycho-physical. This is an extremely important point regarding the general semantic theory of meaning. Meanings or statements evoke emotional as well as intellectual responses or reflexes. When these responses last, they are called semantic states. Ultimately the meanings to each individual depend on the racial meanings called science which he receives through the influence of education, environment, language and structure. Hence these racial meanings called science become

---

[121] *Ibid.,* p. 373.
[122] Anatol Rapoport, "The Criterion of Predictability," *Etc.,* II, 3 (Spring. 1945), p. 135.

physiological semantic factors of the reaction. As Pollock describes the process:

> We may now define the meaning of a symbol bearing in mind the fact that symbols are both uttered and heard. From the point of view of the speaker, a symbol's meaning is the psycho-physiological experience of which the utterance is the conditional response. From the point of view of the hearer, the symbol's meaning is the conditional response of which the symbol is the stimulus. The meaning of the symbol DOG is thus the psycho-physiological experience which leads an individual to utter the word dog as well as the conditional response which the sound or sight or thought of the word dog evokes in an individual. To say that a sign has meaning for an individual in these days is thus simply a verbal short cut for the statement that the individual is conditioned to respond to or with the sign. . . . Semantic reaction is the conditioned response of a human being to or with verbal signs.[123]

Later on he asks: "How does a sign come to have meaning for the individuals in a speech community?" and answers: "because a number of individuals are conditioned to respond in similar ways to the same sign."[124] But he questions whether, strictly speaking, on theoretical grounds, any two members of a speech community ever acquire the same response exactly to any sign, because it is impossible for two individuals to have the same psycho-physiological structure and history. A person knows a word if his semantic reaction is somewhat similar to the reaction of the others in the speech group who react in a similar way. Thus he maintains that "a major part of the reality of language lies not in external signs but in the experience of human beings by whom the signs are produced and received."[125]

As is evident, this stress on the emotive factor in meaning is similar to the emphasis put on emotive language, as distinguished

---

[123] Thomas E. Pollock, *The Nature of Literature* (Princeton: Princeton University Press, 1942), p. 38.
[124] *Ibid.*, p. 44.
[125] *Ibid.*, pp. 46-47. Cf. supra, pp. 120-122.

from referential language, by C. K. Ogden and I. A. Richards, in *The Meaning of Meaning*. Korzybski referred to this book several times in a favorable way in *Science and Sanity*.[126] The Basic Englishers, as Ullman calls them, stress the intension of words while the general semanticists stress the extension of words, but both groups are aware of both aspects. Snowden Arthur shows the similarities between the famous triangle of Ogden and Richards and Korzybski's structural differential by opening out the triangle.

1. The symbol or word of Ogden and Richards becomes the label of Korzybski.

2. The thought or reference is similar to the abstracted characteristics in the structural differential—really the intension of the object.

3. The referent represents extension and the object of the structural differential.

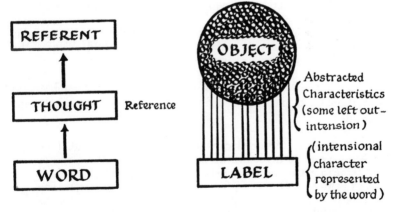

Arthur thinks that Korzybski's analysis is clearer inasmuch as his diagram shows that some characteristics are left out and some are left in, while the triangle does not show either the omission nor what is included.[127] But although Ogden and Richards condemned the definitions of the scholastics according to genus and

---

[126] Korzybski, *Science and Sanity*, pp. 33, 52, 542, 763.

[127] Snowden Arthur, *Vocabulary, Semantics and Intelligence* (Bethesda, Maryland: Lexicon Press, 1952), pp. 36-62.

specific difference, still they wished to give definitions merely in terms of more basic words. They never indicated that, no matter how you define a word intensionally, this definition, according to other words, consists of fundamental characteristics as abstracted by human beings.

We now come to some practical examples given by the general semanticists, of what they consider to be meaningless words or statements and what they consider to be truth and the criterion of truth—two considerations which flow from the theory of meaning as being operationally defined. Although, as shown before, many words are mere noises, strictly speaking, even noises or signs represent some symbolism. The task is to find out in which of the three possible fields the symbolism applies. A symbol carrying its meaning in one field will often be a mere noise in another field. The three fields in which we find symbols are:

1. that of chemistry; physics, or physiology.
2. that of psycho-logics which contains events within our skin or semantic reactions.
3. the pathological field belonging to psychiatry which contains semantic disturbances and to which "we would relegate the older metaphysics of every description."[128]

There are some very practical consequences of the emphasis on operational and extensional definitions as the following quotations indicate:

> To be sure the devil can be extensionally defined. One can point to a picture of one. But this definition is not equivalent to the usual extensional definitions of the devil (Prince of Darkness, Tempter of Humanity, etc.). The term is therefore meaningless because no connection can be established between its verbal definitions and direct experience. . . .
> If you ask many people whether they believe in hell, they will say 'yes.' Many people guide their actions in accordance with a desire to avoid going to hell. So hell is real to them. Therefore it does have some measure of reality.
> Indeed the person who defines hell in this way is ad-

---

[128] Korzybski, *Science and Sanity*, pp. 138-139.

hering to our standards of operational definition. We did imply that any definition is acceptable which connects the term with some observable events in space and time. People's behavior certainly consists of observable events. Therefore an operational definition of hell must be admitted to have been given. There is no argument there. Any term may be arbitrarily defined that is connected with any class of events whatsoever. We allow complete freedom of definition because we recognize that words do not have an inherent meaning. But once one has committed himself to a level of discourse by giving a definition, one must stick to that level. And if one does that, one will find that the way to avoid 'going to hell' is simply not to react to the word as if it stood for anything other than fiction. *The person most important for 'salvation' then becomes the semanticist instead of the priest.*[129]

A similar change takes place in the meaning of truth. In fact there is no longer the two-valued system of either true or false but a four-valued system consisting of true, false, meaningless and indeterminate statements. A statement containing meaningless noises and a propositional function both have a common semantic characteristic: neither of them can be true or false. A propositional function is an infinite-valued statement with one or more variables so that, when single values are assigned to these variables, the expression becomes, in principle, a one-valued proposition. Any statement can mean anything according to the values we here and now give to the terms. Any word also has meaning or is meaningless according to the experience here and now which it represents. There is no meaning for absolute truth, since there can be no extensional definition of truth, just as there are no statements absolutely true or absolutely false. We must define truth operationally according to our knowledge of the moment. The truth value of my assertion changes as the state of my knowledge changes.[130] There are at least four senses of the word *True:*

1. Some mushrooms are poisonous. (If we call this true, it means that it is a report and can be and has been verified.)
2. Sally is the sweetest girl in the world. (If we call this true, it means that we feel the same way towards Sally.)

---

[129] Rapoport, *Science and the Goals of Man,* pp. 158-159. (Italics ours.)
[130] *Ibid.,* p. 160.

3. All men are created equal. (If we call this true, it means that this is a directive which we believe should be obeyed.)

4. (x plus y)^2 equals x^2 plus 2xy plus y^2 (If we call this true it means that this statement is consistent with the system of statements possible to be made in the language called algebra.[131]

Truth is only a sound or set of ink-marks until you define it. One can define it as whatever the leader says is true, what society agrees upon or as what predicts most accurately.[132] As "we recognized the multi-ordinality of words, *truth* becomes as nonsensical as most noisy lines in *Alice in Wonderland*."[133] Eternal verities last only so long as the human nervous system is not altered. Philosophers formulated a two-valued logic and a confusion of the orders of abstraction so that under their influence nearly all men contracted a firm predilection for general statements, universal, as they were called.[134] "Absolute truth is meaningless because no definition of it can be agreed upon."[135]

> We must define truth operationally. Since time-binding makes possible a constant extension of our repertoire of operations, truth is not static or absolute. The world is a dynamic state of affairs and our knowledge about it is always changing. . . . One cannot expect therefore any assertion about the world to retain its truth value as the state of our knowledge changes. No assertion tells all about the world or any portion of it. . . . The truth value of an assertion is measured by how much you are able to predict on the basis of it. In the literature of general semantics, this notion of truth is referred to as the criterion of predictability. . . . To speak the truth means to predict well. . . .[136]

There is a difference between validity and truth-proper. The validity is determined by the relation to a set of assertions and is

[131] Hayakawa, *Language in Thought and Action,* pp. 292-293.
[132] Rapoport, Answer, *Etc.,* VII, 3 (Spring, 1950), pp. 237-238.
[133] Johnson, *People in Quandaries,* p. 157.
[134] Hayakawa, *Language in Thought and Action,* p. 292.
[135] Rapoport, *Science and the Goals of Men,* p. 160.
[136] *Ibid.,* p. 161.

logically derived with no reference to anything in the material world. The material truth of a statement depends on its material consequences. An assertion is operationally true if all three of the following conditions are met:

1. the assertion implies predictions to be tested by conceivable operations. If not, it is meaningless.

2. the operations have been carried out to test the predictions. If not, it is an indeterminate statement.

3. the predictions have been verified by the operations. If not, the assertion is false. If so, the assertion is true and thus we have four different kinds of assertions instead of the two under the Aristotelian system.[137, 138]

The modern concept of truth, then, depends on no transcendental realm of ideas but ultimately on practicality and universal agreement.

> Intellectual problems are ultimately problems of classification and nomenclature. Society regards as true those systems of classification that produce desired results. . . . The scientific test of truth is . . . strictly practical except that the desired results are more severely limited. . . . Science seeks only the most generally useful systems of classification; these it regards, for the time being, until more useful classifications are invented, as true.[139, 140]

---

[137] Rapoport, *Operational Philosophy,* p. 33.

[138] Cf. Alfred Tarski, "The Semantic Conception of Truth and the Foundations of Semantics," *Philosophical and Phenomenological Research,* IV (March, 1941), 342-345, as found in Irving J. Lee, *The Language of Wisdom and Folly* (New York: Harper and Bros., 1949), pp. 67-71 (background readings in semantics).

[139] Hayakawa, *Language in Thought and Action,* pp. 215-217.

[140] Rapoport in his answer to a criticism of his article on "The Criterion of Predictability," *Etc.,* VII (Spring, 1950), pp. 238-239, says: "The emphasis on the relativistic aspects of general semantics is in accordance with the demonstrations of general semantics on the existence of higher invariants rather than on the unqualified relativity of standards. . . . This criterion of higher invariance does not have to be included into the notion of the relativity of truth values. But if it is not included, then the agreement aspect of truth must be abandoned and if it is abandoned what is left? If

Thus symbolism is .of the greatest importance to the general semanticists who are concerned with the idea that "man's greatness and madness rest on his preoccupation with symbols." Good semantic behavior is governed by semantic awareness of the distinction between:

1. symbol and referent or word and thing or map and territory
2. inference and observation
3. valid conclusion and factually true statement
4. the distortions brought by generalizations to our percept.[141]

The emphasis on the return to the actual existent, on the pragmatic value of statements or on the predictability value of the statement leads to the sanest type of behavior because it means "that the neural processes are most closely adjusted to the structure of the universe."[142]

> "Love thy Neighbor" has not been successful as a guide to behavior not because it is contrary to human nature but because it has not yet been defined in terms of behavior on the colloidal level.[143]

At least three general consequences flow from this emphasis on extensional definitions and predictability in order to secure meaning. First, many of the old questions are now meaningless:

> For thousands of years, millions upon millions of humans have used a great deal of their nervous energy in worrying upon delusional questions forced upon them by the pernicious 'is of identity,' such as 'What *is* an object?,' 'What *is* life?,' 'What *is* hell?,' 'What *is* heaven?,' 'What *is* space?,' 'What *is* time?,' and an endless array

---

we wish to keep the agreement aspect we must look for suitable (universal) invariants of the truth notion. Predictability is one proposed by logical positivists and by several general semanticists. The choice has been inspired not so much by moralistic considerations as by pragmatic ones—it works."

[141] Anatol Rapoport, "The Role of Symbols in Human Behavior," *Etc.*, XII, 3 (Spring, 1955), p. 186. Cf. also Korzybski, *Science and Sanity*, p. 84.
[142] Anatol Rapoport, "The Criterion of Predictability," *Etc.*, II (Spring, 1945), p. 135.
[143] *Ibid.*, pp. 135-136.

of such irritants. The answer, based on the human dis-
scriminations of orders of abstractions and so proper
human evaluation, is definite, undeniable, simple and
unique: 'Whatever one might say something' *is,* '*it is not.*'
Whatever we might say belongs to the verbal level and
not to the unspeakable, objective levels.[144]

Second, words can change their meanings and should change
with growing knowledge. Even the most time-honored ones can
and should change. An article by Stuart Carter Dodd in *Etc.* illus-
trates this with regard to three words which are basic in physics,
metaphysics and religion: *time, quality,* and *God.*[145] As he said, a
major thesis in semantics is that the symbols we use for viewing
phenomena largely mold our views. Sometimes, however, it is
necessary to shift either the symbols or their referents while keeping the other constant, or, in other words, changing the name
without changing the meaning or changing the meaning without
changing the name. We will here present his application of this
idea to the word God. His thesis is: Whether God is the chief
force in man's life or not depends on our viewing symbols which
unify or separate God and what we worship.

What men work for and live for defines their goals in
life or what in fact they believe to be good.
Suppose instead of current religious methods of determining 'the good' based on tradition largely, we follow
the semantic method based on more factual research. Re-
ligionists tend to say, "God is defined by such and such
characteristics. Let us worship this God." But semanticists might say, "Whatever we want most in life can be
symbolized by the word God. Let us study men's wants
and then go on to glorify this God. There would be no
need to urge people to worship this most wanted good
for everyone worships this God and only this God now.
The whole problem of religion shifts to making people
want the best and highest goals in life, thus glorifying
their God.[146]

---

[144] Korzybski, *Science and Sanity,* p. 408.
[145] Stuart Carter Dodd, "Three Semantic Exercises: Time, Quality and
'God,'" *Etc.,* XI, 1 (Autumn, 1953), pp. 41-48.
[146] *Ibid.,* p. 45.

There are many beneficial results from this symbolization of man's goals by the word *God;* most important of all is that there will be more agreement on the ultimate ends in human life. Among other results, he feels the following would accrue:

1. this God would become the chief force in man's life
2. this God would be humanity's system of values or goals.
3. this God or system of human goals could be observed and studied by scientific methods.
4. this God would unify religion and science. Science would become one vast research for God
5. this God could be taught in public schools as other sciences. Uncertainty is the alternative hypothesis.
6. this God would evolve slowly while semantic shifts are incomplete. God would grow as man's view grows.
7. this God would reduce the gap between standards as professed and practiced.
8. this God would not be a single unitary entity—but appear as a system of values as sometimes reflected in a frequency distribution from polls.

One of the major problems of science and religion would be then "raising our ends periodically as we reach them, aspiring toward a nobler god."[147]

A third practical consequence is exemplified by an experimental study,[148] and indirectly reveals that the general semanticists' emphasis on the relativity of truth leads to the assertion of the falsity of some statements of great importance to the Christian educator. Weiss' study aimed to test empirically the principles of general semantics and claims to have given evidence of their validity. The chief test was that of 'the *is* of identity,' i.e., that when the structure of the language used by an individual is dissimilar to the structure of the world and the individual is unaware of the dissimilarity, the individual misevaluates and becomes maladjusted. The test consisted of one hundred and six questions which were supposed to be '*is* of identity' questions. The answers to all were false, although the testees did not know this, and Weiss ascer-

---

[147] Dodd, *Etc.,* XI, 1 (Autumn, 1953), pp. 47-48.
[148] Weiss, *An Experimental Study Applying Non-Aristotelian Principles.*

tained that an all-false test did not lessen the validity of the test and is not discovered frequently enough to make a statistically significant difference.[149] He assumed that in process reality, there is no excluded middle. "It is apparent, then, that there is no true or false statement in the absolute sense. True and false are evaluations or judgments which occur inside the skin of the observer."[150] The test was aimed at discovering whether the testee was aware "that there is no absolute standard of truth." Instructions required that the testees mark as false all answers that were not *always* true. "Since in process reality, there is no allness and identity, there can be no always-true response; that is, there cannot be in the world outside our skins."[151] The test was given to a sample of the adolescent population in Lansing—to about two hundred and fifty boys and girls in Lansing Public High Schools and to about two hundred and fifty individuals in correctional institutions in the same area. The criterion of adjustment was teacher-rating as to adjustment and diagnostic ratings as well as the IQ and Mooney scores. Weiss felt that it was safe to conclude the following from his study:

> The results of this study seem to imply that the principles of general semantics which underlie this investigation are sound. They seem to imply further that the reasoning based on these principles is correct, namely that when the structure of the language used by an individual is dissimilar to the structure of the real world and the individual is unaware of the dissimilarity it can lead him into misevaluation and consequent maladjustment.[152]

2. there were no significant differences found between the means of the "is of identity" test scores, and age, sex, church attendance, diagnostic and prognostic ratings, self-ratings categories.

3. a person's use of the "is of identity" is connected with his degree of adjustment to society. This is based on findings that

---

[149] *Ibid.*, p. 34.
[150] *Ibid.*, p. 35.
[151] *Ibid.*, p. 36.
[152] *Ibid.*, p. 78.

institutional boys do use the *"is* of identity" to a greater degree than non-institutional boys as evidenced by the lower mean score on the *"is* of identity test."[153]

Of greater interest to the present study than either the statistical procedures or the conclusions are the questions asked. It must be remembered that Weiss considered *all* of them false, either because they were always false or because they were not always true. Some of them are reproduced here. Those with special implications for the teacher are italicized. The children tested were unaware of the "correct" answers. But these questions are given as an example of the conclusions to which general semantic theory can lead its followers.

Some selected questions from the Weiss Study:

Those you believe to be not always true fill in the dotted lines in the false column. Those always true are to be checked in on the dotted lines in the true column. (According to Weiss, *all* should be marked *FALSE*.)[154]

1. A statement is either true or false.
2. Mules are stubborn.
3. A pig is a dirty animal.
4. *God is everywhere.*
5. A boy who won't fight is a coward.
8. The word dog—is a four-footed animal.
11. A boy who never lies is good.
16. *Adam and Eve were the first human beings.*
17. It takes two to make a bargain.
18. *He that believeth not shall be damned.*
19. The good die young.
20. *There is one basic cause for all effects.* (this violates the general infinite valued notion of causality)
22. Humans can talk.
23. No one wants to die.
24. Americans are not communists.
30. What goes up must come down.
33. A circle is round.
36. A leaf is green.
40. The sky is blue.

---

[153] *Ibid.,* p. 76.
[154] *Ibid.,* p. 91.

45. A house is either frame or brick.
46. A drunkard is a sinner.
48. Everything that is true can be proved.
52. *Everyone is an image of God.*
53. Two heads are better than one.
54. *God is everything good.*
55. A good man never cheats.
56. We must be Christian to be saved.
59. Love is blind.
60. *Jesus was all things to all men.*
64. A mother is the holiest thing alive.
65. All children should be Christians.
67. Prayer is the voice of faith.
70. All socialism threatens democracy.
71. Freedom of speech is good.
72. Anyone who talks against our country should be imprisoned.
75. The voice of the people is the voice of God.
76. We live in the best of all possible worlds.
77. Russia is the worst country in the world.
78. It is never all right to kill.
81. Children should always obey their parents.
86. Telling dirty jokes is bad.
82. Children are born bad.
92. *Better a clean soul than a clean body.*
93. *The Bible is the greatest source of truth.*
95. Love is holy.

SUMMARY ON THE THEORY OF MEANING AND OF SYMBOLISM

I. *The Way Man Secures the Meaning of Things*—By semantic reaction and abstraction.

1. These semantic reactions are not purely intellectual but are of the whole man, including emotional factors as well.

2. These reactions are responses of the nerve organism set up by electrical currents—a type of colloidal behavior which abstracts certain things from the stimuli.

3. Therefore, meanings are not identical existentially with the stimuli. They do correspond but not note for note, in order to be physical reproductions of stimuli. When they are so considered by man, the individual makes wrong judgments, gets into conflicts, and becomes maladjusted.

II. *The Meaning of Words*

1. Words do not fully represent the reality they symbolize.

2. Some words are in reality mere noises since they have no existential correlate.

3. Extensional and operational definitions are the best correlates of reality because they have the smallest gap between them and experience.

4. For the same reason, predictability is the best criterion of truth.

5. Words can change their meanings; and ideas represented by words can change (e.g., the meaning of God).

6. Statements are never always true, but change as society's knowledge changes. The principle of uncertainty or probability in language is the result of the discrepancy between absolute individuals and the generalizing or abstractive character of language. Positive statements are only probable (e.g., Weiss and his "not always true statements").

7. Mathematics is the best language because it represents both the uniqueness of individuals and their similarities which are abstracted by man. Hence devices borrowed from this field will reform language and habits of thought. In a word, the great emphasis is on the relativity of meanings due to the different past experiences of both society and the individual, to the nature of the process world, and to the process of selecting and abstracting by which man gets meanings.

VALUES

It might seem strange to include here even a short section on values, free will and morality. Yet the general semanticists speak of morality and ethics as flowing from their semantic reforms, and their theory of the meaning of words. It is a physiological morality that flows from cortico-thalamic integration.[155]

Most of the general semanticists merely hint at a value system. Hayakawa pleads for a non-Aristotelian morality based on cultural and historical contexts and not on abstract statements

---

[155] Korzybski, *Science and Sanity*, p. 40 and 552.

about human nature. Johnson, on the other hand, quotes Brock Chisholm as laying the blame for all the chaos in the world on morality.[156]

Korzybski alone of this group clarifies his position on the freedom of the will. Although he admits that science is committed to indeterminism, this is due to our lack of knowledge, for it is impossible to discover determined values in all cases. But he claims that, with increased knowledge, the unknown may be determined. He then concludes that determinism is really more fundamental and more general than indeterminism, which is only a particular case. Therefore, in keeping with his desire to have his metaphysics and language based on science, he declares that we must accept an infinite-valued determinism.[157] Again, this is a consequence of meaning theory.

> As words are not the things we speak aloud, and the only link is structural, the human mind must require linguistic structural infinite-valued determinism as a condition of rationality. As soon as we find that any linguistic issues are not deterministic, it is an unmistakable sign that the language or the 'logic' we are using is not similar in structure to the empirical world and so should be changed.[158]

Korzybski asks if the objects on 'moral' and 'ethical' grounds are serious enough to induce us to reinstate in our "semantic attitude the older structurally misleading indeterminism."[159] His answer is negative. In fact he claims that a new and better morality would result if his system were adopted. His infinite-valued determinism is in keeping with his infinite-valued meaning and linguistic system. He claims with this that parents would realize their responsibilities toward the individual and realize "that the actions of parents, society, etc., are, to a large extent, responsible for the future development of the child on quite deterministic psychophysiological grounds. In the old way no one

---

[156] Hayakawa, "Non-Aristotelian Revision of Morality," *Etc.*, III, 3 (Spring, 1946), pp. 161-173.

[157] Johnson, *Your Most Enchanted Listener*, p. 37.

[158] Korzybski, *Science and Sanity*, p. 222.

[159] *Ibid.*, p. 551.

was supposed to be responsible except "the poor victim of free will."[160] Under the new system, the individual would be blamed less and there would be a more thorough investigation of structure, language, system, metaphysics, education, conditions of living, etc. The imparting of the semantic reactions of science in a short period would result in a thoroughly integrated thalamocortical system and morality would be inevitable. Thus the Aristotelian infantile standards of evaluation, such as commercialism, militarism, etc., would be replaced by the non-Aristotelian, adult standards of evaluation.[161]

In one of the latest books by a general semanticist, Bois sums up the new orientation and quotes St. Paul's Epistle on Charity, substituting agape for charity. Other scientific words are also inserted. He concludes:

> I do not ignore the cardinal points of the moral compass.
> I want better instruments to navigate more speedily and
> safely in a world of many more dimensions than our
> forebears could anticipate.[162]

SUMMARY OF THE CARDINAL POINTS OF GENERAL SEMANTICS AS
THEY ARE DIRECTED TOWARD THE THEORY OF MEANING
AND OF SYMBOLISM

I. The Aim

1. To reconstruct the structure of language to correspond more closely to the world as science knows it today.
2. To attack the present Aristotelian language system today because it is based on the three principles of

1. identity   2. contradiction   3. the excluded middle or either-or orientation.

II. The Concept Of Reality—a world of processes and events.

3. "Scientific" knowledge infers that the world is in continual flux, a process of events that are related to each other. This

---

[160] *Ibid.*, p. 552.
[161] *Ibid.*, pp. 553-555.
[162] J. Samuel Bois, *Explorations in Awareness*, p. 202.

leads to the following basic premises of the new structure of language and of general semantics, which are just the opposite of those of the Aristotelian language and which will develop an extensional not an intensional orientation.

a. Non-identity: a world in process means that no thing is ever identical with another thing or even with itself.

b. Non-allness: all living organisms react to this process stimuli by selectivity.

c. Infinite valued orientation and nonelementalism. Statements are never just true or false but can also be meaningless or indeterminate.

III. Concept Of Man—a time-binding class of life:

4. Man alone, of all living organisms, goes on improving from where the previous generations left off. He does this because his means of communication, symbols, can represent things in their absence, in space-time.

5. The most important symbol of man is language.

6. Since life is a form of colloidal behavior, language and reaction to language is a kind of conditional reflex in the nervous organism to the stimulus of electric currents on the colloidal structure of man. The reaction of the total man to the stimulus is called semantic reaction.

7. The symbol function of man should take place in the cortex after sensation has taken place in the thalamus. Thalamic-cortical integration is essential for correct semantic (symbol) reaction in man.

IV. Abstraction

A study of Korzybski's theory of symbolism, meaning and communication of meaning through language involves, first of all, the study of the process of abstraction.

8. Abstraction means a process of selecting, of leaving out.

9. All living organisms abstract in reaction to stimuli.

10. Man has two main levels of abstraction and several subordinate levels.

    a.   the non-verbal levels include that of

        1) the sub-microscopic world
        2) microscopic world
        3) object level

    b.   the verbal levels include

        1) label or description
        2) inference
        3) inferences about inference, etc.

11. Animals can only abstract on the non-verbal level. Man can abstract indefinitely, at higher and higher levels.

12. Science is the highest form of abstraction and actually infers the lowest order of abstract, that of the sub-microscopic level, which has proved a workable hypothesis. Thus man's language and knowledge are basically circular, beginning and ending with scientific hypotheses.

13. Consciousness of the levels of abstraction is necessary to have correct semantic reactions and to avoid confusion and conflict.

V. Symbolism

14. On the verbal level, symbols or words are the lowest form of abstraction.

15. Like all abstractions, words are selective. This leads to three basic premises about words:

    a. the word is not the thing
    b. the word is not all the thing
    c. words are self-reflexive—words can be said about words; inferences can be made about inferences in a higher order of abstraction

16. Since words cannot correspond identically to the world of events and process, the only kind of correspondence possible is that of similarity of structure.

17. Since the world is extensional, the extensional language of mathematics is the best language since it can express generalities without denying or omitting differences.

18. Certain devices, borrowed from mathematics, can be applied to our present language to cultivate the extensional orientation and to make people aware of abstractive nature of their knowledge and their language:

    a. to emphasize non-identity—subscripts: $Smith_1$ $Smith_2$ dates: $Smith_{1940}$ $Smith_{1950}$
    b. to emphasize non-allness—"etc." because you never can say all about anything.
    c. to emphasize non-elementalism—hyphens to show that there is not a dichotomy—mind-body; space-time; intellect-emotions, psycho-logical
    d. to emphasize multi-ordinality—single quotes to show that these words mean different things at different times to different people.

VI. Meanings

19. Meanings of words, then, are best expressed by extensional definitions—i.e., by references to actual existents in the process world.

20. So-called words or noises not referring to actual existents or to self-contradictory 'ideas' are meaningless.

21. Statements and words can have logical existence if they are not self-contradictory.

22. Most metaphysical terms, statements and categories are meaningless since they cannot be extensionally defined.

23. Some words do not have any definite meanings but their meanings are determined by their context and their level of abstraction.

24. Since meanings correspond in structure to the world as man knows it at a given time, meanings of words can change with man's growth in knowledge (e.g., the meaning of God)

25. There are no absolute meanings, no absolute truths; the best criterion of truth is predictability. If a statement, when applied and tested, gives correct predictions, it is true and meaningful. If predictions cannot be made or are not realized, the statement can be false, meaningless or indeterminate.

VII. Values and Morality

26. Morality and truth are relative to the knowledge of society at the present moment.

27. Adult morality and truth are only matters of correct semantic reactions which result from integrated cortico-thalamic action. Children can be trained in this by the simple devices proposed by the general semanticists to make them aware of their abstractions, the levels of their abstractions, and of the relational structure of all the events in this process world.

Thus there is a threefold relativity of knowledge and language because of:

1. the relational character of the world in process
2. the relational character of man's reaction to this—a result of his whole being, emotional, cognitive, environmental and experiential.
3. man's expression of this in words—which is the result of No. 1 and No. 2.

CHAPTER III

DISCUSSION OF GENERAL SEMANTICS THEORY OF MEANING IN THE LIGHT OF THOMISTIC PRINCIPLES

It is evident from the previous chapter that the general semanticists have both raised questions about the problem of meaning which have been raised before, and have given insights into some of the answers which thinkers of other ages have suggested. The key problems resolve themselves into one great paradox: how reconcile the obvious fact that there must be something common, something basic and permanent in reality, in order for science to hypothesize and predict and for the common man to communicate, with the fairly common experience that words sometimes mean different things or have different connotations to different people due to the past experiences of these people and to emotional overtones? The problems subsumed under this paradox and to be discussed in this chapter are listed below:

1. *The problem of change:* The most obvious and persistent observational fact about the universe. How can this fact be reconciled with the equally evident order and structure that is the object of scientific investigation and has enabled man to predict, generalize, hypothesize?

2. *The problem of how man knows:* What is there in man that enables him so to predict and generalize? How does he abstract from the phenomena and flux he observes to form generalizations which seem to correspond fairly well to the order and structure underlying that flux?

3. *The problem of communication—including the meaning of words:* Each man derives and forms by himself the meaning of each event that he experiences. It is the result of his personal structure and experience. How is it, given the fact that each man has acquired ideas and meanings of words from past experiences ultimately unique to him and somewhat unshareable, that he is able to communicate to others and we know that he is? Is there a communality of meaning underlying all those unique meanings?

Would it have any counterpart with the meaning science has hypothesized as underlying and accounting for the order and structure of the universe?

4. *The problem of the conformity of words and thoughts to things:* Given the uniqueness of the world and the fact that, in one sense, the meanings we have are unique since they are acquired from personal past experiences, how adequate and how true can our statements be? Do these statements represent only the changing character of the universe or are there some that can represent its order and structure? Are these, then, absolute enough for science to transmit its findings from generation to generation? How can there be a time-binding class of life if all is relative to the knowledge and speech of the current generation? What is there to *pass on* from generation to generation except a few basic absolutes that defy being classified with the flux and phenomena of the rest of the universe?

No definite answer will be given to these questions because it is the belief that no definite answer can be given apodictically, with the exception of the last question. As was pointed out in the preface, the discussion will be in the light of what this writer feels represents a synthesis of the thoughts of St. Thomas Aquinas on these problems. Where the problems stress aspects not emphasized or fully developed by St. Thomas, contemporary works applying his basic principles, are utilized. This is especially true in the section on symbolism. It was emphasized in the preface, also, that this is not an effort to present what may be considered a definitive Thomistic answer for each of these problems. That would be impossible. Through this discussion of the questions and insights raised by the general semanticists in the light of this synthesis of Thomistic thought, it is hoped that greater and more satisfactory insights will result to the benefit of educators and students.

The defense of Aristotle will not form part of this study. For those who wish to see how his thoughts were misrepresented, and to see what Aristotle really held about the laws of identity, of contradiction and of the excluded middle, a list of suggested readings is given below.[1-8]

---

[1] Aristotle, *The Works of Aristotle,* trans. and ed. by W. D. Ross, 12 vols. (Oxford: Clarendon Press, 1908-1952).

THE PROBLEM OF CHANGE

The general semanticists follow the thought of Heraclitus, Bergson, Whitehead, and others when they affirm that the world is merely a process. No two things are identical; in fact, no one being is identical with itself from moment to moment. There is, they say, underlying the change evident to the senses, no permanent and abiding subject, nothing *which* changes. The denial of an abiding subject or substratum underlying change is the denial of substance. The "static" world of Aristotle, according to the general semanticists, has been replaced by the dynamic world of science, a world of atoms, protons, neutrons, positrons, etc., all in perpetual motion. A deeper examination of this problem of change, however, would lead to the conclusion that the hypotheses of science, do not, in any way, entail the rejection of the metaphysical explanation of change in terms of composite substances. They would, rather, corroborate, on the *scientific* level, this *metaphysical* explanation. It will be necessary at first to dispel false notions concerning what St. Thomas meant by substance. For it may well be that the rejection of the notion of substance by the

---

² ———, *The Basic Works of Aristotle,* ed. Richard McKeon (New York: Random House, 1941).

³ ———, *De Anima,* in the version of William of Moerbeke; and the *Commentary of St. Thomas Aquinas,* trans. Kenelm Foster and Silvester Humphries (London: Routledge and K. Paul, 1951).

⁴ Joseph T. Clark, *Conventional Logic and Modern Logic* (Woodstock, Md.: Woodstock College Press, 1952). That medieval logic, which is based on Aristotelian logic, is not contradictory to modern logic is the thesis of this small book. Father Clark concludes on p. 59: "Whoever purports to be an exponent of scholastic logic and presumes *ab initio* to repudiate or to minimize a calculus of statements, does not know the logical priority of statement calculus to the theory of the syllogism and above all does not know scholastic logic."

⁵ Thomas Greenwood, "Aristotle on Mathematical Constructivity," *The Thomist,* XVII (1954), pp. 84-94.

⁶ ———, "The Character of Aristotelian Logic," *The Thomist,* IV (1942), pp. 221-246.

⁷ ———, "The Unity of Logic," *The Thomist,* VIII (1945), pp. 457-470.

⁸ J. A. MacWilliams, "The Bond Between the Physics and Metaphysics of St. Thomas," *The Modern Schoolman,* XXII (1944-45), pp. 16-23.

modern philosophers and by the general semanticists is often due to a lack of understanding of it as a *metaphysical* principle.

There are several erroneous views concerning what most Thomists hold the nature of substance to be. Some believe that substance is posited as a concrete center around which concrete accidents collect; others, that it is an inert substratum underlying accidents. Some say that persistence is its essential characteristic. But according to St. Thomas, it is not a material entity upholding the characteristics of things; it is a metaphysical reality arrived at by the intellect (not by the senses) in its penetration into the nature of reality.[9] It is a dynamic principle of identity, activity and organization.[10]

---

[9] *In. Metaph.* vii, 2. Here St. Thomas shows that the Greeks failed to recognize the existence or explain the nature of substantial change in the universe because they did not rise above the level of thinking in images.

[10] Raymond Smith, *Whitehead's Concept of Logic* (Westminster, Md.: The Newman Press, 1953), p. 139. Cf. also *Sum. Theo.*, Ia, Q. 4, art. 2 and 3; Ia, Q. 2, art. 3. For a thorough treatment of the whole question cf. Andrew G. Van Nelsen, *The Philosophy of Nature* (Pittsburgh, Pa.: Duquesne University Press, 1953). As Garrigou-Lagrange says in *God, His Existence and His Nature* (trans. by Dom Bede Rose, St. Louis, Missouri: B. Herder Book Co., 1934-36), pp. 176-178: "Substance is the determining principle of identity. . . .

"In its relation to the intellect, substance is but a primary determination of being, necessary for the purpose of rendering intelligible, in the role of being, a group of phenomena which presents itself as autonomous. On the first presentation of any sensible object whatever, such as, e.g., the swaddling clothes in which an infant is wrapped, whilst the sense of sight perceives the color of this object, that of touch its shape and resistance, the intellect acquires a confused knowledge of its *being*—that the object is 'something which is.' This first known object of the intellect becomes more clearly defined as *something which is one and permanent* (a substance) after the intellect has noted the multiplicity of its phenomena and the changes which they undergo. In fact, it is only by reason of this oneness that the multiple becomes intelligible, just as the permanent or the identical explain the transitory; for one of the formulas of the principle of identity is that 'every being is one and the same with itself.' *To say of a being that it is a substance is to assert that it remains one and the same under its multiple and changing phenomena.* The principle of substance, therefore, is simply a determination of the principle of identity, and the idea of substance a determination of the idea of being. In the acquisition of its knowledge, the intellect proceeds from the idea of being—in which that of substance is *de facto* implicitly included—to

The important thing about substance is, not that things inhere in it, but that it does not need anything in which to inhere itself; its *perseity* is more important than its relation to accidents.[11]

> What is, is substance, sustaining itself in itself and in itself sustaining potency and act, causing and sustaining accidents and providing for activity as controlled, whereby the universe as composed of true units continues organized activity and harmony.[12]

The exact meaning of substance will become clearer when the proofs for its existence are considered. Two types of proof will be considered here. The first appealed to the medieval thinkers and considers substance as it is; the second considers substantial change, the object of scientific study, and deduces the need for the metaphysical principle of substance in order to explain this substantial change.

The first proof for St. Thomas is based on the impossibility of infinite regress. Either things exist in themselves or in another. If they exist in themselves, we call them substances. If they exist in another then the things in which they exist are called substances. If they do not exist in themselves there is a further regress

---

the somewhat confused ideas of the manner of being implied in phenomena, multiplicity and change. It seeks to render these new ideas intelligible in the light of the idea of being, and comes to recognize the 'something which is' as one and a permanent subject, as a *being* in the full sense of the word, as *something which exists in itself or subsists* (a substance). The intellect is now in a position to narrow down the concept of the manner of being implied in the phenomenon which cannot be defined except in terms of what exists in itself, for it is *ens entis*, 'an entity of an entity.' Thus the confused concept of the phenomenon adds to the definiteness of the concept of substance, and is in turn more clearly defined by it. (*Sum. Theo.*, Ia, q. 85, a.5.) Therefore the morcellation which separates *being* from the phenomenon is not a utilitarian division of the continuous in sense perception but a division of the intelligible which by reason of the principle of identity is a metaphysical or *a priori* requisite."

[11] I *Sent.* d. XXIII, q. I a. 1; II *Sent.* d. XXXV, q. 2. a. 1 ad. 1; cf. Regis Jolivet, *La Notion de Substance* (Paris: Gabriel Beauchesne, 1929), p. 43.

[12] Robert McCall, *The Reality of Substance* (Washington, D. C.: Catholic University of America Press, 1956), p. 57. Cf. *Sum. Theo.*, I, Q. 11, art. 1, ad 1 and *In Metaph.* XII, lect. 12 n. 2362.

until we must either accept things which have independent existence or conclude to nothing, due to the ever-eluding alternative.[13]

The general semanticists and many modern philosophers and scientists would oppose the foregoing proof on the ground that the scientific hypothesis, "all is in flux," contradicts the idea of things with independent existence. Actually, the assertions that things change and that the world is in flux imply the metaphysical notion of substance. It is not a case of substance versus flux but of substance versus nothing, because becoming is not being and you only have becoming because something exists to become or to change.[14]

A serious consideration of substantial change leads inevitably to the conclusion that this metaphysical principle of identity called substance is necessary as an explanation.[15] It is even referred to in a different way by the general semanticists themselves as a

---

[13] Vincent E. Smith, *Philosophical Frontiers of Physics* (Washington, D. C.: The Catholic University of America Press, 1947), pp. 182-183, points out that modern physics accepts infinite regression. For this reason we feel that the second proof based on the nature of substantial change would be more satisfactory to the general semanticists although Smith has refuted this idea of infinite regression in physics and shown the absurd conclusion to which it leads. See also *De Potentia*, q. 9, art. 1.

[14] *In IV Metaph.* 8 n. 638; *Sum. Theo.*, I, Q. 11, art. 1, ad 1.

[15] As McCall says in *The Reality of Substance*, pp. 110-111: "Nature is the intrinsic source of unified activity. From all that man can discover about a sensible object, what it can and cannot do, what can and cannot be done to it, brings the conclusion that whatever be its specific nature, the nature is the organizational center of the object. *It is the fundamental source of its identity.* It is the very core of resistance against disintegration and consequent loss of identity. . . ." "Not only can the mind know *what* the thing is. It can also know *that* the thing is. And it can know that the thing is in an independent manner.

"This independence of existence, which the nature or essence has by its own right, is further highlighted by the evident dependent character of the nature's properties. The parts, the powers, and the activities which proclaim the presence of some nature which is more than they, and which is their source, proclaim thereby their own dependent nature. They need that more basic something which is the thing in its essential nature—to act as their support. The evident etymology of substance highlights the underlying and supporting role which nature performs for the phenomena. It could not play such a role unless in its own right it was the basis for independent existence."

mathematical construct: "invariance of function," "stable invariants are reality."[16] Let us see how this "invariance of function," this "stable invariant," this principle of identity—in the words of St. Thomas, more dynamic than the "stable invariants" of the general semanticists—is not only necessary for the metaphysics which the general semanticists admit must underlie their theories, but also for a metaphysical explanation of the world in process.

Few deny that there is change in the world. But change implies things to be changed. If there were not *things* to change, man would say that there were *new* things, not that *things changed*.

> Change means that the same thing would be different now than what it was previously. Sometimes, indeed, the same actual thing is different now from what it was before, as in motion according to quantity, quality and place; but sometimes, it is the same being only in potentiality, as in substantial change, the subject of which is matter.[17]

There are indicated in the above passage two kinds of change—substantial and accidental. St. Thomas gives some very keen insights into the nature of change in several places.[18] He shows that everything that changes has some kind of composition whereby something is lacking that the change brings about. In all changes there are three elements:

1. the arrival of something new.
2. a subject to receive the change or to be changed for, if there is nothing that has changed, no *change* has taken place but a new being has come. A ball to be moved must be a ball or it cannot be moved and be described as a ball that has been moved. A child to grow must be a child; the growing does not occur unless there is a subject of growing.
3. the subject's lack of the perfection acquired through the change.

Therefore in change, permanence is implied. The world cannot be considered as wholly fluid, nor as wholly fixed. To explain this

---

[16] Supra, pp. 35-36.

[17] *Sum. Theo.,* I q. 45, art. 2 ad. 2.

[18] *Sum. Theo.,* I. q. 9, art. 1; also *De Veritate,* q. 28. art. 9 and *Quodlibet,* VII, 9.

neither wholly static nor wholly dynamic character of reality, St. Thomas, following Aristotle, stated that there are in reality two component elements,—potency and act.[19] Act is perfection; sometimes it is considered as synonymous with existence. Potency is the capacity to be actual. The actual is what is; the potential is what can be. Motion is in between act and potency or a mixture of the two; it is the fulfillment of what exists potentially in so far as it exists potentially. The subject of motion or change in this universe is called *matter;* the perfection which motion or change begets is called *form* and the lack of the new perfection, privation. All three are necessary for change.

It is impossible to find a more satisfactory metaphysical explanation of the fact of substantial change other than that given by Aristotle and St. Thomas. Now if this explanation is satisfactory and if it rests on the more basic metaphysical principle of substance, it follows that this more basic principle is also satisfactory. Substantial change involves the generation of a new substance; it is not a mere change in size, shape, motion, and appearance, but a basic change, such as that of generation and corruption. These changes are manifest not only in variations from the outside working inward toward the interior of the changing being, but from the interior working outward. Chemical changes in the living and the lifeless, and nuclear transformations in nature and in the laboratory are all substantial changes, since the new substances have a new principle of motion and a new nature. The difference between nature and substance is that *nature* is a universal community of a given kind (often called a second substance since it is found in the mind of man but drawn from individual

---

[19] *Sum. Theo.,* I. q. 48, art. 3. In his commentary on Aristotle's Book XII of the *Metaphysics,* St. Thomas shows that the answer to the question, "Is reality in flux or static?" lies in the concept of potency and act.

"The Philosopher solved their doubts (the 'ancients') by showing how something comes from being and non-being. He holds that being is twofold, actual and potential. Whatever is changed, therefore is changed from potential into actual being; as something potentially white becomes actually white. So in the genus of substance, all things come from being and non-being; from non-being accidentally insofar as something comes from a subject under privation which is said to be non-being, but the thing comes to be *per se* from being in potency."

substances with fundamental similarities).[20] *Substance proper* or first substance is the individually existing thing. All silver has the same nature, but it does not have the same substance. Substance may be taken as a nature existing, a nature that is no longer universal but invested with all the requisites of an existing thing. Already here, we are laying the foundation for the relational knowledge so sought after by the general semanticists.

The act and potency of substantial changes are designated as prime matter and substantial form. The subject of change is called prime matter.[21] If the prime matter were not a reality abiding through the change and appearing in both the old and new beings, substantial change would really mean the annihilation of the old substance and the creation of an entirely new one from nothing. Substantial change would then be not a change but a creation out of nothing, a succession of completely new entities. This abiding element, prime matter, is an undetermined element in substance capable of being determined by an infinite variety of determining elements, the forms. In a substantial change[22] such as the fission of uranium into barium fragments, the change of iron and oxygen

---

[20] Cf. McCall, *The Reality of Substance,* p. 152.

[21] References to prime matter are numerous throughout the works of St. Thomas. It can only be defined in relation to form as potency can only be defined in relation to act. For a notion of what prime matter is cf.: *In VII Metaph.* lect. 2; *In I Phys.* lect. 11; -12; -13. *Sum. Theo.,* I q. 66, art. 1 resp. 3; -I, Q. 77, art. 1 and 2; -I, Q. 84, art. 3 ad. 2; -III, q. 75, art. 3; -I q. 4, art. 1: -Q. 115, art. 1 ad 2; *De Verit,* q. 3, art. 5, ad 3; *De Ente et Essentia,* c. 7/. Some of the writings showing what prime matter is not are: *Sum. Theo.,* I, q. 76, aa. 3, 4; -I, q. 76, art. 6, resp. 1 and 2; -I-II, q. 113, art. 8.

[22] For a more complete exposition of the nature of substantial change according to St. Thomas cf. Sister Mary Consilia O'Brien, *The Antecedents of Being* (Washington, D. C.: Catholic University of America Press, 1939), pp. 78-110.

For a thorough study of the existence and knowability of substance in answer to the modern attacks on this metaphysical principle cf. McCall, *The Reality of Substance,* and Leo Foley, *A Critique of the Philosophy of Being of Alfred North Whitehead in the Light of Thomistic Philosophy* (Washington, D. C.: Catholic University of America Press, 1946).

Our next few pages will discuss substantial change as considered by the modern physicists.

into rust, the identity of the original being is lost and a new identity emerges. This is a transformation far more radical than the accidental change wrought in a piece of marble that is chiseled and sculptured to become a replica, say, of Lincoln. Yet, in an analogous way, one being differs from another by its substantial form, whereas the difference in the marble is by means of the accidental form. The unity and the multiplicity so evident in nature is further evidence that this metaphysical explanation of the bifurcation of nature into prime matter and substantial form is acceptable. It must be emphasized that this is discovered wholly on the *meta*physical level since the physical level only gives evidence of the variations. But man, by recognizing variations, that is differences, implicitly recognizes similarities, because recognition of differences implies similarities from which the differences deviate. So, too, change implies sameness from which the change departs; otherwise, all would be considered the same—one great flux.[23]

Thermodynamics also confirms this theory of matter and form. Only in terms of an existing nature, that is, in terms of a substance as the subject of contraries can that which is conserving be, at the same time, entropic; the empiriological physicist would account for this opposition by a reduction to different principles but, basically, there must be an identifying substrate in which both the principles are rooted. Otherwise there would be realities that obey the first law and escape the second and vice versa. But science shows that there is no escape from either law. In no other way than in the traditional matter-form dualism can the atom be explained. Its conservative principle flows from its form; its divisive and destructive principle from its matter.[24] The stable invariant the general semanticists postulate accounts only for the conservative principle; and this is completely separate from the changing phenomena. Matter and form do not involve a complete dichotomy such as Descartes made. The substantial unity of the entity is

---

[23] Vincent E. Smith, *Philosophical Physics* (New York: Harper and Bros., 1950), pp. 42-80.

[24] Prime matter is a metaphysical concept, the undetermined and determinable element in second matter or physical matter which is always composed of prime matter and substantial form. Physicists and all scientists deal with second matter.

guaranteed by the fact that there are two essential elements in the entity—the one, the subject of change, and the other, the dynamic principle of activity and change, and identity. As Smith points out, changes in the thermodynamical conditions of an object should be analyzed not as it looks but according to its operations under different conditions. Chemical compounds yield the same evidence, frequently, for matter and form. These compounds will turn out to be different substances because they show an inner principle of operating or substantial form which cannot be accounted for by the mechanical linkage of their component elements. In testing for the existence of substantial forms distinct from the ingredients they virtually contain and dominating them, the measurement must not be according to how the thing looks, but according to how it is moved or how it acts. Otherwise, water vapor might seem like hydrogen. It is combustibility, specific gravity, conductivity, magnetic permeability and other such exhibitions of mobility rather than appearance that enable the scientists to discern and distinguish substances.[25]

> The standard for deciding the differences of nature, is, to recall Whitehead, not how a thing looks but how it operates under the same external conditions as some other substances. . . . It is their action and operation that count and two different substances subjected to the same thermal extremes will be moved differently. They will also act differently when subjected to the same process of crystal growing. The principle determining the activity of the atom is within it.[26]

Obviously, too, this principle is anything but static. "To say of a being that it is a substance is to assert that it remains one and the same thing under its multiple and changing phenomena,"[27] directing and organizing the activity. The world then has composite substances, each with an active and a passive element; the former determines the change and the latter receives the determination.

---

[25] Smith, *Philosophical Physics,* pp. 217-224.

[26] *Ibid.,* p. 223.

[27] Reginald Garrigou-Lagrange, *God, His Existence and His Nature,* Vol. I (St. Louis, Mo.: Herder Book Co., 1939), p. 178.

The former is not an inert something underlying appearances but a principle of identity, organization and activity. *Composite substances are the key to the mystery of change.* Through this principle, a further application of the principle of potency and act, the change in the world is accounted for and the order and structure underlying the change is also explained metaphysically. Science can only exist because there are in reality principles whereby the different "events" are determined to act in a certain way. Otherwise there would be nothing to give permanence to the laws of science nor certitude to men. While scientific theories may be temporary, they are intended as approximations towards permanent truth.

> For what is in a continual state of flux cannot be grasped with any degree of certitude, for it passes away ere the mind can form a judgment thereon; according to the saying of Heraclitus, that it is not possible twice to touch a drop of water in a passing torrent.[28]

The metaphysical name given to the principle of identity and activity in each entity in the universe upon which science has built its laws and made its great discoveries, is substance.[29] Therefore, there would seem to be no repugnance between the physical explanation of the universe as a phenomenon of flux and the corresponding metaphysical explanation of substance as responsible for the order manifest in the flux. If, as indicated above,[30] science and the general semanticists transfer the scientific hypothesis of the process world to a metaphysics, it is *they* who have confused the levels of abstraction. In similar manner, the metaphysician can never claim to demonstrate *empirically* what he means by substance,[31] for he, too, would then be confusing the levels of abstraction. Actually, as will be shown more completely later, this metaphysical notion of substance corresponds with the structure of reality as we see it today—a composite of unity and

---

[28] *Sum. Theo.*, I, Q. 84, art. 1.

[29] See supra, pp. 85-86, footnote 10, quoting Garrigou-Lagrange.

[30] Supra, pp. 36-37; 66-75.

[31] Cf. Jolivet, *La Notion de Substance*, p. 42; also E. Nelson, "Substance in Modern Philosophy," *Philosophical Review*, Sept. 1947.

multiplicity, change and permanence. In fact, it is through the substantial *form* that is re-presented in the human mind that man is *informed* concerning the outside world.

Though he may reject the *word* "substance," the scientist bases his generalizations on the fact that, "underneath" the world of constant flux, there are determining, defining and limiting principles which he can know, not directly nor identically as they are in objective reality, but representationally, in a way that is closely related to reality though not identical with it. Substance is both the principle of existence in the being in the ontological order and the principle of knowledge in the knower, that is, in the epistemological order.[32]

Moreover, the common man does not predicate characteristics only of other characteristics, and still less does the scientist do so; but, ultimately of objects. For example, I.Q. scores are attributed to persons, who, it is presumed, are basically the same as when they took the test. Identification of persons does not depend on the changing external characteristics but on the fact that it is assumed that despite the external changes over the years, the person is the same, basically. No educational system would keep records if there were not some permanence underlying the very volatile changes that administrators notice occurring in their students from day to day and from year to year.

This idea that there is a basic abiding principle in the person is found, of course, not only in record keeping or in personnel files. All communication of thought by means of words depends on the implicit recognition of the notion of substance in beings and of a corresponding principle in thought. There can be no significant statements unless this is so.[33] Even the theory of relativity and the higher mathematics of Einstein, so praised by Korzybski, are incompatible with the notion of complete flux. As Vincent E. Smith says:

> The mathematics of Einstein show that he cannot adopt
> the Heraclitean point of view in practice. The relation of

---

[32] *Sum. Theo.*, I, Q. 29, art. 3: "Substance is twofold: considered as essence and as the existent thing."

[33] Aristotle, *Metaph.* 1006a; *In Metaph.*, lect. 6n, 608.

a thing to its specific frame of reference, is, as a relation, absolute; and when one frame of reference is in motion with respect to another, definite equations exist for relating them. The theory of relativity seeks to relationize the absolute but ends by absolutizing the relative.[34]

What science investigates is reality, and this reality, whether science explicitly so views it or not, is a composite of change and permanence. Science can only generalize about the phenomena it observes because of the permanence it implicitly accepts as the substratum of the change. Substance is a dynamic principle of being, not a static one—the source of its activity, development and knowability. As St. Thomas said six centuries ago:

We are wont to call by the name of substance, the first beginning of a thing especially when the whole subsequent thing is virtually contained in the first beginning.[35]

In conclusion, the emphasis on the changing aspects of the world is due, no doubt, to the reaction against the emphasis on the static essences made by past ages. However, there does not seem to be one simple answer—the world is neither wholly in flux nor wholly static. If science wishes to postulate the metaphysics underlying the change it observes, it must take into account the twofold aspect of change.[36] Probably the rejection of the notion of substance by most philosophers and scientists since Locke is due to the connotation of a static, material entity associated with substance. This view has been widespread ever since Descartes made so absolute a split between matter and spirit. The dualism in man is not so irreducible. By the notions of potency and act as reciprocal elements, the one receiving and being determined; the other acting, determining and being limited,

---

[34] Vincent E. Smith, *Philosophical Physics,* p. 328.

[35] *Sum. Theo.,* Ia, Q. 4, art. 1.

[36] For the distinction between the spheres of science and philosophy see J. Owens, "Our Knowledge of Nature," *Proceedings of the American Catholic Philosophical Association* (Washington, D. C.: Catholic University of America Press, 1955), pp. 63-86.

the unity of man and of reality is preserved at the same time that an explanation is given of the dual aspect of that unity—multiplicity amid unity; change amid permanence. Scientists stress change, it is true, but postulate "stable invariants" which do not connote the "organic" relationship to the phenomena that the concepts of potency and act, prime matter and substantial form connote. It would seem then, that this notion of substance as a composite of prime matter and substantial form on the physical level and in the order of essences, and of potency and act, on higher levels, is a less self-contradictory and more satisfactory explanation of science, of communication, and, in the words of the general semanticists themselves, of time-binding activity because it is more in correspondence with observable phenomena and scientific generalizations.

THE PROBLEM OF HOW MAN KNOWS

In setting forth the ideas of general semantics, the explanation of how man knows involved several subtopics: the definition of man as a time-binding class of life, the process of abstraction, and semantic reaction. Obviously, any theory or explanation of how man knows is based on a theory of what this man is. The general semanticists had three main points regarding man's nature:— that he is superior to other classes of life because he alone of all three classes can bind time; second, he, like all living beings, abstracts in his reaction to the external world; third, this reaction is similar to the conditioned reflex of animals, in that it is a reaction of a purely material nervous system aroused by the stimuli or electrical currents on its colloidal structure. This section will consider the first and third points and leave the second for the section on abstraction.

This idea of the three grades of life—plant, animal, and human—was formulated by Aristotle long before Korzybski conceived it. In commenting on this section in Aristotle's *De Anima,* St. Thomas first shows that all living things have as their principle of activity and vitality a substantial form called the soul. This is in keeping with the theory of potency and act, and of prime matter and substantial form. The soul is defined as the substantial form of living beings, the source of all their activity.[37]

> He starts then by saying that to carry out our intention of proving the definition of the soul, we must assume as a kind of principle that things with souls differ from those without souls in being alive. Life is the test; and as life shows itself in several ways, if a thing has life in only one of these ways, it is still said to be alive and to possess a soul.[38]

Now the gradation of life is based on the degree to which the activities of the different entities rise above the limitations of time and space, of changing matter. Actually Korzybski used somewhat the same criteria for his chemistry-binders, space-binders and time-binders but he did not probe as deeply into the consequences of such independence of time which he attributed to man. Nor did he notice, as St. Thomas did, that animals can be further divided into stationary and mobile. Life, St. Thomas says, shows itself in four modes: 1) as intellectual; 2) as sensitive; 3) as the cause of motion or rest in space; 4) as cause of the motion of taking nourishment, decay and growth. . . . There are four such degrees,

> distinguished in the same way as the four modes in which life is manifested: for some living things, i.e., plants, only take nourishment and grow and decay; some have also sensations but are always fixed to one place—such are the inferior animals like shell-fish; some again, i.e., the complete animals like oxen and horses, have, along with sensation, the power to move from place to place; and finally, some, in addition, have mind.[39]

When St. Thomas analyzes the differences in activity he notices that the higher the grade of life the less the dependence on matter. The activities of the plant are limited completely to the material;

---

[37] *Commentary on De Anima,* II, ii. 254, p. 183.
[38] *Ibid.,* p. 184.
[39] *Commentary on De Anima,* II. 11, 255, p. 184. Cf. *Sum. Theo.,* I-II, Q. 5, art. 2, resp. 1.

all activities begin and end outside itself. The animal requires corporeal organs but can complete activities within itself and thus can achieve a relative independence of matter. It has consciousness within itself, while the plant can only take in food within itself. Man can transcend not only space but also time; in some of his activities he does not need a bodily organ—e.g., speculation. Even though in the beginning he derived some symbolic representations from the outside, the thoughts and theories he is framing are beyond any bodily organ until he again will symbolically represent them. His ideas are independent of time. Korzybski saw this difference between the activity of man and that of an animal but he did not see what this difference involved. He saw that the symbolic activity of man distinguished him from animals, but he did not see that, if man can act independent of time, in even one form of activity, he must be independent of time *by nature*. In other words, there is something in man that is not material, not limited by time, independent of matter, or *spiritual*.[40]

It would seem that Korzybski contradicts himself: for, while he maintains an absolute break between animal and man,[41] he describes both in similar ways and ascribes similar activities to both. Both animals and men are living organisms, colloidal in structure. Both are stimulated by electrical currents; both have semantic reactions. In fact, when man does not delay in his semantic reaction and does not wait to form a symbol reaction, he duplicates the signal reaction of the animal.[42] If we are to follow the advice of Whitehead and the traditional way of examining entities by their operations, it would seem that animals and men do have something in common and St. Thomas had some reason, based on the activities of man, for calling him a "rational animal."

St. Thomas attempts to show the basis for what Korzybski maintains—that man is superior to the animals, radically.[43] At the

---

[40] *Ibid.*, I, questions 75-78 form the *Treatise on Man,* in which St. Thomas fully develops this theory of man as a rational animal.

[41] Supra, p. 39.

[42] Signal reactions have been dropped by Hayakawa in *Language in Thought and Action.*

[43] *Sum. Theo.*, I, Q. 58, art. 3.

same time, he includes in his explanation what Korzybski ignores in his *explanation* yet includes in his *description* of man's activities —the fact that man, though superior in some activities, is similar to the animal in many others. Korzybski stresses the superiority of man yet maintains that he is pure matter, similar in structure to the animal, though radically different in activity.[44] The contradiction is resolved, it seems, rather well by St. Thomas when he indicates that man has a substantial form which is independent of matter in some of its activities and yet, as substantial form, is essentially united to prime matter through which it also performs such activities as the plants and animals perform. Thus the ideas of the unity of man, the superiority of man over the animals and his similarity to animals in some respects are all included in the notions of substantial form and prime matter, again a manifestation and application of the basic idea of potency and act, the key idea in the metaphysics and psychology of St. Thomas, an idea further refined by the use of the principle of analogy.

Korzybski, throughout his book, gives evidences of the immateriality of the activities of man which he has observed, but he does not go on to the logical and, it would seem, inevitable conclusion that activities imply powers and if powers are immaterial, the principle of those powers, their source must be immaterial. He says that science is man's highest achievement, that a dog has no science, and that science is the highest degree of abstraction (away from materiality, from the physical object). He also admits that a dog cannot become conscious of abstracting as man can and should.[45] Yet he does not see that, since a material power cannot reflect on itself, this consciousness of one's own activity is a non-material act. An eye does not see itself seeing; nor does an ear hear itself hearing. St. Thomas uses the activity of abstraction from materiality and that of self-reflexiveness or self-consciousness as indications of that independence of matter which is the chief characteristic of spiritual entities.[46]

---

[44] Cf. Alfred Korzybski, "An Outline of General Semantics," *Papers from the First American Congress,* ed. Hansell Baugh, pp. 1-20.

[45] Korzybski, *Science and Sanity,* p. 409, cf. supra, p. 39, footnote 42.

[46] It seems advisable to quote here two of the key selections from St. Thomas in the *Summa Theologica* explaining this activity of man which is

On the surface, then, St. Thomas would seem to state just what Korzybski and the general semanticists were stating regarding the three levels of life. But they differ radically as to the nature of

---

separate from matter and which therefore indicates a radically different nature from all other living beings, that is a radically different substantial form. First he shows that things are known spiritually or materially Ia, Q. 84, art. 2:

> "If it were necessary for the thing known to exist materially in the knower, there would be no reason why things which have a material existence outside the world should be devoid of knowledge; why, for instance, if by fire the soul know fire, that fire also which is outside the world should not have knowledge of fire [should this question be applied to the electrical currents on the colloidal structures?]. We must conclude therefore that material things known must needs exist in the knower. [Ancient philosophers thought that the form of the thing known is in the knower in the same mode as in the thing known]. . . . By matter the form of a thing is determined to some one thing. Wherefore it is clear that knowledge is in inverse ratio of materiality. Plants, not receptive of forms save materially [e.g., nutrition, a substantial or a change of one substantial form for another], have no power of knowledge whatever. (*De Anima* ii, 2.) But the more immaterially a thing receives the form of a thing, the more perfect is its knowledge. Therefore the intellect which abstracts the species not only from matter but also from the individuating functions of matter has more perfect knowledge than the senses which receive the form of the thing known without the matter indeed, but subject to its material conditions."

He says somewhat the same thing in *Sum. Theo.*, Ia, Q. 75, art. 2, showing that the intellect acts independent of matter:

> "By means of the intellect man can have knowledge of all corporal things. Now whatever knows certain things cannot have any of them in its own nature; because that which is in it naturally would impede the knowledge of anything else. . . . A feverish tongue cannot taste sweet. . . . If the intellectual principle contained the nature of a body, it would be unable to know all bodies. Every body has its own determinate nature. We cannot understand by means of a bodily organ since the determinate nature of that organ would impede the knowledge of all bodies. . . .
> "Therefore, the intellectual principle which we call the mind or the intellect has an operation of itself apart from the body. Now only that which subsists can have an operation of itself. . . . A thing operates according to what it is."

Therefore, the conclusion is, that if man operates independent of time and space he is in some way independent of time and space; at the same time, he, in most of his operations operates in dependence on physical conditions so that he obviously is a composite—a rational animal, as Thomas described him.

man—or his structure, as Korzybski would call it. St. Thomas
defines man as a rational animal: *animal,* because he obviously
performs some activities similar to those performed by animals,
and *rational,* because he can rise above the limitations of space
and time, and perceive what holds for all time and all space, the
universal. He can generalize. The criterion for the differentiation
of natures is not how they look to the eye or to the microscope,
but, as Whitehead says, how they act and operate.

There is one other point regarding man that Korzybski stresses
—his unity. This is consistent with his attack on elementalism
and his emphasis on non-elementalism. But the elementalism he so
attacks (e.g., the split of man into mind and body, intellect and
emotions), is not entailed in genuine Aristotelian or Thomistic
psychology. Rather, it is a direct outgrowth of Descartes' splitting
up of man and of Kant's further division of all reality into noumena
and phenomena. Any real understanding of the principles of
potency and act, of prime matter and substantial form would
reveal that the unity of man, his substantial union, is a necessary
consequence of this theory. The separation of man by definition
into rationality and animality is made by the *mind alone;* it is a
logical separation, not a real one. An intellectual distinction does
not imply an existential separation. The basic proof St. Thomas
offers for this idea of the unity of man is the dependence of the
intellect on the senses for the source of knowledge.[47] It is intimately
tied up with the process of abstraction. Man requires the body
not as an organ but as an object since the intellect needs the
phantasms produced by the imagination and the imagination needs
the senses and the senses need the body.[48] This statement would

---

[47] For a more thorough treatment of this whole problem, see Anton Charles
Pegis, *St. Thomas and the Problem of the Soul in the Thirteenth Century*
(Toronto, Canada: St. Michael's College, 1937).

[48] *Sum. Theo.,* I, Q. 84, art. 7: "In the present state of life in which the
soul is united to a passible body, it is impossible for our intellect to understand anything actually except by turning to the phantasm. And of this there
are two indications. First of all, because the intellect, being a power that
does not make use of a corporeal organ would in no way be hindered through
the lesion of a corporeal organ if for its act there were not required the
act of some power that does make use of a corporeal organ. Wherefore it is
clear that for the intellect to understand actually, not only when it acquires

seem to be an excellent example of elementalism, of splitting up man into innumerable "faculties" as was done in some nineteenth century psychologies. However, Thomists do not consider faculties as separate entities but as powers of one man. When, for example, we say our hand can grasp, lift, pound, write, we ascribe different names, verbs, to the different powers of the hand. We do not think of these powers as separate entities, apart from the hand or apart, even, from man. We do not think of the hand as one power plus another. The same is true for the other powers of man. He has the power of seeing, thinking, feeling, loving, etc. We must and do put different labels on these different actions in order to communicate our meanings. The division, then, is chiefly a verbal or logical one, a formal rather than concrete distinction.

Not only does St. Thomas show the unity of man by showing the dependence of man's knowledge, even his intellectual knowledge, on his body, but also by showing that the efficiency of the mind is, in large part, dependent on the perfection of the body. This dependence would not be, if Thomas had held to a real and not merely to a logical separation of body and mind.[49]

> The important point in this matter is that in his theory of the substantial unity of the body and soul, St. Thomas realized that the corporeal constitution of man and its various changes are to be predicated of the *whole man* (italics ours).[50]

Thus we see that both the general semanticists and the Thomists recognize the superiority of man over all other living beings. But,

---

fresh knowledge but also when it applies knowledge already acquired, there is need for the act of the imagination and of the other powers. For when the act of the imagination is hindered by a lesion of the corporeal organ, for instance, in the case of frenzy; or when the memory is hindered; we see that a man is hindered from actually understanding things of which he had previous knowledge. Secondly anyone can experience this of himself that when he tries to understand something he forms certain phantasms to serve him by way of examples. . . . When we wish to help someone to understand something we lay examples before him from which he forms phantasms for the purpose of understanding." Cf. *De Veritate*, XIX, 1.

[49] *Sum. Theol.*, Ia, Q. 85, art. 7; IaIIae, Q. 82, art. 4, res. 1.

[50] Hans Meyer, *The Philosophy of St. Thomas Aquinas,* trans. Fred Eckhoff (St. Louis, Mo.: B. Herder Book Co., 1944), p. 180.

while Korzybski denies that man is an animal, he nevertheless recognizes that man performs some of the actions of an animal. While he admits that man is able, in science and mathematics, to transcend time and space, he does not attribute this power to anything but superior electrical reactions of the colloidal structure of man, which structure is found in the lesser and lower forms of living beings. Therefore this power would be wholly dependent on physical structures for its activity. Thomas, on the other hand, considers man to be a rational animal. He recognizes that some of man's actions are similar to those of animals and that some of the activities transcend the powers of animals, in fact, of all beings immersed in time and space. He calls these activities spiritual and states that they must flow from a spiritual power. Since this spiritual power is in man and has to do with his essence, his substantial form must be spiritual. This relationship points up the nature of man's superiority over all other living organisms or substances. According to the theory of act and potency as applied to substances, the source of activity is the substanial form, which, in living beings, is termed the "soul." The notion of the spirituality of man's soul, i.e., his substantial form, is, therefore, a direct consequence of observing the symbolic, abstractive nature of his knowledge, especially of science which generalizes beyond time and space. His prime matter is the subject of his changes in appearance, dimension, etc., but his soul is the principle of his abiding unity and identity and most characteristic activity—intellectual knowledge. The concept of man as a rational animal is fully consistent with the theory of the universe—based on the theory of act and potency. Korzybski and the general semanticists do not seem to be so consistent and leave many contradictions and questions unanswered:

1. just what is there in the electric currents or the colloidal structure of man that animals have not so that man forms symbols and science and animals do not?
2. why is it said that the reactions in animals and humans exhibit different degrees of conditionality? If *degree,* and not *kind,* why is not a human a degree of animal? Just what is the essential difference between animal and human which is so stressed by the general semantic̓ists?

At present the more satisfactory explanation would seem to be that of St. Thomas who, in saying that man is a rational animal, a substantial union and unity of spiritual soul, as substantial form, and of prime matter, accounts for the fact that some of his operations are shared with the animals and some transcend time and space. An example of this second type of activity is the very "science" which denies the universal character of its content at the same time that it builds its systems on generalizations. Such a concept of man, a further extension of act and potency, is basic to the understanding of abstraction and of the question of the relative and absolute meanings of things, ideas and words.

Abstraction

The term "abstraction" is used both by St. Thomas and by general semanticists to describe the process by which man acquires "knowledge." In general, both groups agree that abstraction has a broad meaning of "selecting." But while both apply it to the problem of how man knows reality, the application is very different. To some scholastics, the problem of how man grasps the abstract, universal aspect of sensible phenomena—which is what science does—is one that will never be solved. They believe that we cannot ever know *how* this is done, although evidence requires the conclusion that it *is* done. But most of them use the hypothesis of an active intellect abstracting the universal from the sensible phenomena. One definition of this process by scholastics is:

> Abstracting—in a general sense, the power of the mind to focus on one note of reality to the exclusion of all other notes. Mostly used in scholastic doctrine to indicate that power of the spiritual intellect to penetrate to the idea, spiritual pattern or nature of an object without regard to how or what the reality may appear in the concrete.[51]

There are two essential differences in the use of the word by the two groups:

1. Abstracting, according to the general semanticists, is an ac-

---

[51] *Sum. Theol.* Vol. III, Glossary, p. 3555. Benziger Bros. edition.

tivity common to all living organisms; to St. Thomas it is found in or attributed only to man—as an activity of his intellect.

2. Abstracting, according to the general semanticists, implies a gradual emptying of reality so that the highest level and the level farthest from the concrete reality is most empty of notes contributing to knowledge. According to St. Thomas, abstracting eliminates the limiting characteristics of phenomena, of matter and enables the mind to get at the "real" reality—the *unchanging universal reality which makes science possible*. Thomas says the organizing principle of identity is left in,[52] that which makes the thing what it is, while what are left out are the external characteristics which can only exist because they have an abiding principle to be their subject. Furthermore to know the individual, the knower must eventually return to the phantasm after it has abstracted the "essence" of it.

The following contrasting quotations may reveal the difference more clearly:

> Our knowlege is the result of nervous abstraction.[53]
> Our intellect both abstracts the intelligible species (idea) from the phantasm inasmuch as it considers the nature of things in universal and yet nevertheless understands these natures in the phantasms since it cannot understand even the things of which it abstracts without turning to the phantasm.[54]

Korzybski attributes the fallibility of sense knowledge to the fact that it is abstractive and also the result of the interaction of observed and observer. While Thomists do not call sense knowledge "abstraction," they, too, recognize that sense knowledge in large part depends on the individual organism. Korzybski says, "We can only agree on colours, shapes, distances, etc., by ignoring the fact that the effect of the same stimulus is different in dif-

[52] *Ibid.*, I, q. 79.
[53] Korzybski, *Science and Sanity,* p. 254.
[54] *Sum. Theo.,* Ia, Q. 85, art. 1, resp. 5.

ferent individuals;[55] a modern scholar of St. Thomas says somewhat the same thing:

> Qualities properly speaking while belonging virtually to the corporeal objects are nevertheless essentially relative to the organs of the subject so that it is impossible to determine in direct fashion by any simple reflection on immediate data just what these qualities are in themselves. . . . The partial relativity of qualities is due to the fact that the sensation depends on the nature of the psychophysiological properties of the organism. . . . A great many current errors are due to confusing the object in itself, the physical object and the psychological object.[56]

Though St. Thomas does not apply the word *abstraction to* sense knowledge he uses it in several different ways when referring to intellectual knowledge. First, there is the simple abstraction which is used in the formation of an idea; then we may consider degrees of abstraction, according to the amount of separation from the conditions of *materiality* (not as the general semanticists call it, from conditions of *reality*). Here again, there is some disagreement today over terminology. Some would consider the highest "degree" of abstraction as separation. We will present below as briefly, simply and clearly as possible, a description of all types of abstraction, described by St. Thomas with other references needed for a deeper understanding of this process.[57]

The process of abstraction by which according to some Thomists[58] the intellect arrives at the universal aspect of sensible phe-

[55] Korzybski, *Science and Sanity*, p. 375.
[56] Ferdinand Van Steenberghen, *Epistemology,* trans. Martin J. Flynn (2nd ed., New York: Joseph F. Wagner, Inc., 1949), pp. 224-234.
[57] Sources on Abstraction are: Aristotle, *De Anima,* III, 4 and 5; *Sum. Theo.*, I. Questions 84, art. 7; 85, art. 1 and 2; 79, art. 2; 54, art. 4; 55, art. 2 and the commentary on *De Anima,* III, 4 and 5.
[58] Robert Edward Brennan, *General Psychology* (New York: The Macmillan Co., 1939), p. 328, describes the conceptual process in the following way: "An object makes an impression, or a series of impressions upon the end organs. The presentations of sense are gathered together into a synthesis which is described in a general way as a phantasm—a term which is somewhat obscure in the writings of Aquinas, but which may be taken to mean

nomena is, briefly, this:

1. a material object or event impinges on one or more sense organs; their reaction is carried by the nervous system to the brain where the sensations from the various receptors—for sight, hearing, touch, etc., are pre-consciously fused into one unified percept or phantasm or image. This image is actually a representation in some way of the object with some of its concrete individuating notes, such as size, shape, color, odor, etc. As such, it cannot form the knowledge known as universal, which transcends time. In this image there is implicitly present a counterpart of the substantial form in the actual concrete object.

2. The active intellect "lights up" this form which is potentially present in the image, and the passive intellect forms the *verbum mentale* or mental word or idea of the concrete object. To know the individual, to make an existential judgment, involves a return to the phantasm. The active intellect postulated by Aristotle and most scholastics is described as the power of the intellect whereby it modifies itself so as to represent in a spiritual manner, or abstract manner, what is concretely depicted in the imagination.[59]

_____

either a perceptual product or its derivative image. In any case, the point about the phantasm which is important for the process of conception is its essentially synthetic character. The disjointed and unconfigured masses of information that arrive in consciousness through the avenues of external sense must first be resolved into unity by the internal senses before the intellect can begin to work on them. The phantasm, therefore, is the starting point in the natural order of all our intellectual operations. Its mere presence is sufficient to arouse the conscious subject to the exercise of the powers of ideation. Immediately upon its appearance active intellect penetrates to its inner core and discloses the essence that lies hidden beneath its surface characteristics. To the product of this abstractive process Aquinas has given the name *species impressa*. The whole purpose and function of such a product is to stimulate passive intellect which, in giving conscious expression to it, produces a *species expressa* or concept."

A theory of this kind avoids two extremes: first that of supposing our knowledge to be a purely material function of mind, like the interaction of physico-chemical events, or a mere complexus of sensations and images; secondly, that of accounting for our higher modes of cognition without any reference whatever to sensory functions.

[60] See also, Wilhelmsen, *Man's Knowledge*, pp. 111-117.

Besides this notion of abstraction, Thomas considers levels of intellectual abstraction, according to the degree of withdrawal of their objects from the sensible order. We are now dealing with scientific objects, objects of scientific knowledge. Now today, some Thomists consider that metaphysics is truly a separation and that the other sciences employ abstraction or scientific distinction. Knowledge is not considered scientific unless it is necessary knowledge, that is knowledge that *must be* as it is, in some manner; scientific knowledge cannot be of the contingent or ephemeral. Change is at the root of natural contingency, matter is at the root of natural change, since, as shown above, it permits things to become other than they were by receiving different substantial forms. Matter, then, is at the base of flux, generation, corruption and change, "if matter is at the root of natural change and change is the root of natural contingency and the contingent is opposed to the necessary, and science is of the necessary, then scientific knowledge is opposed to materiality."[60] The three kinds of scientific objects in relation to their withdrawal from materiality are:

1. those that need sensible matter for existence and for being understood. These are studied by the physical scientists.

2. those that need sensible matter for existence but not for being understood. These are studied by the mathematical scientists.

3. those that do not need sensible matter for existence or for being understood. These are the object of the study of metaphysics.[61,]

Scientific abstraction is a conscious act of discrimination, not the preconscious act of the agent intellect illuminating the species in the phantasm. Once the intellect is brought from potency to act by the species (the potential form which was abstracted by the agent intellect), it then can proceed to judgment or to deeper understanding. If the latter, it will penetrate some essential aspect of reality and will express this penetration in a concept. All con-

[60] *Ibid.*, pp. 192-195; see also *Sum. Theo.*, Q. 79, art. 3 and 4.

[61] See also: William H. Kane, "Abstraction and the Distinction of the Sciences," *The Thomist*, XVII (January, 1954), pp. 43-68, and M. D. Philippe, "Abstraction, Addition, Séparation dans la philosophie d'Aristote," *Revue Thomiste*, XXXII (1948), pp. 461-479.

cepts and definitions are products of one of two ways in which the intellect can grasp the essence:

1. abstraction of the complete essence from particular things possessing that essence—that is the universal nature, abstracted from the particular entities participating in that nature. This is common to all sciences, especially to the natural sciences and is also found on the prescientific level as well.

2. abstraction of a form from the sensible matter in which it exists. This is not a consideration of an essence in isolation from the individuals but of forms that in reality depend on sensible matter for existence. Once abstracted the mind considers these forms in and for themselves as is seen in mathematics.

To abstract is not to falsify, since it is merely means to isolate some aspect away from the existential conditions of things in which the aspect has being. When I consider the circle apart from the ball, I merely consider it in isolation from the ball in which it exists. But if I judged that the circle existed in physical reality the way it existed in my mind I have judged falsely. But abstraction is not judgment.

Metaphysics is judgment and involves separation more than abstraction, according to some of the more recent Scholastics.[62] In every true negative judgment, man separates things or principles actually separated or capable of being separated in existence. In metaphysics, man denies that *being* (the object of metaphysics) is necessarily linked with material being. "Separation is uniquely proper to metaphysics in the sense that the metaphysician can get at his formal object, being, *as* being, only by constantly separating it from the material and other existential conditions in which it is presented to him in sensation."[63] This judgment type of separation is somewhat analogous to the "inference" in the ladder of abstraction of the general semanticists.

There is another slight similarity with Korzybski, regarding this idea of abstraction, and the requirement that knowledge correspond in structure as closely as possible to the structure of reality. Moderate realists, as Thomists term themselves, demand

---

[62] Wilhelmsen, *Man's Knowledge,* p. 196. Cf. *Sum. Theo.,* I, Q. 40, art. 3 and Q. 85, art. 4.

[63] Wilhelmsen, *Man's Knowledge,* p. 196.

also that there be an objective basis for knowledge and, therefore, for the three levels of abstraction. Some Thomists point out that the three levels of abstraction (or two of abstraction and one of separation) correspond to the threefold composition in sensible things; again this is based fundamentally on the composition of potency and act:

1. real composition in sensible things of substance and accident, substance holding itself to accident as potency to act. This is the objective basis of mathematical sciences.

2. real composition of prime matter and substantial form, prime matter holding itself to substantial form as potency to act and this is the object of the philosophy of nature.

3. real composition of essence and existence, the essence holding itself to existence as potency to act, and this is the object of metaphysics.

> In each of these three orders in which there is an increasingly deeper penetration of sensible being, intellect is able to grasp an act (accident, substantial form, existence) apart from this or that potency (substance, prime matter, essence). And thus we have three ascending orders of abstraction each of which has an objective basis in sensible reality as the doctrine of moderate realism demands.[64]

The similarities and differences in the levels of abstraction of both groups can be shown more clearly by listing them in parallel columns. The abstraction ladder of the general semanticists is a composite of that presented by Korzybski and Hayakawa.[65]

THE GENERAL SEMANTICISTS	SYNTHESIS OF THOMISTIC THEORY[66]
Non-Verbal Levels	
1. submicroscopic l e v e l postulated by science.	1. the object impinges on sense organs.

[64] F. G. Connolly, "Abstraction and Modern Realism," *The New Scholasticism,* XXVII (1953), 72-90.

[65] Korzybski, *Science and Sanity,* pp. 376, 384, 447; Hayakawa, *Language in Thought and Action,* p. 165; cf. Wendell Johnson, *People in Quandaries,* pp. 134-167.

[66] Wilhelmsen, *Man's Knowledge,* pp. 96-97; also Brennan, *Thomistic Psychology* (New York: The Macmillan Co., 1941), p. 183 and passages in *Sum. Theo.,* referred to above.

2. the gross macroscopic daily experience level of rough objects manufactured from the event by our lower nervous system.

2. senses react — *sensation*.

3. psychological picture probably manufactured by the higher systems—unspeakable psycho-logical picture (not in Hayakawa's ladder).

3. reactions fused by central sense into a *percept*.

4. the imagination makes a sensible representation of the object with its material conditions—the *Phantasm*.

Verbal Levels

5. verbal label for the object; describes verbally our facts, e.g., Bessie.

5. active intellect illuminates the essence, the universal, and basic similarities by which the object can be identified in relation to other similar objects.
5. passive intellect forms the *concept, mental word* by which man knows the essence.

6. inference — "cow" stands for characteristics we have abstracted as common; characteristics peculiar to each cow left out.

6. intellect reverts to the phantasm and knows the object as *cow,* for example.

7. inference—"livestock" only the characteristics in common with other livestock are considered.

8, 9, other inferences.

10. inference—creeds and other semantic reactions "wealth is good."[67]

11. mathematical knowledge, contains all particulars but not physical content.

12. scientific generalizations—the highest level of abstraction.

11. abstraction from individual matter — the physical sciences.

12. abstraction from all except quantity—mathematics.

13. separation from all except being.—metaphysics.

The chart reveals that both groups consider that abstraction involves omission in one sense or another and a process of going from lower to higher levels. The general semanticists extend the term below the human level to include all forms of knowledge but do not mention the highest form of abstraction described by St. Thomas: that involved in ontology. The general semanticists also apply the word "abstraction" to the process of labelling. St. Thomas speaks of a mental word[68] but it does not seem to resemble the verbal label since it has an intrinsic and necessary connection with the object while the verbal label would seem to be arbitrarily fixed on the object. This question of mental word, concept and of the transition between the non-verbal and verbal levels is the matter of the greatest difference between the ideas of the two groups. The semanticists would make the label a class concept whose primary function is to aid communication. The universal concept reflects the essence, the nature of the object first. The former class concept seems to be arrived at by social agree-

---

[67] Korzybski, *Science and Sanity*, p. 445.

[68] St. Thomas has this to say about the word in *Sum. Theo.*, Ia, Q. 34, art. 1: "First and chiefly the interior concept of the mind is called a word; secondarily, the vocal sound itself, signifying the interior concept is so called; and thirdly, the imagination of the vocal sound is called a word." Thus the signification of the vocal sound, according to St. Thomas is not from consensus of opinion but from the concept it symbolizes vocally.

ment and is more vocal than cognitive. The universal concept has its roots, not in social agreement, but in the object itself. This is obtained by the abstracting activity of the agent intellect. This difference is basic and involves the whole field of meaning, sign, symbol, universals and nominalism. It will be discussed more fully in the next section. What is important to note here is that this is the crux of the difference between the abstraction of the general semanticists and that of St. Thomas. According to the latter, abstraction enables man to *get at* reality. According to the general semanticists, abstraction means *going away from* reality, although occasionally they stress the importance of high-order abstractions. The greatest advance in approaching basic reality is made by the abstracting activity of the agent intellect, according to St. Thomas. At approximately the same level, the general semanticists are claiming that the greatest departure is made from the real—at the juncture between the verbal and non-verbal level when the object gets "in," so to speak, the human being. Finally the percept described by some of the contemporary Thomists seems to be what the general semanticists mean by the "psychological picture."

Summary on the process of abstraction:

1. General semantics "abstraction" begins on the non-verbal level, is practised by both animals and men, and goes up only to mathematics, the highest level.

2. Abstraction as described by St. Thomas starts with man and goes to a third degree, that of metaphysics.

3. The percept of Thomas might have its correlate in the "psychological picture" postulated by Korzybski.

4. Korzybski goes directly from object to label. The Thomists maintain that before the vocal word there is a "mental word" or *concept* formed.

5. The label of the general semanticists is based on a communality of external characteristics while Thomas' universal concept expressed by a word is based on the nature of the object, that is, on intrinsic characteristics held in common by all of a type in all time and space. To show its correspondence with substance, this concept is sometimes called second substance while

the principle of identity in the object it represents is called first substance.[69]

6. The general semanticists hold that abstraction, in leaving out external details, leaves out reality; St. Thomas maintains that abstraction, in leaving out the external details which change in time-space, actually enables man to get at permanent reality underlying all change. But he also states that to know the individual there must be a return to the phantasm. He admits that the intellectual knowledge of the individual is indirect; only the sense-knowledge of the individual is direct.[70]

7. The "inferences" of the general semanticists at times seem to have similarities with the "judgments" described by St. Thomas.

Thus the value of the general semanticists' views regarding abstraction is not in their fundamental conception of the process, which is inadequate, but in the emphasis they put on being aware that knowledge does not and cannot correspond identically with particulars, on the dangers of overgeneralizations, and on the necessity of distinguishing levels of abstraction. Whether these practical values can be adopted by educators without subscribing to the theoretical considerations underlying them is a problem which needs more clarification as it involves a consideration of the third problem—that of meaning and of communication. On the whole, it must be pointed out that both theories of abstraction are only postulated explanations of how man goes from the experienced object to the recognition of it as an abiding member of an abiding class. Such an explanation as that given by St. Thomas cannot be verified absolutely by empirical methods. In fact, as pointed out before, the empirical psychologists admit that "meaning has no material correlate."[71] It is entirely consistent with the theory of act and potency, substantial form and prime matter, that meaning has no material correlate. The hypothesis of an agent intellect to bridge the gap between the material object

---

[69] Brennan, *Thomistic Psychology*, pp. 32 and 283.

[70] *Sum. Theo.*, II, 75, art. 4, I. Q. 85, I, resp. 5; I, Q. 86, art. 1. This principle of identity called substance is related in no way to the "is of identity" described by Korzybski. (See Chapter II.)

[71] Charles Osgood, *Method and Theory in Experimental Psychology* (New York: Oxford University Press, 1953), p. 680.

(whose material conditions stimulate the sense organs), and its essence without material conditions, is a plausible and possible explanation. Declaring that this agent or active intellect illuminates the intentional form in the phantasm so that the passive intellect can be informed by the object in a non-material way, seems to be a more satisfactory explanation of this gap which the general semanticists bridged only by the word or label.

THE PROBLEM OF COMMUNICATION: MEANINGS IN THINGS,
IDEAS AND WORDS

A recent writer has summed up the theory of general semantics regarding language in these words:

> A popularized brand of positivism, a two-bill positivism
> . . . is already the common intellectual diet of millions of
> the semi-educated in the United States and Great Britain. The conviction is abroad in the great universities
> that if language could only be fossilized into rigid mathematical and logical symbols on the level of science and
> reduced to simple statements and exhortations on the
> level of practical life, all our intellectual and social problems would wither away. . . . This position is consistently
> put forward by S. I. Hayakawa in *Language in Thought
> and Action.*[72]

One is tempted to say that Hayakawa himself might well have written the above paragraph and applied it to Aristotelian language habits, although he would have substituted the subject-predicate symbolism of the Aristotelian orientation as the cause of the fossilization of language. In a sense, both accusers would be correct. The general semanticists have condemned the subject-predicate language as the cause of disagreements, conflicts and maladjustments, although they continue to use it. As pointed out above, the basis for this condemnation seems to be the claim that this kind of language conveys the illusion that words are identical with things, through the pernicious use of the word "is." It is difficult to juxtapose the theory of St. Thomas against that of

---

[72] Wilhelmsen, *Man's Knowledge,* p. 50.

the general semanticists since the former stresses that *knowledge* is not identical with reality and the latter point out that *words* are not identical with reality. The general semanticists seem to hold the pragmatic view that the meaning of an object is the human reaction to the thing, and does not lie in any transcendental idea. If so, the human reaction, the word, then is the meaning. The difficulty in any discussion of these two theories of meanings is that any *criticism* of the theory of meaning set forth by St. Thomas is directed against language; and any *exposition* of the same theory of meaning stresses the idea, the concept which symbolizes reality and is, in turn, we may say, symbolized by the word. This is a new development in the attack on knowledge as M. Whitcomb Hess pointed out.[73]

It has seemed best to follow this order in considering this problem:

1. Brief indication that the so-called "laws of Aristotelian language" have been misrepresented and that they are really laws of being, and of thought.

2. Demonstration of the fact that St. Thomas recognized and insisted on the fact that knowledge is not identical with reality.

3. Consideration of sign and symbol as Thomas conceived them, especially as applied to ideas and words.[74]

---

[73] M. Whitcomb Hess in "The Semantic Question," *The New Scholasticism*, XXII (1949), says on pp. 186-206:

"Though the problem of verbal reference which includes that of the symbolism of language was necessarily implicit in the controversy over universals, the symbol side had not itself become a central articulate issue before this present century." He shows that the semanticists have removed the idea from the semantic field, which "means failure to connect words and things logically for semantic relations do not obtain between words and their destinations but only between symbols and ideas. . . . The idea in the word and the truth in the thing must coincide as identical; and when implications in the verbal symbol's conjunction of mind and matter, thoughts and things, ideas and objects are once more recognized as witnessing stable truth and making science possible, a word may be referred to once more as the sign of an idea without the cavil about signs which is so modern."

[74] A few quotations from St. Thomas given here will show that he regarded

4. Consideration of the fact that both St. Thomas and the general semanticists recognized that the meanings of things and of words as known by each man depend largely on the individual's past experiences.

The last problem to be considered is the extent of the variations of meanings held by different men and the possibility of arriving at underlying stable truth, and of communicating this truth. It concerns the fact that in actual day-to-day communication, the connotations attached to words are more important or as important as their denotation.

The general semanticists state that the Aristotelians base their orientation on three principles regarding the accuracy of language:

1. the principle of identity[75]—a word is the thing.

2. the principle of contradiction

3. the principle of the excluded middle—either-or orientation

In turn, it will be recalled, they advocate these principles with regard to language:

1. the principle of non-identity—the word is not the reality.

2. the principle of non-allness—the word is not all of reality.

3. the principle of self-reflexiveness—the word can be used in statements about itself.

---

the concept as a sign of the thing and the word and concept were hardly separated in his mind:

Sum. Theo., I, Q. 29, art. 4, obj. 1.: When we understand a stone, that which the intellect conceives from the thing understood is called the word.

———, II-II, Q. 91, art. 1. We use words in speaking to man in order to tell him our thoughts which are unknown to him.

———, Q. 107, art. 1: The concept of the mind is called the interior word. To speak to another only means to make known the mental concept to another.

———, I, Q. 93, art. 1, resp. 2: With regard to any sort of word, two points may be considered: 1) the word itself, 2) that which is expressed by the word. For the spoken word is something uttered by the mouth of man and expresses that which is signified by the human word. The same applies to the human mental word, which is nothing else than something conceived by the mind by which man expresses his thoughts mentally.

———, II-II, Q. 72, art. 1, obj. 2, resp. 2. Our words if we consider them in their essences, i.e., as audible sounds injure no man except perhaps by jarring on the ear. . . . But considered as signs conveying something to the knowledge of the other, they may do many kinds of harm.

[75] This is not the same thing as substance described on pp. 85-97.

Actually these two sets of principles as their originators meant them are not related even by way of contradicting each other for the three principles of Aristotle stated above do not apply to language at all, but to existing things and to thought.[76] They have logical and ontological aspects but no semantic aspects. The principle of identity according to Aristotle simply meant that whatever is, is itself, and no other thing at the same time in the same respect. "A thing cannot be and not be at the same time in the same respect," is the more basic principle of contradiction. Because of the qualifying phrases, "at the same time" and "in the same respect" this could even refer to the process world. So, too, for the principle of the excluded middle—this is a principle of *being,* really, and not of *language.* Aristotle recognized relations other than those of contradictories but he meant that between being and non-being there is no reality unless you consider potency, capacity for being as an intermediary between being and non-being. He did not so consider it. Neither do followers of St. Thomas advocate the either-or orientation as is evident from the famous scholastic dictum: "Never deny; rarely affirm; always distinguish."

But even were we to dismiss the misrepresentation of Aristotelian principles, the accusation that the Aristotelians or medieval scholars maintained that knowledge is identical with reality is false. No one recognized more clearly nor reiterated more frequently the fact that knowledge does not correspond point to point with reality but that there is a similarity of structure so that man can know. Knowledge, says St. Thomas, is in the knower according to the manner of the knower, not according to the manner of the known.[77] The known has another existence, another presence in the knower, an intentional existence. This is because no material thing could be in another being at the same time in the same way as it exists in itself. Now just how this presence in the knower is accomplished is one of the great problems of psychologists and philosophers and is the cause of great discussion. We do not, of course, pretend to "solve" the problem. What will be

---

[76] Cf. Barrows Dunham, *Man Against Myth* (Boston: Little, Brown and Co., 1947), pp. 233-266.

[77] *Sum. Theo.,* II-II. Q. 1, art. 2.

shown here is that St. Thomas recognized that the knowledge, while bearing a *real* relationship to the object, does not bear an *identical* relationship. A few pertinent quotations from St. Thomas and contemporary scholars on this question might best indicate what is meant here concerning the difference between the conceptual and real order:

> The order of reasoning activity does not exactly coincide with the real order. It is in fact only a conceptual transposition of the real order. Indeed the original element found at the basis of all reasoning is the concept. Now the concept is not a "double" of the datum of experience, it is rather a synthetic and abstract representation of it. Reasoning strives to build up a system of concepts, a conceptual order which will be a transposition of the real order to the level of intellectual immanence, the plane of stability and union. The value of the transposition is the same as the concept. This transposition sacrifices the originality of the concrete thing or individual as such; it sacrifices every element in spatio-temporal reality which cannot be expressed in abstract universal concepts. But, on the other hand, it reduces the diversity and changing flux of my world of experience to the unity and stability of an immanent synthesis in my consciousness. It strives to give me possession of the real order in a final synthetic act.[78]

And St. Thomas said centuries before this:

> The likeness of a thing is received into the intellect according to the mode of the intellect, not according to the mode of the thing. Wherefore something on the part of the thing *corresponds* to the composition and division of the intellect but it *does not exist* in the *same way* in the intellect and in the thing.[79]

Three orders in knowledge can be distinguished:

> 1. at the level of experience, the real order
> 2. at the level of conceptual immanence, the conceptual order

---

[78] Van Steenberghen, *Epistemology,* p. 239.
[79] *Sum. Theo.,* Ia, Q. 85, art. 5, resp. 3.

3. within the conceptual order, the logical order or formal order (inferences about inferences, in general semantics terms).

The real order is that which is independent of our concepts; the
logical order signifies that which is transposed into conceptual
immanence.[80]

Human knowledge is imperfectly objective in three respects
due to the influences of the subjective function: On the level of
perception, the nature of the perceiving organ and the psycho-
physiological tendencies of the subject modify the perceived qualita-
tive differences; on the level of the phantasm, because the data that
are preserved and associated are so preserved and associated according to previous experiences and perceptions; on the conceptual
level, the data transposed under the form of abstract concepts are
so transposed and reconstructed in accordance with the logical
laws proper to conceptual thought.

> In short, the basic imperfection of my knowledge con-
> sists in the irreducible duality of experience and concept
> destined to complete one another naturally but never to
> be identified. . . . The ultimate reason for all the imper-
> fection of man's knowledge may be reduced to the dual-
> ity of man's medium of knowledge (sense and intellect)
> as contrasted with the ineffable unity of the real with
> and in itself.[81]

Now knowledge may be described as "an immanent activity in
which I perfect myself by the conscious possession of the objective and subjective real."[82] This possession cannot be of the actual
thing and therefore must be by some kind of re-presence in the
knower. The nature of this representation has been the subject
of much thought and consideration and involves a deeper insight
into the nature and kinds of signs. Some Thomists say that the
object is present in the knower, not physically, but intentionally,
by virtue of a formal sign. The distinction between physical re-

---

[80] Van Steenberghen, *Epistemology*, pp. 240-241.
[81] *Ibid.*, p. 247.
[82] *Ibid.*, p. 246.

presentation and intentional re-presentation is important. For example, fire manifest by smoke seen against the sky can be said to have three presences: 1) the actual physical presence of its very being; 2) the re-presence, also physical, through the smoke it caused; 3) the intentional re-presence in the mind of the observer as a result of the observer recognizing the fire in the sign it caused. Purely material things can be re-presented physically to others either through spatial contact or the action they exercise on another (e.g., caused smoke). To a knower "things can be recognized in signs of themselves." This represence in the knower is "a mode of existing which is relational as opposed to the mode of existing by which a being exists in and for itself."[83]

We now must consider the nature and kinds of signs as described by commentators on St. Thomas. A sign may be defined as that which represents something other than itself to a knowing power. Three elements are thus included:

1. the element of representation
2. the element of something other than itself
3. the element of representing to a knowing power.

The semanticists eliminate the last element or any consideration of how we know, which is a more fundamental consideration than their emphasis on how we use signs. A sound semantics must be based on a sound analysis of knowing, for semantics discusses words as used, and words as used can only be used *if* there is a user.

Signs may be considered in relation to the knower—a consideration of the greatest importance to the semanticist—and, in relation to the thing signified. As related to the thing signified, signs are either natural or conventional. Natural signs are related to the thing signified causally and, therefore, they have the same signification for all men; for example, smoke is a sign of fire. Conventional signs are those whose relations to the thing signified are made arbitrarily by the agreement of men. Words and traffic

---

[83] Wilhelmsen, *Man's Knowledge*, pp. 82-84. Cf. *Sum. Theo.*, III, Q. 60, art. 4, resp. 1; I, Q. 85, art. 3, resp. 1. "The thing understood is in the intellect by its own likeness."

lights are examples. This difference is illustrated by the following diagram:[84]

signifies by convention   signifies naturally

WORD   CONCEPT   THING

instrumental sign   formal sign

As related to the knowing power, there are two kinds of signs: formal signs and instrumental signs. A formal or intentional sign functions as a means of knowing. It is a form through which an object is represented to our knowing powers. By means of the image or phantasm as formal sign, we have sense knowledge; by means of the concept as formal sign, we have intellectual knowledge. These are the only formal signs we have—the interior signs by which we know. But knowledge is a pure or formal sign and is not a thing in any sense of the word. Instrumental signs exist in their own rights as words do. All signs except formal signs have two realities: a) they are things existing in the natural order—e.g., vocal sounds; b) they are signs. As signs, they represent something other than themselves; as things, they exist in their own right. Not only do they re-present the thing signified, but they present themselves. Knowledge, however, is not an instrument or carrier of meaning. It is the meaning itself.[85] Its whole existence is exhausted in representing the thing to the knower. It "exists merely to help the knower know the thing."[86] The object it signifies is known by the knower before it is itself known in a reflex act. In order to exercise their function as signs, the formal signs are known not by appearing as an object but by disappearing before the object. The concept is not that which is known when we know, but purely the means by which we seize directly the intelligible aspect of things.[87] In the concept, the ob-

---

[84] John A. Oesterle, *Logic* (New York: Prentice-Hall, 1952), p. 8.

[85] Wilhelmsen, *Man's Knowledge,* p. 87.

[86] *Ibid.,* p. 88.

[87] *Sum. Theo.,* I, Q. 27, art. 2, resp. 2. "In our way of understanding we use the word conception to signify that in the word of our intellect is found the likeness of the thing understood, although there be no identity of nature."

ject of intellection is present in a mode of intentional existence in the sense that there is nothing else in the concept than the object thus present. The concept is a formal sign and the intentionality is there in act. We may well ask more about the nature of this presence. Some scholastics asked the question: "What may be that element of the signified which is joined to the sign and present in it as distinct from the sign itself and its own entity?" The answer they gave is: "no other element than the very signified itself in another mode of existence."[88] The correspondence of knowledge to reality is based on this intentional presence of the known reality in the knower. The intentional form, or what is called second substance, is in the mind in another way than the physical form or first substance is in reality, but the correspondence and relationship are very real. This other mode of existence depends on the knower; in animals and in sense organs, the individual form is present with its aspects of materiality but abstracted from the physical elements. In intellectual knowledge, the mode of existence is free from all limitations of materiality.

The birth of an idea, and hence of intellectual life, seems bound up with the discovery of the value of the meaning of a sign.

> To perceive the relationship of meaning is to have an idea, a spiritual sign. Nothing could be more suggestive in this connection than that kind of miracle which is the first awakening of intelligence in blind-deaf-mutes; essentially it depends upon the discovery of the relationship of the meaning of some gesture with regard to a desired object.[89]

Animals use signs without perceiving their meaning, and as far as is known, meaning has no material correlate.

Thus concepts are formal signs of reality; they re-present reality to the knower but according to the manner of the knower, in another mode of existence. St. Thomas and general semanticists are in agreement that knowledge is not a complete identical pres-

---

[88] Jacques Maritain, *Ransoming the Time*, trans. Harry Lorin Binsse (New York: Charles Scribner's Sons, 1941), pp. 217-220.
[89] *Ibid.*, p. 220.

entation of reality[90] and can be made even less adequate if either the powers of coming into contact with reality are injured or our emotions interfere with the process.

Words are even less direct symbols of reality.[91] Words signify concepts which, in turn, signify "events" or "entities" or "relations" in the world. This double signification and two-step removal from reality on the part of the symbols which make up language is not clearly pointed out by the general semanticists. The ladder of abstraction does not account for words as being separate from human knowledge. The triangle of Ogden and Richards, while not indicating the abstractive nature of both words and thoughts, at least includes thought.

In order to clarify the ideas regarding symbol and meaning it is necessary first to consider a little more the distinction between words and concepts in order to show their relationship and to show how they differ. Fundamentally, as was pointed out above, words are conventional and instrumental signs while concepts are natural and formal signs.

Words, it is true, signify concepts; but one word can signify either one or many concepts. Man signifies one concept; bark signifies two—the sound made by dogs and the covering of trees. Two words can signify the same concept—dog in English signifies in the broad sense the same thing as "chien" in French. Words express and communicate concepts but they are not identical with concepts, still less, with the objective reality signified by the concept. From experience, man knows that often words fail to express what he means and also that his ideas fail to grasp the totality of reality. But concepts re-present more adequately than words because they are less limited by the material conditions of space-time. The semanticists are correct in seeing that there is no necessary connection between the sound called forth by the symbol "man" and the *concept* of man or the *reality,* man. But they imply that since words are arbitrary signs which can and do change what they signify, according as men agree by custom or decree to change them, so, too, does the meaning or the reality

---

[90] *Sum. Theo.,* I, Q. 85, art. 1.
[91] *Sum. Theo.,* Ia, Q. 107, art. 1; I, Q. 93, art. 1, resp. 2; I, Q. 34, art. 1.

represented by the words.[92] Thus they would change the idea of
God.[93] Current semantic analysis is inadequate because there is
no way of connecting with the person who knows as he knows
nor of explaining why meanings are independent of words. A
"modern" semanticist denies or ignores the role of formal sign
and therefore the problem of knowledge becomes for him either
unsolvable, non-existent, or a question of the "correct" response
to a stimulus without meaning. The behavioristic stimulus-response
theory seems to lie implicitly under all of the semanticists' descriptions of direct reaction of word to thing. But the important relation is *not* between *word* and *thing*. In fact, Ogden and Richards
have a dotted base line to show that this relation is arbitrary and
conventional. The important relation is between *mind* and *object*.
The semanticists do not go further into this problem, beyond the
word to the idea. They fail perhaps because such a lack of a
material correlate admitted by empirical psychologists is not consistent with the idea of living protoplasm with a colloidal structure
being stimulated by electric currents. The lack of material correlate
leads to the hypothesis that perhaps a non-material principle is
the source of this kind of activity.

But general semanticists and most Thomists agree that words,
as instrumental signs, have the following limitations which are
important for communication.

> 1. Any instrumental sign involves ambiguity which
> must be solved in order to have communication.
> 2. Words depend on the precise signification the user
> of the words wishes to convey through his words. Nor
> does the user depend solely on words to express his
> meaning or "ideas." He knows that what he is signifying
> through words may be ambiguous to others. He wishes
> to communicate concepts which he intends to signify
> instrumentally to some one else and the words may fail
> him or they may mean other things to his listener.[94]

---

[92] Oesterle, *Logic*, pp. 4-8. Cf. Aristotle, *De Interpretatione,* 16 a. 3.
[93] Supra, pp. 71-72.
[94] John Oesterle, "Another Approach to the Problem of Meaning," *The
Thomist,* VI (1944), pp. 233-263.

This leads to a conclusion not mentioned by the semanticists: words are not the true causes of communication but ideas are.[95] Simultaneous translations going on at United Nations sessions have different words all communicating, it is hoped, the same ideas. Words, then, are meaningless sounds, not when they have no objective reality which can be pointed out, but when there are no *ideas* which they symbolize. The ideas, in turn, must represent some reality, either logical or real, but this need not be observable by the senses. Great literature is full of ideas not observable by the senses.[96] Current emphasis is on the relation of the words to the listener and to the speaker. Proper semantic reactions refer only to this relation. Yet the cause of disagreement is less that of confusion over words than of the differences of meanings these words convey to different people. Two people may talk about the same thing using the same word but have entirely different meanings and therefore there is no real communication between them even though each hear the other using the same word. St. Thomas gives an example of this, which is particularly interesting in view of the article quoted above on the meaning of the word *God*. He says:

> The idea in the intellect is the likeness of what is in the thing as is said in Periherm i. But the word animal applied to a true animal and to a picture of one, is equivocal. Therefore this name God applied to the true God and to God in opinion is applied equivocally. . . .
>
> This name God in the three aforesaid significations is taken neither univocally nor equivocally, but analogically. This is apparent from this reason:—Univocal terms mean absolutely the same thing, but equivocal terms absolutely different; whereas in analogical terms a word taken in one signification must be placed in the definition of the same word taken in other senses.
>
> The multiplication of names does not depend on the predication of the name but on the signification; for this name, *man*, of whomsoever it is predicated whether truly or falsely, is predicated in one sense. But it would be

[95] *Ibid.,* p. 247.
[96] Cf. George Alexander Carver, Jr., *Aesthetics and the Problem of Meaning* (New Haven: Yale University Press, 1952).

multiplied if, by the same *man* we meant to signify different things; for instance, if one meant to signify by this name *man,* what man really is, and another meant to signify by the same name, a stone or something else. Hence it is evident that a Catholic saying that an idol is not God contradicts the pagan asserting that it is God; because each of them uses this name God to signify the true God. For when the pagan says an idol is God he does not use this name as meaning God in opinion, for he would then speak the truth as also Catholics sometimes use the name in that sense as in the Psalm: All the gods of gentiles are demons. . . .

Neither a Catholic nor a pagan knows the very nature of God as it is in itself. So a pagan can take this name God in the same way when he says an idol is God as the Catholic does in saying an idol is not God. But if anyone should be quite ignorant of God altogether, he could not even name Him unless perhaps as we use names the meanings of which we know not.[97]

Thus St. Thomas and general semanticists agree also that words mean different things to different people. In the above examples an analogical usage is involved. The former's explanation of this fact is consistent with the theories of abstraction, of the substantial unity of man and of the nature of man as rational animal. The whole psychological theory of knowledge and judgment also throws light on the role of the pre-conscious and the symbolic in man's emotional and cognoscitive life.[98] All ideas are ultimately drawn from the matter contained in phantasms.[99] Over the years,

---

[97] *Sum. Theo.,* I, Q. 13, art. 10. St. Thomas holds that with respect to true universals, the concept is identical in all who arrive at them, if *considered purely as concept.* If the intellect does come to the fully abstracted meaning or essence of a thing, it will be the same essence as another human intellect would get under the same conditions although the *meaning* in the *broad* sense of the general semanticists would be different. The general semanticists use *meaning* as if it were defined as the *total personal reaction to something* whereas St. Thomas uses his *significatio* as the *completely abstracted part* of that *total* reaction. The concept, e.g., of "circularity" purely as concept is identical in all who arrive at it, but the impact may be very different to a philosopher, a mathematician and a basketball player.

[98] Wilhelmsen, *Man's Knowledge,* p. 114.

[99] *Sum. Theo.,* II-II, Q. 175, art. 4; -I, Q. 12, art. 12.

man accumulates various phantasms which contribute to his idea, say of "an American." Therefore his idea of "an American" is colored by his past experiences with Americans as represented in his phantasms and stored in his memory, his unconscious or preconscious as well as present habitually in his intellect. When he says "An American is peace-loving," the subject of that sentence is a symbolization of what is in the memory and is not a new meaning. In the new judgment the old phantasms are used by the intellect. In previous judgments or acts of knowing the phantasms probably did refer to something else. This prior meaning is latent within the phantasm and pervades it even as it is used in a new judgment. Hence, in any new judgment, the predicate is working through a large body of inarticulate knowledge.[100]

It is this latent knowledge, which is proper to each individual, that is at the root of the disagreements which the general semanticists are trying to eliminate. Our knowledge of any subject is gradually built up over the years by experiences which enrich the subject with more and more meaning. The difficulty in communication, therefore, lies not in the words themselves, but in the fact that these words symbolize ideas which have been colored by the individual past experiences of each man. Misunderstandings arise from the diverse symbolic meanings attached to the same word. The word "atom" to a nuclear physicist and to the man in the street sounds the same but contains very different meanings due to the very different experiences of the two men with the reality and the thought of the reality symbolized by the word. It seems difficult to see, then, how there can be absolute clarity in a world in which meaning involves the past experiences as well as the present. Words rarely denote only; they usually connote different aspects to different men. In order to have such clarity, complete communication would entail an actual physical exchange of phantasms and of experiences. It would actually entail one man's

---

[100] Frederick Wilhelmsen, "The Philosopher and the Myth," *The Modern Schoolman*, XXXII (November 1954), p. 46. Cf. *Sum. Theo.*, II-II, Q. 173, art. 2: Just as the various arrangements of the letters of the alphabet convey various ideas so the various coordinations of phantasms produce various intelligible species.

becoming the other. "The closest mankind can ever come to
mastering the symbolic is to live in a common culture, worship
at the same altar and face a like destiny."[101]

Thus the relativity of connotation as due to the past experiences
of man is one point about which St. Thomas and some contemporary Thomists and general semanticists are in agreement.
It would seem, then, that there can not be any absolute truth and
we are faced with either scepticism or a relativism that would
make the children in our schools even more insecure than they are
today. If meanings change from age to age, and from culture to
culture, even from man to man, it is difficult to see how any
knowledge can be transmitted from age to age that would be
helpful. We are faced, then, with the fourth problem: the truth
of man's knowledge. How relative are the meanings ascribed by
men to words, and more basically, how closely do the meanings
of things grasped by men, conform to that reality? Is there any
guarantee that there is a communality of knowledge for all ages?

Conformity of ideas to reality and of words to ideas:

The problems of the relativity of man's knowledge (due to the
fact that it is so colored by past experiences), and of the need
for some kind of communality of knowledge from age to age are
really entailed in the question of universals. It is raised here by
the general semanticists because of the fact that "class concept"
seems to be the result of common experience and, as neo-
nominalists, they would deny that there is any basis for this
concept in reality. Hence class concepts change their meanings
with each age and culture. Actually the general semanticists are
correct in saying that the class concept is not in individuals. They
are right, too, in saying that Smith is not identical with the "class,
man." That such is not the import of the classical tradition, however, is shown by this fact: Aristotle and, later, St. Thomas insisted that a universal affirmative proposition cannot be reversed
(as to the subject-predicate relationship) and remain true. Herein,
by the way, is an explicit Aristotelian denial of the "is of

---

[101] Wilhelmsen, *Man's Knowledge of Reality*, pp. 113-115. Cf. supra, pp.
47, 62, 68.

identity," if taken in reference to a particular-universal relationship. That is you cannot say man is Smith. The proposition did not imply an identity but a *membership in a class*. The class concept has some verification in the individual, but not the verification of class identity. There is something in the individual whereby it belongs to a class. It participates in the reality of a class; it is an "imitation" of the class reality though in a singular fashion.[102] The universal can be predicated of it though not in its formal sense of class. It is here that St. Thomas supplemented the doctrine of intrinsic forms or the principles of existence, the substantial forms, with the doctrine of extrinsic forms which are, of course, the ground of universals, the "non-existent" exemplars of all existents. In other words, things that exist today reveal order and conform to a certain pattern to which science can somewhat penetrate. But any pattern or order is the result of thought. There-fore, these existents, so patterned and ordered and structured, must be the result of thought. Since, obviously, they are not the artifacts of man, they are not the result of the thought of man. But they must be the result of some intellect, *some* knowledge, other-wise they would not be so ordered. Thomists say that these patterns do not exist except fundamentally in the infinity of God. These pat-terns or natures cannot be known experimentally for empirical knowledge is only of the actions of existents in the physical order. These patterns are in the mind of God as the plan of a house is in the architect's mind before he begins to put the house into existence. Oddly enought, this thesis (that we cannot think of the natures in plants or man without thinking also that these "natures" are called into being by thought) has received emphatic and perhaps unexpected support in the principles of modern existentialism. Both St. Thomas and Sartre could be said to hold the same premise: things have an essential nature only in so far as they are fashioned by thought.[103] For example, we can speak of the nature of a letter opener only because of the fact that man exists and has a constructive intellect which can invent and has invented

---

[102] *Sum. Theo.*, I, Q. 85, art. 3, resp. 1 also—Ia, Q. 44, art. 3, resp. 3: "It is not necessary that universals should exist outside the particulars in order to be their exemplars."

[103] *Sum. Theo.*, I, Q. 18, art. 4, resp. 2.

the letter opener. Sartre denies the evidence of order and pattern in the world because he has first denied God. Therefore he says: "There is no such thing as human nature because there exists no God to think it creatively."[104] But what St. Thomas does is to start from the evidence of pattern and order present in the objective world. Pattern, design, and order come only from an intellect. No human intellect patterned and ordered the universe; therefore this pattern and order is present in a supreme intellect, in the mind of God. It is the presence of these exemplars, models, patterns in the mind of God that is the security of man's knowledge. St. Thomas postulates three universals: the pattern or *universal* in the mind of God before the entity ever exists and according to which it is, so to speak, constructed; 2) the pattern in the thing itself, the substantial form which is the dynamic principle directing and organizing the activity and development of the existent thing in accord with the exemplar; 3) the universal which men have abstracted from the existent, the concept which is formed as a result of the activity of the human intellect drawing out of the phantasm the form that was potentially present in it.[105] When men then reflect on this, the formal universal idea that results is the essence, not only of the particular existent, Tom, but of *man* as such. Because this idea of "man" as such is derived from the passing existent, it would be relative only to that passing existent, were it not for the fact that the passing or contingent existent, in turn, is patterned after a model which transcends time and space. Such is the basis for the communality of knowledge from age to age and from culture to culture. The reality and character of things consist in their being creatively thought or known by the Creator. True is a synonym for real. The essence of all things as creatures is that they are formed after an archetypal pattern which dwells in the absolutely creative mind of God.

We must remember that we can never properly grasp this conformity of the original model in God and the created being which is the existent thing. St. Thomas said that thinkers have

---

[104] Pieper, *The Silence of St. Thomas,* p. 52, quoting Sartre.

[105] *Sum. Theo.,* I, Q. 15, art. 1-3; Q. 75, art. 3, resp. 1 and Q. 44, art. 3, resp. 3.

not and will never succeed in finding the essence of a single fly[106] because we can never fully grasp these likenesses of the divine ideas precisely as likenesses. Nor can we know God directly from these likenesses. Things are unknowable to man, because they are themselves all too knowable, and because of the weakness of man's power of knowing. While it may be said truly, however, that the design and essence of natural things cannot be wholly grasped by the human mind, they are knowable to a certain extent. Man's intellectual power enables him to penetrate to the essence of things; science has had insights into and made assertions about the nature of things which, though, not exhaustive, are true. Science, as science, can give fairly definitive answers if it *keeps* to the sphere of science—to the measurable and observable, to, for example, the chemical composition of paper or the structure of an atom. But when the question is "what is this object?" in the sense of "what is this portion of material reality in its *truth* and *essence?*" no adequate answers can be given by science, first of all, nor by philosophers, although the latter will give metaphysical explanations that are more adequate than those of science since they do endeavor to get at the essences. But no human mind can completely grasp real things to know them as fully as they are knowable. In this, the general semanticists agree with St. Thomas. But only the latter points out that it is a philosophical problem that cannot be answered by science in terms of material correlatives. The answer transcends the highest level of abstraction of the general semanticists, that of science, and belongs to philosophy. A finite spirit is unable to acquire, in the last resort, such a comprehensive knowledge "because the knowability of Being which we are attempting to transform into knowledge, consists in its being creatively thought by the Creator."[107] It is not up to science, once it recognizes its inability to penetrate into the deepest secrets of the universe, to say that there are no such secrets. It can know that there is a pattern; it can measure the pattern and express in symbolic terms the structure. But the foundations and cause of this pattern are beyond the measuring

---

[106] Pieper, *The Silence of St. Thomas*, p. 64, quoting St. Thomas on *The Apostles' Creed*, chap. 1.

[107] Pieper, *The Silence of St. Thomas*, p. 97.

tools and methods of science. To deny the underlying model means to deny the pattern and this, science cannot do, because its body of knowledge is precisely of this pattern.

The problem and the paradox of human knowledge, that it is "at the same time true and not fully sufficient,"[108] has been seen by general semanticists and by others centuries before them. The inadequacy of human knowledge has been emphasized by the former and the inference is that the truth of the knowledge of man is completely relative, we might almost say, absolutely relative. The criterion of truth they present, in keeping with their positivist foundations, is that of predictability on the empirical level and of freedom from self-contradiction on the logical level. Such a criterion could be justified if the ideas of men were *their constructs only,* without any basis in things. Ever since Kant proposed his categories, truth has come more and more to mean what is decided upon by men either through custom or decrees. In one sense, St. Thomas agrees. Truth, he says is the equation of thought and thing; the conformity of mind to reality. The question is *what mind.* Things are placed between the creative knowledge of God and the non-creative, reality-conformed knowledge of man. The structure of reality is a system in which the archetypes and the copies are both embraced. *Things* are ontologically true if they are conformed to the archetypes or their eternal patterns. And *man's knowledge* is true if it is conformed to the existent thing. There is a double concept of the truth of things. The first denotes the creative fashioning of things by God; the second, their intrinsic knowability for the human mind. The creative fashioning by God makes it possible for things to be known by men. Were they not creatively thought by God, they could not be known by men; in an analogous manner, because a plan of a house has been thought of by man, it can be known by other men. The difference is that the plan of the house and the house are not created out of nothing; it will be made out of other existent things combined in a new way. The creative knowledge of God creates the very elements out of which the existents are made. However, because of the dual aspects of truth, that of the con-

---

[108] *Ibid.,* p. 54 and cf. *Sum. Theo.,* I, Q. 16, art. 1.

formity of things to their models and of man's mind to things, there are, in the second sense, many truths. St. Thomas, even says that there are as many truths as there are men:

> If therefore we speak of truth as it exists in the intellect, according to its proper nature, then there are many truths in many created intellects; and even in one and the same intellect according to the number of things known.[109]

Nor are men's *statements* eternally true:

> Because our intellect is not eternal, neither is the truth of enunciable propositions which are formed by us eternal.[110]
> . . . Hence in one way truth varies on the part of the intellect from the fact that a change of opinion occurs about a thing which in itself has not changed and in another way when the thing is changed but not the opinion; and in either way there can be a change from true to false.[111]

The "truth," so-called, of our intellects can change. For example, the statements: "the earth is the center of the universe" was once considered true and is now regarded as false. Man's intellect before the fifteenth century was not conformed to reality concerning this fact. Science discovered the reality and in so doing corrected man's knowledge so that men say that the former statement, once held to be true, is now false.

These considerations can help to clarify two points of the general semanticists concerning the meaning of words: the operational and extensional definitions and the multi-ordinality of some words. St. Thomas preferred "intensional" definitions because he found them more consistent with the theory that the substantial form is the principle of identity and this substantial form is represented in human knowledge by the concept.

> The concept conveyed by a word is its definition. Words do not signify the intelligible species [ideas] themselves,

---

[109] *Sum. Theo.,* Ia, Q. 16, art. 5; Ia, Q. 21, art. 2.

[110] *Ibid.,* Ia, Q. 16, art. 7.

[111] *Ibid.,* also I, Q. 85, art. 6.

> but that which the intellect forms for itself for the pur-
> pose of judging of external things.[112]

Definitions by ideas are considered the forms themselves apart
from the thing itself. The form or likeness of the house pre-exists
in the mind of the builder. This is what is expressed by the
intensional definition or the essential definition. Sometimes it is
impossible to arrive at an intensional definition, especially of
physical things. In that case, the extensional definition, called
nominal since it merely designates the particular to which the
name is applied but does not specify the essence through genus
and difference, is perfectly acceptable. So, too, is a definition from
the effects, which may, in one sense, be called an operational
definition.[113]

The multi-ordinal terms of the general semanticists seem to
change their meanings as they range up and down the levels of
abstraction. These are similar to analogous terms in the philosophy of St. Thomas with this significant difference. Multi-
ordinal terms have no transferred significance, but derive it all
from context. Analogous terms have common meaning which
changes as it is applied to other levels of being, in *proportion* to
the level of being.

> Whenever anything is predicated of many things analogi-
> cally, it is found in only one of them according to its
> proper nature and from this one the rest are de-
> nominated.[114]

Aquinas uses the isomorphic theory and suggests that there is an
identity not between the contents meant by both analogical terms
but between some relations holding between the first term and
its thing on one side and the second term and its thing on the
other. The relations are not identical.[115]

This acknowledgment by St. Thomas of the variations in human

---

[112] *Sum. Theo.*, I, Q. 85, art. 3.
[113] *Ibid.*, Q. 29, art. 1, resp. 3; Q. 2, art. 2, resp. 2.
[114] *Ibid.*, Q. 16, art. 5.
[115] I. M. Bochenski, "On Analogy," *The Thomist*, II (1948), pp. 424-447.

knowledge is an incomplete presentation of his theory of truth while it sums up the whole position of the semanticists. The human intellect can and does change in its knowledge of reality and therefore what men stated as true one year may not be stated as true in the next. There are no eternal truths *in* created intellects, which are not eternal. Moreover, given the limitations of human knowledge, the conformity of the human mind to the reality is a growing conformity as more and more of the reality is revealed through the discoveries of science. In this sense, because man's knowledge is relative to his age, the truth, as expressed by man, is relative and cumulative. But we are not condemned then to the uneasy uncertainty of complete relativism. The universe still runs according to the same plan and order it did one thousand years ago. What has changed is man's *knowledge* of the universe, not the *universe* itself, nor the plan according to which it is structured. Moreover, Einsteinian and Newtonian physics differ less than we are often led to suppose. There is not chaos in the universe but evidence of an order which all the greatest minds in the world of all time have not yet succeeded in fathoming. The hypothesis of probability is not because the universe is not ordered according to a model or archetype, but because man has not yet succeeded in discovering all the aspects of the order. As Korzybski himself pointed out in another context, "indeterminism is but a part of a larger determinism." Science holds ultimately to that fact that the universe is determined to a definite plan. The indeterminism is a way of saying that man has not discovered the plan. But the order present in the universe makes possible the confidence of scientists in their predictions. This unchanging order is found in the universals *ante rem,* in the archetypes. *They* would not *be,* were there no eternal intellect to conceive them.

> But if we speak of truth as it is in things, then all things are true by one primary truth; to which each one is assimilated according to its own entity. And thus although the essences and forms of things are many, the truth of the divine intellect is one in conformity to which all things are said to be true.[116]

---

[116] *Sum. Theo.,* Ia, Q. 16, art. 6.

It is the truth of *things* that cannot change, and the truth of things is in the Mind that is not subject to change or to time.

> Universals are independent of place and time. It does not follow from this that they are eternal except in an intellect if one exists that is eternal.[117]

The question then of the changing meanings of things and of words is not a simple one. Things *can* change their meanings if we consider these meanings as being known by men who color them with past sense and emotional experiences; things in *themselves, in their deepest nature* or *meaning* remain *unchanged* although their external appearances may change. The same thing is true for words. *Words* may change their meanings according to the age and culture and background of experience of the society using them; but the *things* which they represent, not the knowledge of them by the individual man, still have an *unchanging meaning in the sense that they are conformed fundamentally to the model or pattern which is unchangeable.* The closer man's knowledge is conformed to these archetypes, the closer the correspondence of his idea to the exemplar, and the closer words can express this knowledge man has, the truer will be his statements. Absolute identity of human thought to thing, of word to thought is impossible, given the number of factors that go into the process by which man gets the thought and associates a word with the thought.

However, it often happens that even after man's knowledge has been corrected to conform to reality, such as the fact that the earth goes around the sun and not vice versa, man still retains the old language form, such as saying "The sun rises in the East"; "sunrise" and "sunset." Most people use the phrases, however, realizing that they do not hold literally. The general semanticists are wise in stressing that, while reform of language probably is impossible, awareness of the incorrectness of language is absolutely necessary. Thus it seems that the subject-predicate form of language is the most convenient for communication, but awareness of the fact that the statement "the grass is green" is

---

[117] *Sum. Theo.*, Ia, Q. 16, art. 4, resp. 3; also art. 8; also I, Q. 85, art. 3, resp. 1 and I, Q. 44, art. 3.

a relative statement, relative to my perception of the grass, is advisable. There is agreement in general on this statement but just what "green" connotes to each person probably differs somewhat due to differences in nervous systems. The danger is that in stressing the relativity of meanings and of truth as known by men (because of varying connotations) awareness is not maintained or developed, of the fact that underlying a very changing world and a very inadequate knowledge of it by men, is the fact that things are in an order and that order is eternal. One may also lose sight of the basic possibility of objective knowledge. Therefore, things are essentially knowable because they have their intelligibility, their inner clarity and lucidity, their power to reveal themselves to the inquiring mind of the scientist, from God Who has creatively thought them. It is not consistent to argue away the idea that things have been creatively thought by God and then go on, as science is doing, to understand or try to understand and know these things and discuss how they can be known by the human mind.

Summary: It can be seen that the fact that each man's knowledge is colored by his past (and that his use of words is also colored by emotional experiences with those words) raises a problem about which the semanticists are rightfully concerned. This problem involves an understanding of the way by which man gets meanings and of the reasons why the connotation of words so differs among men. Like St. Thomas, general semanticists see that the past experiences of each man largely color with emotional overtones the meanings he has of things, and of words. No satisfactory scientific answer can be given concerning the way man gets meanings nor concerning the correspondence of human thought to thing, of human words to thought and to thing. These questions invade the realm of philosophy. A proper balance between the *realization* of the stability of the truth of things because they are creatively known by God and the *awareness* of the *variations* in the degrees of knowledge by men (in the sense that the past experiences of men differ considerably and that knowledge is in the knower according to the mode of the *knower, not of the known*) is both needed and valuable. Educators should point out these facts to their students. The general semanticists have much to contribute towards the second point, but their system, avowedly a materialistic one, cannot help with regard to the first point. Rather than deny the existence of stable truth underlying the whole universe in virtue of its conformity to the archetypes in God, which denial is a philosophical one, it would seem better to stop short of either denial or affirmation, if they are to keep within the limits imposed by themselves in stating that theirs is a scientific discipline.

GENERAL SUMMARY

I. *THE PROBLEM OF CHANGE*: How can change be reconciled with the equally observable order and structure present in the universe according to which science predicts and generalizes? Both groups admit change:

GENERAL SEMANTICISTS

ST. THOMAS
(A SYNTHESIS)

1. Reality is a process of events in continual flux, according to the hypotheses of scientists.

1. Change implies a permanent metaphysical principle, both of existence and of knowledge. It is called substance and is a dynamic principle of activity, organization and identity, directing the changes which are manifest in the phenomenal world.

II. *THE PROBLEM OF HOW MAN KNOWS*: What is there in man that enables him to predict and generalize in a way that corresponds fairly well to the order and structure and activity of the universe? Both groups use the process of abstraction.

1. *Man* is a mere nervous organism whose colloidal structure is stimulated by electrical currents. Truly human activity (symbol-reactions) involves the

1. Man is a rational animal sharing with the animals the powers of sensation, locomotion and emotion, able to soar beyond the source of his knowledge in the

integrated response of thalamic-cortical regions while retarded animalistic behavior (sign-reactions) is the response of the thalamus only.

physical world, to generalize, infer, create beauty, organize science largely through the medium of symbols, especially language.

2. *Abstraction*:

means selection and is carried on by all living organisms in response to stimuli. It is on two main levels — non-verbal and verbal. Animals can only abstract on the non-verbal level; man has no limits to his levels of abstraction. Abstraction means leaving out aspects of reality. It goes from non-verbal level direct to the word.

means the selective and separating process of the human intellect alone whereby it gradually leaves out phenomena and illuminates the form or abiding principle of identity in each. Abstraction means getting to the abiding reality underlying all phenomena. It goes from the non-verbal level to the idea; the word comes later and is not part of the process of abstraction.

III. *THE PROBLEM OF COMMUNICATION*: the meaning of symbols and words. How adequate and accurate are the symbols by which man gets and expresses meanings? Both groups point to the inadequacy of words to express reality.

1. *Symbols*: words are instrumental signs whereby the thing is known, signified and clarified for communication purposes. Meanings of words vary according to cultures and individuals.

1. Words are instrumental signs representing or symbolizing ideas. Ideas are formal signs whereby the object is known. The object is known according to the manner of the knower. Past experiences stored in the imagination and memory "color" meanings for individuals.

2. *Meanings*: W o r d s have meanings as determined by society. Words without corre-

2. Words do change their meanings according to the usages of society. Men's knowledge also

sponding physical reality are meaningless s o u n d s. Communication is through, by, and of words alone. Extensional definitions are the only valid definitions.

changes. But things have meanings in themselves beyond what men know and say of them. Intensional definitions best represent t h e s e meanings, though extensional definitions are sometimes needed.

IV. *THE PROBLEM OF TRUTH*: Given the variations in man's knowledge and expression how can there be an abiding body of knowledge on which to build science?

1. Truth is only what society or predictability indicate. Morality is equally relative.

1. Truth in men's minds is relative to each human mind since truth is the conformity of mind to thing. But things are eternally true to the order and structure of the universe planned by God from all *eternity*. This order is the basis for the confidence of science that it can know and manipulate the universe. It is the basis, too, for the natural law, an *inner* principle shown by reason, according to which man must act if he is to conform to the human archetype in the Divine Intellect.

CHAPTER IV

THE EDUCATIONAL IMPLICATIONS OF GENERAL SEMANTICS

It is difficult to assess accurately the nature and extent of the influence of general semantics in education because, first, there are such conflicting opinions as to the nature of this influence; and, second, the number of the fields which general semanticists claim to have influenced and which contain references to the works of Korzybski and Hayakawa is so great. This chapter will attempt to give some indication as to the extent of the influence by presenting the facts concerning the number and content of articles published referring to general semantics on the four levels of education—primary, secondary, college and graduate or teacher training. At the end, some general conclusions as to the age level and fields where general semantics are most influential, and the advantages and disadvantages of such influence will be drawn.

This will not be a complete and exhaustive examination of all the texts and articles, but it is hoped that it will be sufficiently comprehensive to give a fairly good indication of the importance of general semantics and the reasons why it cannot be ignored by educators. The sources of information in general were:

1. Articles listed in the *Reader's Guide to Periodical Literature* and *Education Index* since 1933.

2. References indicated by the Library of Congress Card Catalogue and the Union Catalogue.

3. References given by the general semanticists themselves from the Institute of General Semantics, in the *General Semantics Bulletin* and *Etc.*

In order not to wander too far afield, a certain amount of selectivity had to be exercised. Although many articles were examined, they all are not treated here, either because they dealt with the semantics of I. A. Richards and C. K. Ogden, or because their content is summarized in other articles which are treated. Whenever both the principles of general semantics and those of the "Basic Englishers" were discussed, as is usually the case in high school texts, the books are listed. One general trend may be noted here. The articles and books after 1950 are less extreme in tone—those of the opponents and the proponents of general semantics as well. The former are less virulent in their criticism; the latter are less exaggerated in their claims as to the panacea-nature of general semantics.

ON THE ELEMENTARY LEVEL

There are no texts for the elementary grades containing pure general semantics principles or even an adaptation of them. However, from 1938 to 1955 some excellent articles have appeared on the application of the principles of general semantics to reading readiness and to reading problems by such authorities as Lou La Brant, Emmett Betts, and Nila Banton Smith in such periodicals as *Education, Elementary English, Elementary School Journal, Educational Research* and *Modern Language Journal.*

The majority of these articles stress the need for enabling the children to get the meanings of words by actually experiencing the objects or situations which the words symbolize and also for making the children realize that words can have different meanings or shades of meanings.[1,2] Sara Michie explicitly referred to the influence of M. Kendig, at present director of the Institute of General Semantics under whom she taught in the Barstow School in Kansas City. Miss Michie stresses the non-Aristotelian scientific method as well as the relativity of word meanings. "A word has absolutely no meaning outside its context."[3] The need to develop the language of relativity in kindergarten was advocated by Osburn, Huntington and Meeks who also attacked the Aristotelian language, "the evil produced by the Aristotelian primary substance"[4] which emphasized the subject-predicate form of proposi-

---

[1] Lou La Brant, "Words for Peace," *Education,* LXVIII (May, 1948), pp. 546-549.

[2] Helen Bachman Knipp, "Development of Thinking and of Concepts," *Elementary English,* XXVIII (May, 1951), pp. 290-297.

[3] Sarah Michie, "A New General Language Curriculum for the Eighth Grade," *Modern Language Journal,* XXII (Feb., 1938), p. 347.

[4] W. J. Osburn, Muriel Huntington, and Viola Meeks, "The Language of Relativity as Related to Reading Readiness," *Journal of Education Research,* XXXIX (April, 1946), pp. 583-601.

tion. These articles, mostly attacking the Aristotelian language and written before 1950, were not as fruitful as those applying general semantics to reading readiness.

Betts traces the history of semantics in his article presented at the annual institute on reading at Temple University in January 1949.[5] He distinguishes Ogden and Richards from the general semanticists by saying that the former, concerned more with linguistics, tend to emphasize word-to-word relationships in their discussions of meanings while the latter stress word-fact relationships and word-person relationships. He also maintains that the foundations of the reading program should deal with Pragmatics, Semantics, and Syntactics as described and defined by Morris. After describing the levels of abstraction according to Korzybski, he points out the danger of high level abstractions and the difficulties of multi-ordinal terms. "At all school levels children must be directed toward developing the learner's awareness of shifts in meaning of tone."[6] Like most of the other writers, he also incorporates some of the theories of C. K. Ogden and I. A. Richards —for example, the four categories of meaning—literal or sense meaning, feeling or mood of the writer, tone or attitude of the reader toward the writer, and intent or purpose of the writer. He, too, distinguishes between referential and emotive types of language. He lists as the outcome of a systematic study of the semantic dimensions of language what could well be applied to any educational program incorporating the ideas of general semantics:

1. articulate awareness of the symbolic nature of language and of the process of abstraction.
2. consciousness of the levels of abstractions, especially of the dangers of "fictions"—those without physical referents.
3. recognition of shifts of meaning according to the whole context of the word and according to metaphorical uses.
4. ability to identify and to interpret the connotations and denotations of words.

---

[5] Emmett Albert Betts, "Reading: Semantic Approach," *Education*, XLIX (May, 1949), pp. 527-555.
[6] *Ibid.*, p. 541.

   5. ability to discriminate between referential and emotive language.[7]

The main purpose in reading readiness programs is, according to Nila B. Smith, to establish referents. She points out the good effects of the emphasis on semantics[8] on reading readiness programs:

   1. wider use of first hand experiences as aids in teaching reading—"The word is not the thing but a symbol of the experience."
   2. increased use of visual aids.
   3. more attention to contextual influences especially in polysemantic words or words of multiple meanings.
   4. clarification of the different levels of abstraction.
   5. new types of reading tests which contain items which will ask the child to:
   a. determine meanings of the same words in different contexts
   b. select words which name a class
   c. underline words which affect feelings, give facts, reflect the author's feelings or ideas.[9]

Two texts for Elementary Teachers which incorporate the principles of the levels of abstraction and the context theory of word meaning and show dependence on general semantics are:

Lou La Brant, et al., *Your Language* (New York: McGraw-Hill Book Co., 1956).
Virgil E. Herrick and Leland B. Jacobs, ed., *Children and the Language Arts* (Englewood Cliffs, N. J.: Prentice-Hall, Inc., 1955).

Lou La Brant gives even more explanation of the general semantics principles, as applied to the teaching of English in general, in her *We Teach English* (New York: Harcourt, Brace and Co.,

---

[7] *Ibid.*, pp. 553-555.

[8] Nila Banton Smith, "How Will the Semantic Emphasis Affect Reading Instruction?" *Education*, CXIX (May, 1949), pp. 556-561.

[9] Nila Banton Smith, "Reading Readiness: Semantic Implications," *Elementary English*, XXVI (December, 1949), p. 548.

1951). The National Council of Teachers of English also devoted
a section on "Teaching Reading and Semantics" in volume one
of their series on teaching English.[10] Hayakawa was a member
of one of the committees and all of the chief books by the general
semanticists are listed in the bibliography as recommended reading, as well as several articles from *Etc*. In reviewing the book,
Etc. felt that insufficient attention was paid to general semantics
as such but laid the blame on the lack of concerted effort by the
general semanticists to go into the practical educational area. The
comment is interesting: "Perhaps we have not defined and accepted a responsibility to make it unlikely that one will graduate
in our educational system without an opportunity to experience
the general semantics orientation as a fundamental guide—not to
what one thinks about life but to how one uses his thinking
machinery."[11]

ON THE SECONDARY LEVEL

There are two texts for junior and senior high schools presenting directly, but on the level of the adolescent, the principles of
general semantics regarding the meanings of words.[12, 13] The more
recent high school texts on language, English and communication
are beginning to have chapters on critical thinking, the distinction
between emotive, directive and informative language; the levels
of abstraction and the difference between inference and report.[14]

---

[10] *The English Language Arts,* prepared by the Commission on the English
Curriculum of the National Council of Teachers of English (New York:
Appleton-Century-Crofts, Inc., 1952).

[11] Col. Ed. Smith, review of *The English Language Arts,* Vol. I, *Etc.*,
XIV, 3 (Spring, 1957), p. 227.

[12] Robert Herman More, *General Semantics in the High School Program*
(Columbus, Ohio: The Ohio State University Press, 1945).

[13] Catherine Minteer, *Words and What They Do To You*: beginning
lessons in general semantics for junior and senior high school (Evanston,
Ill.: Row, Peterson and Co., 1953).

[14] Two of the more typical and more recent texts are:
Joseph C. Blumenthal, Robert Frank and Louis Zahner, *Living Language*
(New York: Harcourt, Brace and Co., 1953), Grades IX-XII in four
volumes. This was recommended in *Etc.,* XII, 1 (Autumn, 1954), p. 62.
Thomas Clark Pollock, Marion C. Sheridan, Francis Ledbitter, Ronald C.

This trend is due to the influence of C. K. Ogden and I. A. Richards and to that of the general semanticists as well, since the bibliographies of these texts usually contain the books of the former as well as those of Korzybski, Hayakawa and sometimes of Johnson and Lee.[15]

Minteer's book is not used as a text but as an auxiliary for the teacher.[16] Although the author states that "successful teachers have always applied the principles of general semantics in their teaching methods," she experimented to see what would be the effects of a planned course on the elementary or junior high school level. The results indicated that there was an improvement in the pupil's ability to express himself and in pupil-teacher relations. Her text gives a lesson for each of the basic general semantics principles with resource readings listed for the teacher such as the works of Lee, Hayakawa, Chase, Johnson and Korzybski. Not only are the general semantics principles and devices presented, but there is even a chapter (XII) explaining the process world to the students so that they could see the need to date all their statements.

While advocating that language study should be based on general semantics, Moore presents a mixture of Korzybski and I. A. Richards. He emphasizes the need for finding the referents and avoiding or distinguishing at least, high level abstractions, the context theory of word meaning and the distinction between emotive and referential language.

The articles in periodicals discussed the application of general semantics in such fields as English, science, mathematics and the

Doll, *The Art of Communication,* 4 volumes (New York: The Macmillan Co., 1955). This book gives Korzybski's levels of abstraction and emphasizes the intensional definitions recommended by Richards as well as his idea of distinguishing emotive and referential language.

[15] Texts for teachers also recommend the works of these general semanticists. For example:

John J. De Boer, Walter V. Kaulfers and Helen Rand Miller, *Teaching Secondary English* (New York: McGraw-Hill Book Co., Inc., 1951).

Holland D. Robert, Walter V. Kaulfers, and Grayson N. Kefauver, *English for Social Living* (New York: McGraw Hill Book Co., Inc., 1943).

[16] From a letter from the publishers, Row, Peterson and Co. (May 21, 1957).

social sciences. The articles are listed and annotated in the bibliography. The most prolific writer was Charles I. Glicksberg who wrote at least four articles in six years urging the adoption of general semantics principles, alleging that it is the application of scientific ways of thinking to the problem of communication. He prophesied a slow but sure adoption of its principles "when the aim of instruction will be not to cover a given amount of subject matter but to change the student's linguistic habits and his methods of evaluation."[17] He also claimed that general semantics would achieve its greatest measure of success in the teaching of science on the secondary level, for the habit of scientific thinking engendered by it would result in a corresponding mastery of language.[18] In several articles he emphasizes the relativity of word meanings and of ideas:

> There is no such universal abstraction as 'truth' or 'race' or 'God' or 'love.' Truth, like love is a matter of degree—Bertrand Russell says people who speak with reference to Truth would be better to speak of fact.[19]

As a result, the teacher should "strive to point out that most of the generally accepted truths which have been dinned into their ears do not possess absolute unconditional validity" but are relative to the given situation at a given time.[20] That words can mean just what the speaker intends, no more and no less, is one of his chief ideas and seems to refer to *ideas* beyond the *words,* which notion is not part of the Korzybski system. Like Rapoport, he is willing to go to scientific discipline for everything and to "depend on that for his salvation."[21]

---

[17] Charles I. Glicksberg, "Methodology in Semantics," *School Review,* LIII (Nov., 1945), pp. 552.

[18] ———, "General Semantics and the Science of Man," *Science Monthly,* LXII (May, 1946), pp. 440-446.

[19] ———, "General Semantics in the Classroom," *English Journal,* XXXIV

[19] ———, "General Semantics in the Classroom," *English Journal,* XXXIV (October, 1944), reproduced in *Etc.,* II, 4 (Summer 1945), pp. 221-227.

[20] ———, "Semantic Revolution and the Teaching of English," *Harvard Educational Review,* X (March, 1940), pp. 150-163.

[21] *Ibid.,* p. 163.

Two articles reviewed, which advocate application of general semantics to the teaching of science,[22, 23] as well as the article on mathematics,[24] merely stress the necessity for the relativistic orientation and for the distinction between the word and the object which would avoid the reification so common in the contemporary teaching of these two subjects.

The other articles all point to the growing interest in general semantics and to the recognition of the fact that the study of semantics must and will be soon introduced into high school English and social studies programs.[25] The most recent summary of the status of semantics and of general semantics in the high school programs was given by Richard Corbin to the National Association of Secondary School Principals in 1955. He pointed out the widespread danger of the misuse of language.

> It is no exaggeration to say that language has ranked in importance above all other weapons in their [our enemies] arsenals.[26]

Although he recognized that "there are certain *moral* and *intellectual dangers* to be faced in the teaching of semantics" he felt that they were no greater than the dangers in a gym class and were merely different in *kind*.[27] Even though a teacher may have used some of the semantic practices in the past, she must form a philosophical view on the subject of semantics before she can be ready to select the matters to be taught. Because, more than ever now, young people need to know not only about the mechanics and style of language but also about the process by which "mean-

---

[22] Phillip Frank, "Science Teaching and the Humanities," *Etc.*, IV, 1 (Autumn, 1946), pp. 1-24.

[23] Wendell Johnson, "General Semantics and the Science Teacher," *Etc.*, IV, 4 (Summer, 1946), pp. 275-284.

[24] Robert S. Fouch, "The Unsanity of Mathematics and Its Teaching," *Etc.*, XI, 2 (Winter, 1954), pp. 113-121.

[25] See annotated bibliography at the end.

[26] Richard Corbin, "Semantics in the Secondary School," *Bulletin of The National Association of Secondary School Principals,* XXXIX (1955), pp. 50-55.

[27] *Ibid.*, p. 53 (italics ours).

ing is produced," he listed five linguistic insights needed by high school students:

1. understanding of the symbolic nature of language;
2. understanding of the nature of differences;
3. understanding of the process of abstraction and the relativeness of the meanings of many words;
4. understanding of the nature of judgment and inference;
5. understanding of the nature of metaphor.[28]

He indicated that more space in high school textbooks is being devoted to semantics (without actually labelling it as such) and that some high schools even adopted Hayakawa's *Language in Thought and Action* for their more mature students. He recommended for further reading, the books by Hayakawa, Lee, Chase, Ogden and Richards, Walpole, Thomas, the N.E.A. and Minteer. He, too, thought that English and social studies provided the most likely setting for training in semantics.

Thomas[29] alone of all the writers, referred to the opposition aroused in the pupil by what they considered the revolutionary ideas in *Language in Thought and Action*. He therefore adopted the devices advocated but led the children to form the principles inductively themselves. He developed this idea more fully in his book for high school teachers of English.[30] In his annotated bibliography which includes the standard works of general semantics he warned against the eclecticism of Chase. Most of the books for secondary teachers of English combine the principles of Ogden and Richards with those of general semantics. Practically all contain references to emotive and referential language which is the contribution of the former writers, and to the levels of abstraction which idea is taken from Korzybski. The Progressive Educational

---

[28] *Ibid.*, pp. 54-55.

[29] Cleveland A. Thomas, "Exploring Language in Senior English," *English Journal*, XLII, 5 (May, 1953), pp. 250-255. Mr. Thomas was Dean of Faculty and head of the English Department, North Shore Country Day School, Winnetka, Ill.

[30] ———, *Language Power for Youth* (New York: Appleton-Century-Crofts, Inc., 1955).

Association lists a bibliography[31] with comments, some of which is reproduced here to show the connection with operational definitions and with logical positivism:

Chase. *The Tyranny of Words*: This book, full of contradictions and lacking in complete understanding of the problem, still offers some stimulation to the teacher who has been conventional in approach to teaching English. It may be used in comparison with the position of Richards. Many might become aware of Richard's meanings through attempting to discover whether or not Chase had Richard's point of view.

Jesperson. *Language*.

C. K. Ogden. *Bentham's Theory of Fictions*
    The Meaning of Meaning (with Ivor A. Richards)

P. W. Bridgman. *The Logic of Modern Physics*
    The Nature of Physical Theory. These books form an important contribution to the technique of definition of terms through operations for which they stand. Empirical in approach, they are representatives of what is perhaps a contemporary trend in science, language and general philosophy.

Ayer. *Language, Truth and Logic*. In this work the author applies an empiricism not dissimilar to Bridgman's to philosophical and ethical questions. He states clearly the position of the empiricists upon the question of the basis of the meaning of words.

Korzybski. *Science and Sanity*. The general reader will find this book far more than an "introduction." It is a detailed and in places a technical treatise upon the psychology and psychiatry of language.

It is evident that there is a growing realization among secondary educators today that there is a need for greater emphasis on critical thinking and on the meaning—denotative and connotative —of words. Departments of Education and School Boards are already incorporating into English curricula sections on critical

---

[31] Progressive Education Association: Commission on Secondary School Curriculum, *Language in General Education*. A Report of the Committee on the Function of English in General Education for the Commission on Secondary School Curriculum (New York: Appleton-Century Co., Inc., 1940).

thinking and on the shifting meanings of words.[32] But Richard
Corbin pointed out the dangers of this movement in showing that
philosophy is implied in this new trend, and also that there are
certain moral and intellectual dangers equal to those of a physical
nature in an athletics program. Despite what he says, only a pure
materialist can consider that these dangers are to be discounted
in the same manner as the risks in physical education courses are
discounted. To destroy in the child the security that comes from
knowing that there is some unchanging truth, in fact to tell the
child that there is no ground for absolute truth, is quite different
from the breaking of bones and may cause irreparable damage
to a whole generation by its inculcation of a completely relativistic
spirit. If children are to be given *Language in Thought and Action*
or if teachers are to give them the principles present there and
in *Science and Sanity,* it seems only just that they should also
be told the exact way in which truth is relative, and how there
is an underlying basis for all men's knowledge that in no way
depends on man's knowledge of reality. Only then can the very
commendable exercises of general semantics bear the fruit they
could bear. Teaching semantics on the high school level must be
done carefully, guarding against the absolute destruction both of
values and of the idea of unchanging truth. This unchanging truth
underlies the changes in the universe and is responsible for its
order, as well as for the scientist's confidence in his power to
predict and manipulate the universe for man's benefit. Both extreme absolutism and extreme relativism are to be avoided especially on this level, since all is considered black or white by the
adolescent. Discrimination and power to distinguish between the

---

[32] In a talk given on July 5, 1957, at Duke University, and on July 10,
1957, at Indiana University, Arno Jewett, specialist for language arts in
the U. S. Office of Education, told of the results of his study of current
courses of language arts throughout the country. Over one half the state
and local courses include a unit on critical thinking. Units on elementary
semantics are also included, largely due to the popularizations of the works
of Korzybski, C. K. Ogden, I. A. Richards and Bloomfield. Hayakawa's
Language in Thought and Action is used frequently in grade 12. There are
usually sections on the nature of meaning, the dynamics of language, the
levels of abstraction and the use of language for social control.

emotive content of a man's statement and fact content does not necessitate destruction of all values.

By far the greatest number of textbooks and articles on general semantics are written for the college level, for courses in English, speech or communication. As far as is known, there are seven texts which directly present general semantics principles and acknowledge their great dependence on *Science and Sanity*. The publishing houses of several of these books kindly furnished information regarding the colleges which purchased these texts in class orders in 1955-1957. It can be safely said that general semantics is being taught, by means of these books, in courses in at least one hundred and eighty-five institutions of higher education, forty-two per cent of these being privately controlled institutions. The seven texts are listed below in chronological order of their publication:

1. Irving J. Lee, *Language Habits in Human Affairs,* 1941, used in twenty-nine colleges.

2. Wendell Johnson, *People in Quandaries,* 1946, used in thirty-one colleges.

3. Samuel Hayakawa, *Language in Thought and Action,* 1949, used in eighty-two colleges.

4. Kenneth S. Keyes, Jr., *How to Develop Your Thinking Ability* (New York: McGraw Hill Book Co., 1950).

5. Zollette Sandro, *Basic Principles of General Semantics* with Exercises and Discussions, 1953.

6. Elwood Murray, Raymond Barnard, and Jaspar Garland, *Integrative Speech*: The Function of Oral Communication in Human Affairs (New York: Dryden Press, 1953), used in seventeen colleges, 1956-57.

7. J. Samuel Bois, *Explorations in Awareness* (New York: Harper Bros., Inc., 1957), used in five colleges.

Other texts which, while not strictly based on general semantics principles, acknowledge their indebtedness to them or quote from Korzybski, Rapoport or Hayakawa are:

1. William G. Leary and James S. Smith, *Thought and Statement* (New York: Harcourt Brace and Co., Inc., 1951), used in thirty-eight colleges.

2. Wilbur E. Moore, *Speech*: *Code, Meaning and Communication* (New York: McGraw-Hill Co., 1955).

3. Norman T. Newton, *An Approach to Design* (Cambridge, Mass.: Addison Wesley Press, Inc., 1951).

4. J. Ruesch and G. Bateson, *Communication*: *The Social Matrix of Society* (New York: Norton Press, 1951).

5. Donald E. Hayden and Paul E. Alworth, *A Semantics Workbook* (San Francisco: Fearon Publications, 1956).

6. Doris Garey, *Putting Words in Their Places* (Chicago: Scott Foresman and Co., 1957).

Although the most important and extensive influence of general semantics has been in the field of the language arts, there have been other fields into which general semantics has ventured and where it has had some impact on the college or graduate level. The proceedings from the Second American Congress on General Semantics[33] gave papers indicating how general semantics had been applied in psychiatry, dentistry, speech education, etc. A few of the more recent articles showing the effect of general semantics in the fields of psychology and linguistics will be summarized here.

In linguistics, William G. Leary claims that general semantics should be introduced into Smith and Trager's courses for the training of Foreign Service Personnel.[34] He quotes a letter from Dr. Smith in which the latter admits that, though they accept the idea of the influence of language on the beliefs of men, their principles are not equivalent to those of general semantics but "large phases of the activity of general semantics would be included within metalinguistics as we use the term."[35]

Through the metalinguistics and information issues, the editors of *Etc.* are endeavoring to show the relationships of the ideas of general semantics with theories of cybernetics and linguistics, especially the theory that language affects the metaphysics of a

---

[33] M. Kendig (ed.), *Second Congress on General Semantics,* University of Denver, 1941 (Chicago: Institute of General Semantics, 1943).

[34] William G. Leary, "Studies in Language and Culture in the Training of Foreign Service Personnel: The School of Languages and Linguistics of the United States Department of State," *Etc.,* IX (1952), pp. 192-202.

[35] *Loc. cit.,* letter to Mr. John Caffrey, July 17, 1951.

society and that communication is a reflex activity of a servo-mechanism, a kind of feedback.

The power of general semantics to improve mental health is developed by Ruth Strang.[36] She quotes Chase and Morris as promising that general semantics would help to encourage the objective analysis of problems and the objective appraisal of statements. Maslow stresses the need that psychology has to be extensive rather than generalized, to study the single, unique person rather than a passive generalized picture of man, which he claims, is due to the stimulus-response theories. In psychology, he says, there is a particular danger for intellectuals to become absorbed, as they might well do in all sciences, with abstractions, words, concepts and to ignore the concrete. As a remedy, he explicitly advises turning to the general semanticists and to the artist, both of whom stress the raw experiences of the individual.[37]

Hayakawa recently drew a portrait of the fully functioning personality developed by combining the negative characteristics urged by Korzybski with the more positive ones proposed by Carl Rogers and Maslow. Korzybski's description includes the following elements for the sane person who

1. does not confuse levels of abstraction;
2. does not treat the map as if it were the territory;
3. does not copy animals in their reactions and therefore is not a *dog*matist nor a *cat*egorist (the puns are Korzybski's);
4. does not treat as identical all things that have the same name;
5. does not exhibit two-valued orientations in which absolute good is pitted against absolute evil;
6. does not confuse reports with inferences, inferences with judgmental states;
7. is cautious about applying generalizations to particulars.[38]

[36] Ruth Strang, "Many-Sided Aspects of Mental Health," *Mental Health in Modern Education,* Fifty-Fourth Yearbook of the National Society for the Study of Education, Part II (Chicago: University of Chicago Press, 1955), pp. 46-49.

[37] Abraham H. Maslow, "Toward a Humanistic Psychology," *Etc.,* XIV, 1 (Autumn, 1956), pp. 10-22.

[38] S. I. Hayakawa, "The Fully Functioning Personality," *Etc.,* XIII (Spring, 1956), pp. 169-181.

When the more positive ideas of Maslow and Rogers are united with the above negative ideas, such as the idea of self-concept, concern with social reality rather than with social façade, and creativeness, we shall get not only sane but ethical personalities.

> The unsane individual is moral only with the greatest of effort and often he behaves unmorally and viciously with the best of moral intentions. Whereas to the fully functioning personality as Rogers, Maslow and Korzybski see him, morality and ethics come naturally as the result of proper evaluation. A person who is fully open to his own feelings and deeply aware of other people as well can hardly act blindly and selfishly. He is deeply socialized, as Dr. Rogers says because one of his own deepest needs is for affiliation and communication with others. When he is most fully himself, he cannot help but be most deeply identified with others too and therefore his orientation is social in the best sense.[39]

This linking of sanity with morality is similar to Korzybski's statement that a fully thalamo-cortical integrated person would be moral, a theory that has important implication for educators.[40] No indication is made as to how and why morality and ethics would come naturally to the fully functioning personality. Most educators have yet to experience that morality and ethics do come "naturally" to their pupils. The testimony of literature and the experience of teachers do not corroborate the prediction of Hayakawa that morality is *easy* to acquire or abide by once the personality is fully functioning on the *biological* level implied by him.

Other writers speaking for college courses and students point out the influence that general semantics can have on art and vice versa. Norman T. Newton of the Harvard Graduate School of Design claims that in Korzybski's work there is implicit: "a solid basis for a twentieth century attitude toward the creative arts."[41] Throughout his book, he says that he hopes to show art students

---

[39] *Ibid.*, p. 180.

[40] Korzybski, *Science and Sanity*, p. 180.

[41] Norman T. Newton, *An Approach to Design* (Cambridge, Mass.: Addison-Wesley Press, Inc., 1951), p. x.

that the process of design is related to the whole of human experience. He maintains that the works of Dewey, Einstein, Korzybski, Bridgman and Ames are concerned with and give the modern point of view on the relations between human beings and their environment: "the very stuff of which the fabric of design is made."[42] There are many of Korzybski's ideas explained here, especially the idea of a world in process and the attack on Aristotelian absolutes.

> It has been said that we cling to our vain search for these invariable fixities not for just some aspect of testable invariant relation but for complete "absolutes," permanent, unchanging, somehow utterly independent of any relation what ever to anything else . . . because we need them for our security. . . . Yet where in a world of process can one find an empirical something that never changes in any respect? . . . We hear such wheezes as "You can't change human nature," when in fact there is no such wholesale thing. There are humans; each has his own attitudes and tendencies and we are continually changing these within ourselves and others.[43]

There are other articles, on art, too, both in *Etc.* and in the *General Semantics Bulletin*.[44] Northrop pointed out the limitations of the Aristotelian way of treating aesthetic qualities as predicates of natural substances which has prevented man from appreciating the aesthetic immediacy of art. He advocates teaching on all levels, even the lowest grades:

1. impressionistic art to give the silent level aesthetic sensitivity.
2. the logic of relations to understand Western mathe-

---

[42] *Ibid.*, p. viii.

[43] *Ibid.*, pp. 56-57. St. Thomas never claimed that the permanent abiding principle of substance was *empirically* discoverable. It is a metaphysical principle, cf. supra, pp. 88-94. Moreover, human nature *as such* does not exist. Individuals exist who *share* human nature; if not, what basis is there for ascribing the same name to fifty men? See supra, pp. 130-139.

[44] Oliver Bloodstein, "General Semantics and Modern Art," *Etc.*, I, 1 (August, 1943), pp. 12-23.

matics, science, norms and values and to train the children
to see that no two sensed sunsets are identical.[45]

Thus, even in articles for art students, the relativistic attitude
is encouraged to the extreme. The attack on human nature, as
such, has the greatest implication since it leads more directly to
relativistic morals dependent on social mores rather than on
correspondence to laws which derive from the nature itself. Only
by acting according to human nature can man develop and reach
human perfection, just as all physical nature can develop only
by acting in accord with certain laws inherent in its nature.

By far, the greatest number of articles and texts influenced by
general semantics are in the field of English and the language arts.
As pointed out above, the oversimplified claims of Korzybski and
his followers in the nineteen forties and the somewhat vitriolic
criticism of these claims at the same time gave way to a more
balanced criticism and a presentation of general semantics principles as modified or as united with those of I. A. Richards. Only
two examples of the earlier writing will be summarized here.
Robert S. Crane had writen in 1942 a very strong criticism of
general semantics condemning it as a dogmatic *a priori* metaphysical construction whose negative principles are inferences de-
signed to reduce all arguments to verbiage. He claimed that it
is especially destructive of any appreciation of literature since
Korzybski himself said that literature, speeches, family quarrels
usually give the best example of improper evaluation.[46] His attack
and the answer were both written in the *College English Journal.*
In April, 1943, Francis Chisholm answered this attack. He admitted
the metaphysical bases of general semantics if that means that
general semantics, "like all coherent intelligent structures has
undefined terms and operations," without any reference to an
"ontological theory."[47] General semantics, he said, considers words

[45] F. S. C. Northrop, "Mathematical Physics and Korzybski Semantics,"
General Semantics Bulletin, No. 16-17 (1955), pp. 7-14. Alfred Korzybski
Memorial Lecture.

[46] R. S. Crane, "College English and the Teaching of Prose Literature,"
College English, IV (October, 1942), p. 219.

[47] Francis P. Chisholm, "Some Misconceptions About General Semantics,"
College English, IV (April, 1943), pp. 412-416.

and things, both of which are "constructed by the trained activity
of the nervous system." He goes on to restate Korzybski's theory
that the real facts are never known directly but only through
scientific inference as corrected and guaranteed by predictability.
Thus he admits, as Korzybski had done, the circular nature of
human reasoning. He criticizes Mr. Crane's theory of language
because it does not include the fact that linguistic formulations
organize our outlook on life situations and suggest courses of
action. He closed with a denial that general semantics was seeking
a battle between ancient and modern thought, but affirmed that
it intends positively to evaluate art in the light of new twentieth
century insights into nature and man. Hayakawa and Johnson
positively affirm the value of literature as giving a kind of vicarious
experience. They say literature is being therefore somewhat
extensional, because it helps readers to develop the extensional
orientation by more contact with life experiences.[48]

A later and more balanced criticism appeared in *College English*
in 1952.[49] The author, P. P. Hallie, pointed out the immense
influence exerted by Hayakawa in *Language in Thought and
Action* in use now in so many freshman English courses (at 82
institutions of higher learning). "For its readableness, power of
stimulating thought and correcting impulsive usage of language,
it is perhaps unequalled by any recent books on the subject of
semantics."[50] But he himself experienced the dangers that resulted
from the theoretical weaknesses of general semantics which he
claimed took the form of half-truths. One weakness is the stress
on the need for extensional meanings, for referents. The implication is that there is no possibility of agreement in the intensional
world. He quotes one student as saying:

> Hayakawa says that if you can't point to something like
> a tape measure to settle your argument, then it's all a
> matter of opinion and anybody can be right.[51]

---

[48] S. I. Hayakawa, *Language in Thought and Action,* pp. 143-155.
[49] P. P. Hallie, "Criticism of General Semantics," *College English,* XIV
(October, 1952), pp. 17-23.
[50] *Ibid.,* p. 17.
[51] *Ibid.,* p. 19.

On tests, Hallie says the students often describe the intensional as that "which you cannot agree on."[52] He then goes on to show that general semantics ignores the power of logic, the power of the human mind really to draw conclusions from premises without looking at any particular external objects. The general semanticists consider logic not as a set of rules for correct thinking but as a set of rules for governing consistency in the use of language.[53] He concludes by recognizing some of the great contributions of general semanticists—their pointing-out of the important distinction between words and things and actions to which the words refer but, as he says:

> The popularity of Hayakawa's book makes it all the more important that the faults in general semantics theory of the mechanisms of communication be no longer ignored by teachers or students of language.

When a student says that if he cannot point to a tape measure then all is opinion,

> it must be emphatically pointed out to him that there are bases for agreement other than the external observations and not the least of these is logic.[54]

It is this emphasis on the necessity for empirical corroboration of statements that is, at once, one of the dangers and one of the contributions of the college texts in general semantics. To develop in the student an awareness of the difference between an inference and a report should not result in destroying the value of the inference for the student. The same is true regarding the distinction between factual and emotive-evaluative statements, but here the danger may be greater. The seven texts listed above all contain sections relating to truth and values or morality. Hayakawa's theory of morality has already been indicated.[55] One of the latest

---

[52] *Ibid.*, p. 20.

[53] Cf. Hayakawa, *Language in Thought and Action,* p. 240 and Korzybski, *Science and Sanity,* p. 79.

[54] Hallie, *College English,* XIV (October, 1952), p. 23.

[55] Hayakawa, "Non-Aristotelian Revision of Morality," *Etc.,* 1946; see supra, pp. 76-78.

textbooks for freshman English courses contains a chapter on "Reality" with subsections on private and public morality. Private morality, it is said, is what is fair and public morality is what is convenient for society. Often what is convenient for society may not be considered "fair" by and for the individual and, therefore, this concept of fairness has a special kind of "reality." In trying to get at moral questions the student is given this advice:

> Generally speaking, the least valuable way will be the flat assertion that such-and-such is *really* "right" or *really* "wrong"; for this assertion cannot be effectively supported. On the other hand, if we say, "This is why I think such-and-such will be a practical convenience to the group," or "This is why I think such-and-such would be fair," we have made a statement which lends itself to support by cognitive details. Though "proof" is often impossible the thoughtful consideration of relevant facts is both possible and essential.[56]

It may well be asked why a consideration of morality should be in a text for a course in freshman English. The justification lies in the fact that the student must be trained to distinguish cognitive and non-cognitive statements, or factual and emotive-evaluative statements. It is claimed that statements about morals belong to the second class. Perhaps the idea of the ethical use of *good* as being a purely emotive one is taken more from Ogden and Richards than from the general semanticists.[57] But what is important here is that courses in English are using textbooks which do not confine themselves to mere words but penetrate into the nature of thought, truth, morality and, since thought can only be true in so far as it is conformed to reality, into metaphysics. These texts *have* done so and are doing so; the question now is, *must* they do so?

---

[56] Doris B. Garey, *Putting Words in Their Places* (Chicago: Scott Foresman and Co., 1957). In the preface the author refers to the seminar in general semantics with the late Alfred Korzybski which she attended in the summer of 1949 and which "planted the seeds of the present undertaking." She also speaks of her indebtedness to Dr. S. I. Hayakawa who introduced her to general semantics through his *Language in Action* and read the manuscript of the book and made many valuable suggestions (p. v).

[57] C. K. Ogden and I. A. Richards, *The Meaning of Meaning*, pp. 124-125.

e their knowledge of things, *things* do not change in
te meanings. Man's knowledge of man changes but the
f human nature remain unchanged despite his knowl-
rwise, science would be unable to have a continuous
owledge which is building up on past knowledge. The
g description of man depends not only on what man
on the fact that the reality symbolized by his language
stable. Just what is stable and what is relative, as
implicitly even by science, must be made clear even
school level if we are to have our children leave
any confidence in the power of the human mind to
. If the level of abstraction ladder is presented, either
resented as a device to clarify the distinction between
tements of man without any reference to the exact
which man does this and the exact nature of the
ld, or it must be correctly described, not as leaving
ut as leaving out the external appearances which are
to true knowledge. The connection between time-
getting down to the essentials of a thing, which are
all ages in all places, i.e., universal ideas, should be

he college level that general semantics has had its
ence, where both the advantages and the dangers are
tainly, the emphasis on awareness of the very rela-
r of language in all four areas of communication
eading, speaking and writing) is needed in this day
ia of communication and propaganda. Whether the
sed by the general semanticists are inextricably bound
ntology, ethics, epistemology and psychology of Kor-
question. In general, the errors seem to be not so much
od questions and pointing out important problems.
ie in the answers—which never indicate the full
ey stress that communication seems to be largely a
nditional response and, in a sense, they are correct.
they account for the "thinking" done for days and
reat scientists without an observable stimulus? They
nging character of the world but ignore the fact that
just pure change; there must be some*thing* that

Another indication that the adoption of the general semantics theory of meaning does not confine itself merely to words but entails the adoption of some of the epistemological and evaluative (ethical) ideas is evident from a report given of a symposium at the 1953 convention of the American Psychological Association in Cleveland.[58] J. Worth Osburn of the University of Washington spoke of his experiences in using *People in Quandaries* with some one hundred and seventy teachers. He listed and explained the following educational implications to be derived from the adoption of general semantics by teachers:

1. Time-binding as applied as a definition of man
2. Semantic blockage
3. Consciousness of abstracting
4. The language of relativity
5. Semantic reactions.

He is of the opinion that religious scruples can prevent a person from deriving profit from general semantics:

> Occasionally still there is a teacher who cannot profit from general semantics because of religious scruples. One woman for example still believes that misbehavior among school children is due to their having been "born in iniquity and conceived in sin."[59]

It would seem then, that critics are right in pointing out that the theoretical notions underlying general semantics are important. Before going into a discussion as to whether or not the practical advantages to be derived from general semantics can be divorced from the theoretical foundations, it is necessary to consider just what are those practical contributions to the field of higher education in particular. This influence is more than that indicated by the number of courses which have the general semantics texts in colleges since there are twenty teachers' colleges included. As a result, many minds, younger and more easily

---

[58] J. Worth Osburn, "Report of Symposium," *General Semantics Bulletin*, No. 12-13 (1953), pp. 69-71.

[59] *Ibid.*, p. 70.

influenced, will be subjected to the principles of general semantics, implicitly and explicitly, whether applied only to language or developed to include a world view. The positive contributions of these college texts for a better use of language are summarized below:

1. emphasis on the shifting meanings of words as used by different speakers and writers according to their backgrounds of experience and to the context of the words themselves. The listener or reader, too, receives these words and colors his meaning of them by his past experiences.

2. emphasis on the inadequacy of words to convey fully the meaning of the speaker.

3. emphasis on the distinction between emotive language and directive and referential or informative language.

4. emphasis on the distinction between reports and inferences.

5. emphasis on the dangers of over-generalization and use of extremely abstract language; the need to distinguish the levels of abstraction.

6. emphasis on greater accuracy of language and on the use of more concrete referents.

Underlying these contributions to better communication are the theoretical considerations usually referred to in an incomplete way in the texts:

1. misrepresentation of and scorn for traditional thought rather than showing that it has inadequacies as well as very valuable points.

2. inculcation of an ambivalent attitude in the student by
   a. the denial of an unchanging principle of identity and organization in all reality which is responsible for the order and structure so evident in reality.
   b. the praise of science which is based on the principle that there is the organizing principle which contributes to the order it seeks to discover.

3. this denial of substance as a metaphysical principle both in reality and as the subject of human knowledge leads further to the denial of any objective law founded in human nature and necessary for man to obey in order to develop and perfect himself, in order, really, to be a fully functioning personality.

4. misunderstanding of the nature of human thought. Thought,

---

according to the general sema action given in response to the an object. This behaviorist exp the obvious and frequent situat ferent words from men of diff general agreement as to wha operative research so marked communality of *thought* rather

5. the educational implicati attitude towards knowledge ar theories of general semantics a in the texts, are shown most c ing meanings of the word *Go* mulated by Weiss at the Univ answers to his questions were is, he assumed that God is not is good, death is not forever. the meaning of these stateme sort of absolutism Weiss wa justment.

SU

The greatest problem of ge college level. On all levels, th tions. On the elementary or general semanticists is on prov the meaning of words, or on On the high school level, the e is on critical thinking, on aw especially these three: the cha of abstractions and the confus guage. Even on these lower tributions can be offset by t teaching too superficially the levels of abstraction. While

Supra, pp. 71-72.
Supra, pp. 72-75.

---

men chang their ultima essentials edge. Othe body of kn time-bindin is, but also is basically recognized on the hig school with grasp realit it must be different st process by process wor out reality non-essentia binding and the same fo indicated.

It is on greatest infl greatest. Ce tive charact (listening, of mass me devices prop up with the zybski is the in asking g The errors situation. Th matter of co But how car months by g stress the ch no change i

changes. They stress the relative character of man's knowledge because the world is so full of change and because he is so different from every other man, but they fail to see that there must be an abiding identity in things and a communality of knowledge in man reflecting that abiding principle of identity, or else we would have neither communication nor science. They stress the relative nature of morality due to changing circumstances but they fail to see that there must be, is, and has been, a certain basic concept of human law derived from the very nature of man himself and present, in general, throughout all ages. This alone can explain the sense of "fairness" in man which conflicts often with his "convenience."

The question is, can both sides of the answers be given by the general semanticists without changing the whole system? Are the practical devices leading to awareness of language confusions only possible with the present theoretical bases of general semantics? Hardly anyone would give an affirmative answer to the second question. Chapter III indicated that Thomists had long ago recognized and stated many of the pitfalls emphasized by the general semanticists. They showed that language and meanings depend on the past experiences of man;[62] that different words can mean different things to different men;[63] that neither language nor knowledge is identical with reality;[64] the scholastic maxim, "never deny; rarely affirm; always distinguish" is a medieval way, if you wish, of warning against the dangers of over-generalization.[65] It is possible, then, to preserve the positive contributions of general semantics without subscribing to its metaphysics. But there is a second question: Do texts on the meanings of words always lead to considerations of first, reality, second, of the way man thinks, therefore, of what man is, as distinguished from or similar to animals, and of the meaning of values? If so, then, some kind of metaphysics is going to "seep" through in all textbooks treating the topic of meaning of words. But if, as suggested, general semantics errs more in what it leaves out than in what it states,

---

[62] Supra, pp. 128-130.
[63] Supra, pp. 126-129.
[64] Supra, pp. 119-125.
[65] Supra, pp. 130-131.

it might be that it could complete each of the main ideas and thus increase its educational value. Something like the following might be possible.

1. Show the world in flux, but show the other side. Show the complete picture of change which implies a *subject* of the change. Thus clarify the notion of substance as a dynamic metaphysical principle of organization and activity and knowledge, rather than as an inert physical principle.

2. Show the nature of abstraction as getting away from change and materiality to ultimate reality.

3. Show that, while man surpasses animals in far more than degree of knowledge, he shares with animals certain activities such as seeing, hearing, etc.

4. Show that, while truth is relative if the relation of things to men's minds is considered, there is an abiding truth in things, because they have been creatively thought by God and all man's quest for knowledge is a quest to grasp this abiding truth to which all nature conforms as a house conforms to its architect's blueprints.

5. Show that the basis of human morality is in this blueprint, or model, so to speak, according to which all men are made and according to which all men must act in order to act humanly. Morality has its basis beyond time and space although its applications are relative to each situation and each age and place.

CHAPTER V

Summary and Conclusion

We have seen the rise and development of the movement known as general semantics from its inception with the publication of *Science and Sanity* to the present day when one of its periodicals has found its way into libraries all over the world. We have traced the genesis of the principles of general semantics in the logical positivism of the Vienna School, in the general scientific trend and in the non-Aristotelian philosophy of such men as Whitehead and Russell as well as in the operationism of P. W. Bridgman.

We have attempted to outline the chief theories of general semantics since both the general semanticists themselves and their critics are convinced that any theory of meaning has epistemological and metaphysical bases.

1. This system criticizes Aristotelian philosophy but falsely presents it, so that the criticism is not of the actual Aristotelian theories.

2. It states that the world, according to scientific *inference*, is a process of events in which no event is identical, either with itself or with another event. This hypothetical construct of science upon which the whole theory of the universe is built seems to be correct, if one-sided, inasmuch as science has verified predictions made according to it.

3. It states that man, in this process world, is a time-binding class of life one quarter of an inch of cortex removed from animals. All living organisms including man are "nothing but" colloidal structures open to stimuli by other events and responding through electric[1] current responses called semantic reactions. Animals have only signal reactions. When men delay in order to have an integrated thalamo-cortical reaction they have symbol

---

[1] Strictly speaking, neural impulses are not electric. They travel at a much slower speed than an electric current. In physiology, "colloidal" also has a more restricted usage than Korzybski gave it.

reactions. Insanity results from failure to rise above primitive animalistic signal reactions. Morality and sanity result from habitual symbol reactions.

Its theory of meaning and symbolism is based on the theory of the process world, and of man as a symbolizer who responds to the stimuli of these events and communicates these responses through words, which, because they are abstractions, do not identically correspond to the process reality.

We pointed out the basic metaphysical and epistemological inconsistencies present in these theories as they were evident in the light of Thomistic principles.

1. the neglect of the idea of substance as a metaphysical principle of existence and of knowledge.

2. the description of man's mental and/or verbal activity as mere stimulus-response activity similar to that of animals while at the same time there was emphasis on the distinct difference between animals and men in higher level abstraction.

3. the omission, in the description of the process of human knowledge, of the formation of an idea. Therefore, there was no explanation given for classifying man as time-binding, that is rising above the limits of time and space, and, hence, of matter and of all material conditions. The *ideas* of man are the only activities of man that give the clue to such a time-binding characteristic. This, in turn, leads to the conclusion that man's power to time-bind must transcend matter and, therefore, is non-material or spiritual. A spiritual activity implies a spiritual power which in turn implies a spiritual source or principle of that power—the human soul, a spiritual soul.

4. the praise of the language of mathematics and science as closest in structure to reality, yet the admission that, as the highest level of abstraction, it has no physical content and consists only of "fictions".

5. the theory of the complete relativity of knowledge, truth, values, yet praise for science which is based on the concept of an underlying structure or design (and there can be no design without essences)[2] of the universe capable of being known by all men in all times.

---

[2] Pieper, *The Silence of St. Thomas*, p. 94.

6. condemnation of the either-or orientation while declaring that *either* we adopt general semantics *or* run the risk of an unsane world.

The educational implications on all levels were discussed. General semantics principles have been applied with great profit to reading-readiness programs on the elementary level and to the improvement of critical thinking on the high school level. Only one report was made concerning the improvement of the pupils' use of words and of pupil-teacher relationships as a result of the application of these principles. On the college level, the disadvantages are derived from the epistemological and metaphysical inconsistencies cited above. The fact that texts incorporating these principles are used in so many colleges indicates that professors have found them helpful, while at the same time, they have not been bothered by the theoretical inconsistencies pointed out, even before this study, by Black and Carroll.[3] Suggestions were made whereby the advantages to be derived from the new stress on awareness of the relativity of word meanings, of which every good teacher must be aware and which was pointed out six centuries ago by Thomas Aquinas, could be freed of the epistemological inconsistencies, which otherwise would endanger the students.

In short, general semanticists have pointed to some very important problems and alerted the educational world to the necessity for developing awareness of the personal element in word meanings and in all communication. The dangers lie not in the questions they raised but in their answers. Their answers invaded the realm of metaphysics and epistemology when they claimed to be a purely empirical discipline.[4] And in so doing, they did not penetrate far enough and gave incomplete and misleading answers.

Thus, two questions are left unanswered at the end of this study, regarding general semantics. First, is there any way of empirically checking on the value of the general semantics devices for a more accurate use of language? Secondly, must textbooks on meanings and uses of words necessarily include sections on the meaning of Truth and Morality? If so, it is important for educators to see that the questions are treated impartially, not just

---

[3] Supra, pp. 20-21.
[4] Supra, p. 1 and p. 5.

from the viewpoint of the scientists or logical positivists. It would seem that, in the world of today, the tendency for science to develop its theories into a *weltanschauung* almost immediately, makes the necessity for vigilance, impartiality, and knowledge of epistemology and metaphysics imperative.

The basic omission of the principle of substance both on the existential and on the cognitive levels led to the notions regarding the external changeability of man, truth and morality as representing the whole picture. But there was a more basic omission implicit in all this emphasis on reality. It is the omission of the premise "that things have an essential nature only in so far as they are fashioned by thought."[5] That all reality is creatively thought by God and can be so known by man to an ever-increasing degree from age to age and century to century, is a major challenge and inspiration of every true educator.

---

[5] Pieper, *The Silence of St. Thomas,* p. 52.

APPENDIX

1. *Alfred Korzybski,* 1935, presented to the First American Congress on General Semantics this statement:

   General Semantics formulates a new experimental branch of natural science underlying an empirical theory of human evaluations and orientations involving a definite neurological mechanism present in all humans.

2. Alfred Korzybski, 1941, preface to the second edition of *Science and Sanity,* p. xi.

   General Semantics is not any philosophy or psychology or logic in the ordinary sense. It is a new extensional discipline which explains and trains us how to use our nervous systems most efficiently. . . . It is the formulation of a new non-Aristotelian system or orientation which affects every branch of science and of life.

3. Irving J. Lee, 1941, in *Language Habits in Human Affairs,* p. 8.

   The body of data and method leading to habits of adequate language-fact relationship Korzybski called General Semantics.

4. S. I. Hayakawa, 1945, "General Semantics: An Introductory Lecture," *Etc.,* II, pp. 160-169.

   General Semantics is: 1) the study or correction of human responses to symbols, symbol system, sign systems and sign situations; or 2) a study of how a human nervous system works and ought to work; 3) an educational theory whose aim is to study the evaluational processes of human beings; 4) ultimately a non-verbal discipline of silence, of dissolving away the encrusted verbalizations and abstractions, dogmas and creeds that envelop most of us like layers of barnacles.

   Note: Korzybski has this to say in his *Manhood of Humanity,* p. 279, concerning wrong definitions of Semantics and General Semantics:

   For example in the Dictionary of World Literature, 'General Semantics' appears under the term Semantics. The two disciplines are confused, and even my 'extensional devices' are called 'semantic devices' whereas such a thing does not exist. In Vol. III, No. 4 of *Etc.* [by Hayakawa], there appears a five-page glossary of terms used in General Semantics, all of them fully explained in *Science and Sanity.* Practically every 'definition' misses the main point and trend of my work. For instance, what is said in the glossary about the use of the term 'semantic' in my '*General* Semantics,' i.e., in a new theory of *values,* is entirely misleading. Such initial errors lead automatically to further more aggravated misinterpretations. It would not be an overstatement to say that definitions of 'semantics' and 'General Semantics' and other terms printed in this glossary must be considered as seriously misinforming the public.

   The most recent example is an article on 'Semantics, General

Semantics' in *Ten Eventful Years,* an *Encyclopedia Britannica* publication, which considerably increased the confusion (also by Hayakawa). It is not even mentioned that 'semantics' is a branch of philology nor is there any clarifying discrimination made between the noun 'semantics' and the adjective 'semantic.' Moreover, it has many misstatements and even falsifications of my work and the work of others, and some statements make no sense.

This may be the explanation of the transfer by Korzybski from Chicago to Lakeville, Conn., in 1946 and of the development of two organizations and two publications.

5. Wendell Johnson, 1946, in *People in Quandaries,* p. 33.

General Semantics may be regarded as a systematic attempt to formulate the general method of science in such a way that it might be applied generally in daily life.

6. Alfred Korzybski, 1947, in *An Introduction to Non-Aristotelian Systems.*

General Semantics is a general theory of non-elementalistic evaluation. It has little to do with 'meanings' of words as such. It deals with the nervous reactions of the human organism-as-a-whole-in-an-environment and depends on undefined terms.

7. Russell Meyers, M.D., 1948, "The Nervous System and General Semantics," *Etc.,* V, pp. 231-245:

Its ultimate goal is nothing less than the construction of an applied anthropology, an empirical science of man emphasizing the processes of evaluation as dynamic and inseparable components of individual behavior.

8. Alfred Korzybski, 1948, Preface to the third edition of *Science and Sanity,* p. viii.

General Semantics turned out to be an empirical natural science of non-elementalistic evaluation, which takes into account the living individual, not divorcing him from his reactions altogether, nor from his neuro-linguistic and neuro-semantic environments, but allocating him in a *plenum* of some values, no matter what.

9. Alfred Korzybski, 1949, *American Peoples Encyclopedia.*

[General Semantics is a] general theory of evaluation which in application turned out to be an empirical science giving methods for general human adjustment in our private, public and professional lives.

10. S. I. Hayakawa, 1950, "New Techniques of Agreement," *Etc.,* VIII, pp. 3-12. pp. 3-12.

General Semantics is an extraordinary provocative study of the act of interpretation or evaluation. . . . A system of Alfred Korzybski purporting to describe and prescribe for wider application the linguistic assumptions underlying science.

11. Nicholas Rashevsky, 1951.

As I see it, General Semantics is a movement the purpose of which is to make every rank and file intelligent individual appreciate and use in daily life the rigorous methods of scientific thinking.

12. J. S. Bois, 1954, in *General Semantics Bulletin,* No. 14-15.

   The new discipline is not limited to language; it covers the study and overhauling of other methods of thinking-feeling such as mathematics, logic, personal attitudes and habits acquired from individual experiences.

13. S. I. Hayakawa, 1954, in preface to *Language, Meaning and Maturity,* p. viii.

   What is central to General Semantics is the exploration pioneered by Alfred Korzybski . . . of what might be called the linguistic (neuro-semantic) unconscious as one of the important determinants of human thought and behavior.

14. J. S. Bois, 1957, in *Explorations in Awareness,* p. 36.

   General Semantics can be viewed as a program of guided awareness, of educated consciousness of what is going on in the world and within ourselves.

Meetings on General Semantics

1935—First Congress at Ellensburg, Washington.

1941—Second Congress at Denver, Colorado.

1949—Third Congress at Denver, Colorado.

1951—Conference on General Semantics at the University of Chicago.

1954—Conference on General Semantics at Washington University, St. Louis, Missouri.

1958—International Conference on General Semantics at Mexico City College, Mexico City, Mexico.

1960—International Conference on General Semantics at the University of Hawaii, Honolulu, Hawaii.

1963—International Conference on General Semantics at New York University, New York.

BIBLIOGRAPHY

Allport, Gordon. *The Nature of Prejudice*. Cambridge, Mass.: Addison Wesley Publishing Co., 1954, 537 pp.

Aquinas, Thomas. *Basic Writings of St. Thomas Aquinas*. Edited by Anton C. Pegis. New York: Random House, 1945, 2 vols. 1129 pp.

——. *Opera Omnia*. Vives ed. 34 vols. Paris, 1872-1880.

——. *Summa Theologica*. 3 vols. Translated by the Fathers of the English Dominican Province. New York: Benziger Bros., Inc., 1947-49.

Ardley, Gavin. *Aquinas and Kant: The Foundations of the Modern Sciences*. New York: Longmans, Green and Co., 1950, 256 pp.

Aristotle. *The Basic Works of Aristotle*. Edited by Richard McKeon. New York: Random House, 1941, 1487 pp.

——. *De Anima*. In the version of William of Moerbeke; and the Commentary of St. Thomas Aquinas. Translated by Kenelm Foster and Silvester Humphries. London: Routledge and Kegan Paul, 1951, 504 pp.

——. *The Works of Aristotle*. 12 vols. Translated by W. D. Ross. Oxford: Clarendon Press, 1908-1952.

Arthur, Snowden. *Vocabulary, Semantics and Intelligence*. Bethesda, Md.: Lexicon Press, 1952, 115 pp.

Ayer, Alfred Jules. *Language, Truth and Logic*. New York: Dover Publications, 1950, 160 pp.

Babin, A. Eugene. *The Theory of Opposition in Aristotle*. Notre Dame, Ind., University of Notre Dame Press, 1940, 104 pp.

Bachelard, Gaston. *La Philosophie du Non: Essai d'une philosophique du nouvel esprit scientifique*. Paris: Presses Universitaires de France, 1940, 145 pp.

Bell, Eric T. *The Search for Truth*. New York: Reynal and Hitchcock, 1934, 279 pp.

Bergmann, Gustav. *The Metaphysics of Logical Positivism*. New York: Longmans, Green and Co., 1954, 341 pp.

Black, Max. *Language and Philosophy: Studies in Method*. Ithaca: Cornell University Press, 1949, 264 pp.

Blake, Robert R., and Glenn V. Ramsey (eds.). *Perception: An Approach to Personality*. New York: The Ronald Press, 1951, 442 pp.

Bloch, Bernard and Trager, George L. *Outline of Linguistic Analysis*. Baltimore: Waverly Press, 1942, 82 pp.

Bloomfield, Leonard. *Language*. New York: Henry Holt and Co., 1933, 566 pp.

Blumenthal, Joseph C., Robert Frank and Louis Zahner. *Viewing Language*. 4 vols. New York: Harcourt, Brace and Co., 1953.

Bois, J. Samuel. *Explorations in Awareness.* New York: Harper and Bros., 1957, 212 pp.

Bonfante, Julian Hugo. *Semantics.* Princeton: Princeton University Press, 1950, 39 pp.

Bram, Joseph. *Language and Society.* Garden City: Doubleday, 1955, 66 pp.

Bréal, Michel. *Semantics: Studies in the Science of Meaning.* Translated by Mrs. Henry Cust. New York: Henry Holt and Co., 1900, 341 pp.

Brennan, Robert Edward. *Thomistic Psychology.* New York: The Macmillan Co., 1941, 401 pp.

Bridgman, P. W. *The Logic of Modern Physics.* New York: The Macmillan Co., 1932, 228 pp.

Briggs, Harold E. (ed.). *Language—Man—Society: Readings in Communication.* New York: Rinehart and Co., 1949, 707 pp.

Brin, Joseph Gottland. *Introduction to Functional Semantics.* Boston: Tudor Press, 1949, 201 pp.

Britton, Karl. *Communication: A Philosophical Study of Language.* New York: Harcourt, Brace and Co., 1939, 290 pp.

Bryant, Margaret M. *Modern English and Its Heritage.* New York: The Macmillan Co., 1948, 401 pp.

Burke, Kenneth. *A Grammar of Motives.* New York: Prentice Hall, Inc., 1945, 530 pp.

———. *The Philosophy of Literary Form.* University, La.: Louisiana State University Press, 1941, 455 pp.

Carnap, Rudolf. *Foundations of Logic and Mathematics.* (International Encyclopedia of Unified Science.) Chicago: University of Chicago Press, 1939, 71 pp. Vol. 1, no. 3.

———. *Introduction to Semantics.* Cambridge, Mass.: Harvard University Press, 1942, 263 pp.

———. *Meaning and Necessity, a study in semantics and modal logic.* Chicago: The University of Chicago Press, 1947, 210 pp.

———. *Philosophy and Logical Syntax.* London: Kegan Paul, French, Trubner and Co., 1935, 100 pp.

Carroll, John. *The Study of Language.* Cambridge, Mass.: Harvard University Press, 1953, 289 pp.

Carver, George Alexander, Jr. *Aesthetics and the Problem of Meaning.* New Haven: Yale University Press, 1952, 90 pp.

Cassirer, Ernst. *An Essay on Man.* New Haven: Yale University Press, 1944, 237 pp.

———. *Language and Myth.* Translated by Susanne K. Langer. New York: Harper and Bros., 1946, 103 pp.

Chase, Stuart. *The Power of Words.* New York: Harcourt, Brace and Co., 1954, 308 pp.

———. *The Proper Study of Mankind.* New York: Harper and Bros., 1948, 311 pp.

———. *Roads to Agreement.* New York: Harper and Bros., 1951, 250 pp.

————. *The Tyranny of Words*. New York: Harcourt, Brace and Co., 1938, 396 pp.

Chisholm, Francis Perry. *Introductory Lectures on General Semantics*. Chicago: The Institute of General Semantics, 1944, 139 pp.

Clark, Joseph T. *Conventional Logic and Modern Logic: A Prelude to Transition*. Woodstock, Md.: Woodstock College Press, 1952. 109 pp.

Coffey, P. *Ontology*. New York: Peter Smith, 1938, 439 pp.

Copleston, Frederick C. *Contemporary Philosophy. Studies in Logical Positivism and Existentialism*. Westminster, Md.: The Newman Press, 1956, 230 pp.

Cornforth, Maurice Campbell. *Science versus Idealism: In Defense of Philosophy versus Positivism and Pragmatism*. London: Lawrence and Wishart, 1955, 267 pp.

DeBoer, John J., Walter V. Kaulfers and Helen Rand Miller. *Teaching Secondary English*. New York: McGraw Hill Book Co., Inc., 1951, 427 pp.

Doob, Leonard William. *Social Psychology*. New York: Henry Holt and Co., 1952, 583 pp.

Dunham, Barrows. *Man Against Myth*. New York: Little Brown and Co., 1947, 320 pp.

Economides, Antony M. *A Non-Aristotelian Study of Philosophy*. Lakeville, Conn.: Institute of General Semantics, 1947, 140 pp.

Edman, Irwin. *Philosopher's Quest,* New York: The Viking Press, 1947, 275 pp.

Eldridge, Francis Reed. *General Semantics*. Washington, 1949, 86 pp. Based on a series of lectures by Capt. J. A. Saunders at the Department of Agriculture Graduate School as well as on the study of *Science and Sanity*.

The English Arts in the Secondary School. 3 vols. Prepared by the Commission on the English Curriculum of the National Council of Teachers of English. New York: Appleton-Century-Crofts, Inc., 1952-1956.

Flew, Antony Garrard Newton (ed.). *Essays in Conceptual Analysis*. London: Macmillan and Co., Ltd., 1956, 265 pp.

————. *Logic and Language*. New York: Philosophical Library, 1953, 242 pp.

Foley, Leo A. *A Critique of the Philosophy of Being of Alfred North Whitehead in the Light of Thomistic Philosophy*. Washington, D. C.: The Catholic University of America Press, 1946, 169 pp.

Gardner, Martin. *In the Name of Science*. New York: George P. Putnam Sons, 1952, 320 pp.

Garey, Doris. *Putting Words in Their Places*. Chicago: Scott, Foresman and Co., 1957, 390 pp.

Garrigou-Lagrange, Reginald. *God, His Existence and His Nature*. 2 vols. Translated from the 5th French edition by Dom. Bede Rose. St. Louis, Mo.: B. Herder Book Co., 1934-36.

General Semantics: Papers from the First American Congress for General Semantics held at Ellensburg, Washington, March 1 and 2, 1935. Collected and Arranged by Hansell Baugh. New York: Arrow Editions, 1938, 111 pp.

Goldberg, Isaac. *The Wonder of Words.* New York: D. Appleton-Century Co., Inc., 1939, 485 pp.

Hayakawa, S. I. *Language in Action.* New York: Harcourt, Brace and Co., 1941, 106 pp.

——. *Language in Thought and Action.* New York: Harcourt, Brace and Co., 1949, 307 pp.

—— (ed.). *Language, Meaning and Maturity.* New York: Harper and Bros., 1954, 364 pp.

Hayden, Donald E. and Alworth, E. Paul. *A Semantics Workbook.* San Francisco: Fearon Publishing Co., 1956.

Herrick, Virgil E. and Jacobs, Leland B. (ed.). *Children and the Language Arts.* Englewood Cliffs, N. J.: Prentice-Hall, Inc., 1955, 524 pp.

Johnson, Alexander Bryan. *A Treatise on Language,* 1836. Edited with a critical essay on his philosophy of language by David Rynin. Berkeley: University of California Press, 1947, 443 pp.

Jespersen, Otto. *Language; Its Nature, Development and Origin.* London: Allen and Unwin, Ltd., 1922, 448 pp.

Joad, Cyril Edwin. *A Critique of Logical Positivism.* Chicago: University of Chicago Press, 1950, 154 pp.

Johnson, Wendell. *Language and Speech Hygiene.* Chicago: Institute of General Semantics, 1939, 54 pp.

——. *People in Quandaries.* New York: Harper Bros., 1946, 532 pp.

——. *Your Most Enchanted Listener.* New York: Harper and Bros., 1956, 215 pp.

Jolivet, Régis. *La Notion de Substance.* Paris: Gabriel Beauchesne, 1929, 335 pp.

Jorgensen, Jorgen. *The Development of Logical Empiricism.* Chicago: University of Chicago Press, 1951, 100 pp.

Kecskemeti, Paul. *Meaning, Communication and Value.* Chicago: University of Chicago Press, 1952, 349 pp.

Kelley, Earl C. *Education for What Is Real.* New York: Harper and Bros., 1947, 114 pp.

Kendig, M. (ed.). *Papers from the Second Congress on General Semantics;* held at the University of Denver, 1941. Chicago: Institute of General Semantics, 1943, 593 pp.

—— (ed.). *Papers from the Third Congress on General Semantics* at the University of Denver, 1949. Lakeville, Conn.: Institute of General Semantics, 1949, 111 pp.

——. Language Reorientation of High School Curriculum and Scientific Control of Neuro-linguistic Mechanisms for Better Mental Health and Scholastic Achievement. Lakeville, Conn.: Institute of General Semantics, 1935, 15 pp.

Keyes, Kenneth S., Jr. *How to Develop Your Thinking Ability.* New York: McGraw Hill, 1950, 246 pp.

Keyser, Cassius J. *Mathematical Philosophy.* New York: E. P. Dutton and Co., 1923, 466 pp.

Korzybski, Alfred. *General Semantics: An Introduction to Non-Aristotelian Systems.* Lakeville, Conn.: Institute of General Semantics, 1947, 806 pp.

———. *Manhood of Humanity.* 2nd ed. Lakeville, Conn.: International Non-Aristotelian Library Publishing Co., 1950, 326 pp.

———. *A Memorandum.* Chicago: Institute of General Semantics, 1940.

———. *Science and Sanity.* 3rd ed. with new preface. Lakeville, Conn.: International Non-Aristotelian Library Publishing Co., 1948, 806 pp.

———. Time-Binding: The General Theory. Two papers, 1924-1926. Lakeville, Conn.: Institute of General Semantics, 1940, 38 pp.

Language in General Education. A Report of the Committee on the Function of English in General Education for the Commission on Secondary School Curriculum. New York: D. Appleton-Century Co., Inc., 1940.

La Brant, Lou, Margaret Anderson and Ed. L. Baldridge. *Your Language.* New York: McGraw Hill Book Co., Inc., 1956. 3 vols. 434 pp. ea.

La Brant. *We Teach English.* New York: Harcourt, Brace and Co., 1951, 342 pp.

Langer, Susanne K. *An Introduction to Symbolic Logic.* Boston: Houghton Mifflin Co., 1937, 363 pp.

———. *Philosophy in a New Key.* Cambridge, Mass.: Harvard University Press, 1942, 313 pp.

Leary, Wm. G. and Smith, James Steel. *Think Before You Write.* New York: Harcourt, Brace and Co., 1951, 490 pp.
    Textbook anthology for College English represents the practical and logical revolutionary outcome of the effect of such works as Hayakawa's *Language in Thought and Action* on restless teachers of freshman composition.

———. *Thought and Statement.* New York: Harcourt, Brace and Co., 1955, 538 pp.

Lee, Irving J. *Customs and Crises in Communication.* New York: Harper and Bros., 1954, 334 pp.

———. *Language Habits in Human Affairs: an introduction to general semantics.* New York: Harper and Bros., 1941, 278 pp.

———. *The Language of Wisdom and Folly; Background Readings in Semantics.* New York: Harper and Bros., 1949, 361 pp.

Lewis, Clarence Irvine. *A Survey of Symbolic Logic.* Berkeley: University of California Press, 1918, 406 pp.

Lindgren, Henry Clay. *Meaning: Antidote to Anxiety.* New York: Thomas Nelson and Sons, 1956, 271 pp.

———. *Mental Health in Education.* New York: Henry Holt and Co., 1954, 561 pp.

Linsky, Leonard (ed.). *Semantics and the Philosophy of Language.* Urbana: University of Illinois Press, 1952, 289 pp.

Lundberg, George A. *Foundations of Sociology.* New York: The Macmillan Co., 1939, 556 pp.

McCall, Robert E. *The Reality of Substance.* Washington, D. C.: Catholic University of America Press, 1956, 202 pp.

McCarthy, Ephrem. *The Logical Empiricism of Alfred J. Ayer.* Philosophical Studies. Dublin: Educational Company of Ireland, 1953, 71 pp.

Nicholl, Donald. *Recent Thought in Focus.* London: Sheed and Ward, 1952, 250 pp.

Mandelbaum, David G. (ed.). *Language, Culture and Personality: Selected Writings of Edward Sapir.* Berkeley: University of California Press, 1949, 617 pp.

Maloney, Cornelius Leo. *Logical Positivism and American Education.* Washington: Catholic University of America Press, 1951, 21 pp.

Maritain, Jacques. *Ransoming the Time.* Translated by Harry Lorin Binsse. New York: Charles Scribner's Sons, 1941, 322 pp.

Marx, Melvin H. *Psychological Theory: Contemporary Readings.* New York: The Macmillan Co., 1956.

Maslow, Abraham H. *Motivation and Personality.* New York: Harper and Bros., 1954, 411 pp.

Mencken, H. L. *The American Language:* Supplement I. New York: Alfred A. Knopf, 1945.

Meyer, Hans. *The Philosophy of St. Thomas Aquinas.* Translated by Rev. Frederick Eckhoff. St. Louis, Mo.: B. Herder Book Co., 1944, 581 pp.

Miller, George A. *Language and Communication.* New York: McGraw-Hill Book Co., 1951, 298 pp.

Minteer, Catherine. *Words and What They Do to You: Beginning Lessons in General Semantics for Junior and Senior High School.* Evanston, Ill.: Row Peterson, 1953, 128 pp.

Mises, Richard von. *Positivism, A Study in Human Understanding.* Cambridge, Mass.: Harvard University Press, 1951, 404 pp.

Moore, Robert Herman. *General Semantics in the High School Program.* Columbus: The Ohio State University Press, 1945, 169 pp.

Moore, Wilbur E. *Speech: Code, Meaning and Communication.* New York: McGraw-Hill Book Co., 1955, 430 pp.
  College text which draws heavily on Korzybski's formulations and emphasizes the fact that the synthesizing core lies in the field of General Semantics.

Morris, Charles William. *Foundations of the Theory of Signs.* Chicago: University of Chicago Press, 1938, 59 pp.

————. *Logical Positivism, Pragmatism and Scientific Empiricism.* Paris: Hermann et cie, 1937, 71 pp.

————. *Signs, Language and Behavior.* New York: Prentice Hall, Inc., 1946, 365 pp.

————, *The Open Self*. New York: Prentice Hall, 1948, 179 pp.

Murphy, Arthur E. *The Uses of Reason*. New York: The Macmillan Co., 1943, 346 pp.

Murray, Elwood, Raymond H. Burnard, J. V. Garland, in collaboration with Guthrie E. Jansen. *Integrative Speech*. New York: Dryden Press, 1953, 617 pp.
> Textbook which attempts to relate speech to social problems, through psychology, group dynamics, general semantics, etc.

Nesbit, Francis Ford. *Language, Meaning and Reality*. New York: Exposition Press, 1955, 181 pp.

Newton, Norman T. *An Approach To Design*. Cambridge, Mass.: Addison-Wesley Press, Inc., 1951, 144 pp.

Northrop, F. S. C. *The Logic of the Sciences and Humanities*. New York: The Macmillan Co., 1948, 402 pp.

O'Brien, Sister Mary Consilia. *The Antecedents of Being*. Washington, D. C.: Catholic University of America Press, 1939, 202 pp.

Ogden, Charles K., and Ivor Armstrong Richards. *The Meaning of Meaning*. 16th ed. New York: Harcourt, Brace and Co., 1949, 280 pp.

Osgood, Charles E. *Method and Theory in Experimental Psychology*. New York: Oxford University Press, 1953, 800 pp.

Oesterle, John A. *Logic: the art of defining and reasoning*. New York: Prentice-Hall, 1952, 232 pp.

Owens, Joseph. *The Doctrine of Being in the Aristotelian Metaphysics*. Toronto: The Pontifical Institute of Medieval Studies, 1951, 461 pp.

Pegis, Anton Charles. *St. Thomas and the Problem of the Soul in the Thirteenth Century*. Toronto: St. Michael's College, 1934, 213 pp.

Peirce, Charles Saunders. *Collected Papers*. Cambridge, Mass.: Harvard University Press, 1931, vols. 1-4.

Persky, Phillip. *Bibliography of General Semantics since 1933*. Unpublished Master's thesis, University of Kansas, 1949.

Philbrick, Frederick Arthur. *Understanding English*. New York: The Macmillan Co., 1942, 209 pp.

Piaget, Jean. *The Child's Conception of the World*. New York: Harcourt, Brace and Co., 1929, 397 pp.

————. *The Language and Thought of the Child*. New York: Harcourt, Brace and Co., 1926.

Pieper, Joseph. *The Silence of St. Thomas*. Translated by John Murray and Daniel O'Connor. New York: Pantheon Books, Inc., 1957, 122 pp.

Pollock, Thomas C., Marion Sheridan, Frances Ledbitter, Ronald C. Doll. *The Art of Communicating*. New York: The Macmillan Co., 1955, 449 pp.
> High school text for four years contains sections on abstracting and defining.

Pollock, Thomas Clark. *The Nature of Literature*. Princeton: Princeton University Press, 1942, 218 pp.

———— *A Theory of Meaning Analyzed*: A Critique of I. A. Richard's

Theory of Language and Literature. Chicago: Institute of General Semantics, 1942, 46 pp.

Rapoport, Anatol. *Operational Philosophy.* New York: Harper and Bros., 1953, 258 pp.

———. *Science and the Goals of Man.* New York: Harper and Bros., 1950, 262 pp.

Reichenbach, Hans. *The Rise of Scientific Philosophy.* Berkeley: University of California Press, 1951, 333 pp.

Reiss, Samuel. *The Rise of Words and Their Meanings.* New York: Philosophical Library, 1950, 301 pp.

———. *The Universe of Meaning.* New York: Philosophical Library, 1953, 227 pp.

Renoirte, Fernand. *Cosmology*: Elements of a Critique of the Sciences and of Cosmology. Translated from the second revised edition by James F. Coffey. New York: Joseph Wagner, Inc., 1950, 256 pp.

Richards, Ivor Armstrong. *Interpretation in Teaching.* New York: Harcourt, Brace and Co., 1938, 420 pp.

Roberts, Holland D., Walter Kaulfers and Grayson N. Kefauver (eds.). *English for Social Living.* New York: McGraw-Hill Book Co., Inc., 1943, 366 pp.

Ruesch, Jurgen, and Gregory Bateson. *Communication: The Social Matrix of Society.* New York: Norton Press, 1951, 314 pp.

Russell, Bertrand. *An Inquiry into Meaning and Truth.* London: Allen and Unwin, Ltd., 1940, 352 pp.

Sapir, Edward. *Language.* New York: Harcourt, Brace and Co., 1921, 258 pp.

de Saussure, Fernand. *Cours de Linguistique Générale.* Lausanne, 1916, 331 pp.

Schlauch, Margaret. *The Gift of Language.* New York: Dover Publications, 1956, 342 pp.

———. *The Gift of Tongues.* New York: The Viking Press, 1942, 342 pp.

Schlipp, Paul A. (ed.). *The Philosophy of Bertrand Russell.* Evanston, Ill.: Northwestern University, 1944.

Searles, Herbert Leon. *Logic and Scientific Methods.* 2nd ed. New York: The Ronald Press Co., 1956, 378 pp.

Shannon, Claude E. and Weaver, Warren. *The Mathematical Theory of Communication.* Urbana, Ill.: University of Illinois Press, 1949, 117 pp.

Smith, Henry Lee, Jr., *Linguistic Science and the Teaching of English.* Cambridge, Mass.: Harvard University Press, 1956, 61 pp.

Smith, Raymond. *Whitehead's Concept of Logic.* Westminster, Md.: The Newman Press, 1953, 179 pp.

Smith, Vincent Edward. *Idea Men of Today.* Milwaukee: The Bruce Publishing Co., 1950, 434 pp.

———. *The Philosophical Frontiers of Physics.* Washington, D. C.: Catholic University of America Press, 1947, 210 pp.

————. *Philosophical Physics*. New York: Harper and Bros., 1950, 472 pp.

Sondel, Bess. *Communication: Written and Oral*. Chicago: University of Chicago Press, 1943, 17 pp.

Strickland, Ruth G. *The Language Arts in the Elementary School*. Boston: Heath Co., 1951, 370 pp.

Sullivan, James Bacon. *An Examination of First Principles in Thought and Being in the Light of Aristotle and Aquinas*. Washington, D. C.: Catholic University of America Press, 1939, 150 pp.

Thomas, Cleveland A. *Language Power for Youth*. New York: Appleton-Century-Crofts, Inc., 1955, 269 pp.

Ullman, Stephan. *The Principles of Semantics*. Glasgow: Jackson Sons and Co., 1951, 314 pp.

————. *Words and Their Use*. London: Frederick Muller, 1951, 108 pp.

Urban, Wilbur Marshall. *Language and Reality*: the philosophy of language and the principles of symbolism. London: Allen and Unwin, 1951, 755 pp.

Vaihinger, Hans. *The Philosophy of As If*. Translated by C. K. Ogden. New York: Harcourt, Brace and Co., 1925, 370 pp.

Van Melsen, Andrew G. *The Philosophy of Nature*. Pittsburgh, Pa.: Duquesne University Press, 1953, 253 pp.

Van Steenberghen, Fernand. *Epistemology*. Translated by Rev. Martin J. Flynn from the second revised edition. New York: Joseph F. Wagner, Inc., 1949, 324 pp.

Vogt, William. *Road to Survival*. New York: William Sloane Associates, Inc., 1948, 335 pp.

Walpole, Hugh R. *Semantics*. New York: W. W. Norton and Co., Inc., 1941, 264 pp.

Weinberg, Julius Rudolph. *An Examination of Logical Positivism*. London: International Library of Psychology, Philosophy and Scientific Method. London: K. Paul, Trench, Trubner & Co., 1950, 311 pp.

Weiss, Thomas Michael. *An Experimental Study Applying Non-Aristotelian Principles in the Measurement of Adjustment and Maladjustment*. Ann Arbor: University of Michigan Microfilms, 1954.

Welby, Viola. *What Is Meaning?* London: The Macmillan Co., Ltd., 1903, 321 pp.

Whitehead, Alfred North. *The Aims of Education*. New York: The Macmillan Co., 1929, 247 pp.

————. *Adventures of Ideas*. New York: The Macmillan Co., 1933, 392 pp.

————. *Process and Reality*. New York: The Macmillan Co., 1929, 509 pp.

————. *Science and the Modern World*. New York: Pelican Mentor Books, 1948, 212 pp.

Whorf, Benjamin Lee. *Four Articles on Metalinguistics*. Washington, D. C.: Foreign Service Institute, 1949, 38 pp.

Wiener, Norbert. *Cybernetics*. New York: John Wiley and Sons, 1948, 194 pp.

————. *The Human Use of Human Beings: Cybernetics and Society*. Garden City, N. Y.: Doubleday, 1954, 199 pp.

Wilhelmsen, Frederick D. *Man's Knowledge of Reality: An Introduction to Thomistic Epistemology*. Englewood Cliffs, New Jersey: Prentice-Hall, Inc., 1956, 215 pp.

Wilson, John. *Language and the Pursuit of Truth*. Cambridge: Cambridge University Press, 1956.

Wittgenstein, Ludwig. *Philosophical Investigations*. New York: The Macmillan Co., 1953, 232 pp.

————. *Tractatus Logico-Philosophicus*. New York: Harcourt, Brace and Co., 1922, 189 pp.

Witty, Paul and La Brant, Lou. *Teaching the People's Language*. New York: Hinds, Hayden, and Eldridge, Inc., 1946, 36 pp.

Zollette, Sandro. *Basic Principles of General Semantics*. Philadelphia: Drexel Institute of Technology, 1955, 70 pp.

PERIODICALS AND ARTICLES

Allers, Rudolf. "On Intellectual Operations," *The New Scholasticism*, XXVI (Jan., 1952), pp. 1-6.

Aly, Bower. "The Rhetoric of Semantics," *Quarterly Journal of Speech*, XXX (February, 1944), pp. 23-30.
This article attacks General Semantics.

Anderson, Jeanette. "A Critique of General Semantics. Two Times Two Is the Same for Everybody. But One Never Is—," *Quarterly Journal of Speech*, XXIX (April, 1943), pp. 187-195.
This is a virulent attack on General Semantics.

Baron, Rebekah J. "Some First Steps in Beginning to Train Senior High School Students in the Method of General Semantics," *General Semantics Bulletin*, nos. 12-13 (1953), pp. 67-73.

Barone, Francisco. "Semantico," *Archivio di Filosofia*, no. 3 (1955), pp. 407-418.

Black, Max. "Limitations of a Behavioristic Semeiotic," *Philosophical Review*, LVI (May, 1947), pp. 258-272.

Betts, Emmett Albert. "Reading: Semantic Approach," *Education*, LXIX (May, 1949), pp. 527-555.
This article shows the application of general semantics to elementary reading.

Bloodstein, Oliver. "General Semantics and Modern Art," *Etc.*, I (Aug. 1943), pp. 12-23.

Bochenski, I. M. "On Analogy," *The Thomist*, II (1948), pp. 424-447.

Bures, Charles E. "A Critique of Hayakawa's *Language in Thought and Action*," *Etc.*, IX (Autumn, 1952), pp. 35-43.

Burke, Kenneth. "Linguistic Approach to Problems of Education," *Modern Philosophies and Education*, Fifty-Fourth Yearbook of the National

Society for the Study of Education, Part I (Chicago: University of Chicago Press, 1955), pp. 259-303.

Busse, W. F. "Too Much Korzybski," *Etc.,* XIV (Winter, 1956), p. 155.

Brewer, Joseph. "Education and the Modern World," *Papers from The First American Congress for General Semantics,* ed. Hansell Baugh. New York: Arrow Editions, 1938, pp. 54-58.

Bykhovsky, B. "The Morass of Modern Bourgeois Philosophy," *Etc.,* VI (Autumn, 1948), pp. 1-15. Translated from the Russian by Anatol Rapoport. Taken from *The Bolshevik: A Theoretical Political Journal,* XXIV (Aug. 30, 1947).

Callahan, J. Calvin. "Semantics-Pedantic Antics?" *Quarterly Journal of Speech,* XXXI (February, 1945), pp. 77-79.
This article defends the use of such books as that by Hayakawa.

Camp, N. Harry. "How Language Affects Behavior," *Education,* LXX (April, 1950), pp. 471-491.
This advocates use of general semantics principles in guidance programs.

Campbell, Douglas Gorden. "General Semantics in Education, Counseling and Therapy," *National Education Association Proceedings,* 1939, pp. 518-524.

Carhart, Raymond. "A Speech Teacher Looks at General Semantics," *Quarterly Journal of Speech,* XXVIII (October, 1942), pp. 332-338.
This article defends general semantics.

Carter, Elton S. "On the Nature of General Semantics," *General Semantics Bulletin,* nos. 16-17 (1955), pp. 98-99.
This is taken from a syllabus of a course, "Introduction to General Semantics," given at Penn State University to juniors, seniors and graduate students.

Cassirer, Ernst. "The Influence of Language," *Journal of Philosophy,* XXXIX (June, 1942), pp. 309-327.

Case, Keith E. "General Semantics: A Technique in Reading Social Relationships," *Fourteenth Yearbook of the Claremont Reading Conferences,* 1949, pp. 55-67.

Chase, Stuart. "General Semantics and Social Science," *General Semantics Bulletin,* nos. 12 and 13 (1953), pp. 21-22.

——. "Korzybski and Semantics," *Saturday Review of Literature,* XXXVII (June 19, 1954), pp. 11-12.

——. "Reading Words," *Nineteenth Yearbook of the Claremont College Reading Conference,* 1954, pp. 103-114.

Chisholm, Francis P. "General Semantics in Reading Instruction," *Etc.,* V (Summer, 1948), pp. 268-275.

——. "Some Misconceptions about General Semantics," *College English,* IV (April, 1943), pp. 412-416.

Clarke, Richard A. "General Semantics in Art Education," *School Review,* LVI (December, 1948), pp. 600-605.

Connolly, F. G. "Abstraction and Moderate Realism," *The New Scholasticism,* XXVII (1953), pp. 72-90.

Corbin, Richard. "Semantics in the Secondary School," *Bulletin of the National Association of Secondary School Principals,* XXXIX (September, 1955), pp. 50-55.

————. "Will Semantics Help?" *English Journal,* XLIII (March, 1954), pp. 130-134.

Crane, R. S. "Semantics and the Teaching of Prose Literature," *College English,* IV (October, 1942), pp. 12-19.

Dettering, Richard. "The Learning of Symbolic Behavior and Its Importance to Education," *Etc.,* XIV (Autumn, 1956), pp. 23-27.

————. "What Phonetic Writing Did to Meaning," *Etc.,* XII (Winter, 1955), pp. 121-136.

Dix, John P. "Semantics Applied in Civic Instruction in Junior High School," *Social Studies,* XXX (November, 1939), pp. 303-305.

Dolch, Edward William. "Depth of Meaning," *Education,* LXIX (May, 1949), pp. 562-566.

Eastman, Max. "Showing up Semantics," *The Freeman,* IV (May 31, 1954), pp. 639-641.
This is one of the more recent attacks on general semantics.

Embler, Weller. "Language and Truth," *Etc.,* XIII (Winter, 1956), pp. 93-105.

Fiegl, Herbert. "Aims of Education for Our Age of Science: Reflections of a Logical Empiricist," *Modern Philosophies and Education,* The Fifty-fourth Yearbook of the National Society for the Study of Education, Part I. Chicago: The University of Chicago Press, 1955, pp. 304-341.

Fishman, Joshua A. "A Review of *Language, Meaning and Maturity,*" *Etc.,* XIII (Spring, 1956), pp. 225-232.

Foley, Leo A. "The Persistence of the Aristotelian Physical Method," *The New Scholasticism,* XXVII (1953), pp. 160-175.

Fouch, S. Robert. "The Unsanity of Mathematics and Its Teaching," *Etc.,* XI (Winter, 1954), pp. 113-121.

Frank, Philipp. "Science Teaching and the Humanities," *Etc.,* IV (Autumn, 1946), pp. 1-24.

Geach, Peter Thomas. "Subject and Predicate," *Mind,* LIX (October, 1950), pp. 461-482.

Glicksberg, Charles I. "Educational Implications of Semantics," *School Review,* XLIX (December, 1941), pp. 744-745.

————. "General Semantics and Psychoanalysis: Korzybski and Freud," *Etc.,* I (August, 1943), pp. 33-40.

————. "General Semantics and the Science of Man," *Science Monthly,* LXII (May, 1946), pp. 44-46.

————. "General Semantics in the Classroom," *Etc.,* II (Summer, 1945), pp. 221-227.

————. "Methodology in Semantics," *School Review,* LIII (November, 1945), pp. 545-553.

————. "Semantic Revolution and the Teaching of English," *Harvard Educational Review*, X (March, 1940), pp. 150-163.

————. "What Semantics Means to the College Teacher," *Harvard Educational Review*, XIV (October, 1944), pp. 300-309.

Glatstein, Irwin Lee. "Semantics, Too, Has a Past," *Quarterly Journal of Speech*, XXXII (February, 1946), pp. 48-51.

Green, Rosemary M. "The Role of Semantics in a Secondary Reading Program," *Education*, LXIX (May, 1949), pp. 590-594.

Greenwood, Thomas. "Aristotle on Mathematical Constructibility," *The Thomist*, XVII (1954), pp. 84-94.

————. "The Character of Aristotelian Logic," *The Thomist*, IV (1942), pp. 221-246.

————. "The Unity of Logic," *The Thomist*, VIII (1945), pp. 457-470.

Hackett, Herbert. "Language as Communication: A Frame of Reference," *Etc.*, XI (Summer, 1954), pp. 290-298.

Hallie, P. P. "A Criticism of General Semantics," *College English*, XIV (October, 1952), pp. 17-23.

Hayakawa, Samuel I. "The Aims and Tasks of General Semantics: Implications of the Timebinding Theory," *Etc.*, VIII (Summer, 1951), pp. 243-253.

————. "Danger in Being Rigid-Minded," *Science Digest*, XXVIII (September, 1950), pp. 45-46.

————. "The Fully Functioning Personality," *Etc.*, XIII (Spring, 1956), pp. 169-181.

————. "General Semantics: An Introductory Lecture," *Etc.*, II (Spring, 1945), pp. 160-169.

————. "General Semantics and Propaganda," *Public Opinion Quarterly* (April, 1939), pp. 197-208.

————. "How Right Is the Dictionary?" *Science Digest*, XXVII (March, 1950), pp. 44-47.

————. "Linguistics and the Future: Some Implications of General Semantics," *Etc.*, I (Spring, 1944), pp. 148-153.

————. "Linguistic Science and the Teaching of Composition," *Etc.*, VII (Winter, 1950), pp. 97-103.

————. "Meaning of Semantics," *The New Republic*, XCIX (August 2, 1939), pp. 354-357.

————. "New Techniques of Agreement," *Etc.*, VIII (Autumn, 1950), pp. 3-12.

————. "Non-Aristotelian Revision of Morality," *Etc.*, III (Spring, 1946), pp. 161-173.

————. "Poetry and Advertising," *Poetry*, LXVII (January, 1940), pp. 204-212.

————. "Poetry and Science," *Etc.*, I (Summer, 1944), pp. 216-224.

————. "Recognizing Stereotypes as Substitutes for Thought," *English Journal*, XXXVIII (March, 1949), pp. 155-156.

——. "Reply to Charles Bures' criticism of Hayakawa's *Language in Thought and Action," Etc.,* IX (Autumn, 1952), pp. 43-50.

——. "Semantics, General Semantics: An Attempt at Definition," *Etc.,* II (Winter, 1944), pp. 116-120.

——. "Semantics," *Etc.,* IX (Autumn, 1952), pp. 1-12.

——. "Semantics, General Semantics," *Etc.,* IV (Spring, 1947), pp. 161-170. Reprint from *Ten Eventful Years,* pub. *Encyclopedia Britannica.*

——. "The Task of the Listener," *Etc.,* VII (Autumn, 1949), pp. 9-17.

——. "What Is Meant by Aristotelian Structure of Language?" *Etc.,* V (Summer, 1948), pp. 225-230.

Hayakawa, S. I and Rapoport, Anatol. "Terms in General Semantics: A Glossary," *Etc.* (Summer, 1946), pp. 279-283.

Hess, M. Whitcomb. "The Poet and the Semanticist," *Catholic World,* CLXXIII (September, 1951), pp. 441-445.

——. "The Semantic Question," *The New Scholasticism,* XXIII (1949), pp. 186-206.

Humphrey, George. "There Is No Problem of Meaning," *British Journal of Psychology,* XLII (1951), pp. 238-245.

Jacobson, Howard Boone. "Extensional Methods in Training for Journalism," *General Semantics Bulletin,* nos. 16-17 (1955), pp. 40-47.

Johnson, Wendell. "General Semantics and the Science Teacher," *Etc.,* IV (Summer, 1947), pp. 275-284.

——. "The Society for General Semantics" (editorial), *Etc.,* III (Winter, 1946), pp. 140-143.

——. "The Spoken Word and the Great Unsaid," *Etc.,* XI (Autumn, 1953), pp. 28-40.

Jones, Howard L. "Elementary Semantics and the Social Studies," *Social Studies,* XLII (May, 1951), pp. 213-216.
This advocates the study of semantics as defined by S. I. Hayakawa.

Kane, William H. "Abstraction and the Distinction of the Sciences," *The Thomist,* XVII (January, 1954), pp. 143-168.

Kantor, J. R. "The Role of Language in Logic and Science," *The Journal of Philosophy,* XXXV, 17 (1938), pp. 449-463.

Kecskemeti, Paul. "A Review of General Semantics," *New Leader,* XXXVIII (April 25, 1955), pp. 24-26.

Keyser, Cassius. "Mathematics and the Science of Semantics," *Scripta Mathematica,* II (1934), pp. 247-260.

Kisker, George W. "Linguistic and Semantic Factors in the Psychodynamics of War," *Journal of Social Psychology,* XVII (February, 1943), pp. 69-75.

Knipp, Helen Bachman. "The Development of Thinking and of Concepts," *Elementary English,* XXVIII (May, 1951), pp. 290-297.

Korzybski, Alfred. "The Brotherhood of Doctrines," *Etc.,* I (Autumn, 1943), pp. 51-57.

——. "An Extensional Analysis of the Process of Abstracting from an Electro-Colloidal, Non-Aristotelian Point of View," *General Semantics Bulletin,* nos. 3-4 (1950-51), pp. 9-12.

——. "Extensionalization in Mathematics. Mathematical Physics and General Education." Paper presented before the Mathematics Section of the American Association for the Advancement of Science, St. Louis, Mo., Jan. 2, 1936. *General Semantics,* New York: Arrow Editions, 1938.

——. "Fate and Freedom," *The Mathematics Teacher* (May, 1923). Also in Lee, *The Language of Wisdom and Folly,* pp. 29-293.

——. "Foreword" to *A Theory of Meaning Analyzed* by Thomas C. Pollock. Chicago: Institute of General Semantics, 1942.

——. "General Semantics: Toward a New General System of Evaluation and Predictability in Solving Human Problems," *American Peoples Encyclopedia.* Chicago: Spencer Press, 1949, vol. IX, 357-362.

——. "An Outline of General Semantics," Papers from the First American Congress on General Semantics, edited by Hansell Baugh. New York: Arrow Editions, 1938.

——. "The Role of Language in the Perceptual Processes," in *Perception: An Approach to Personality.* Edited by Robert R. Blake and Glen V. Ramsey. New York: The Ronald Press Co., 1951, pp. 170-205.

——. "Time-Binding and Human Potentialities," transcribed from a sound mirror recording of the lecture given at Hunter College, New York, for the New York Society for General Semantics. Edited and arranged by Ralph Hamilton. *General Semantics Bulletin,* no. 3 (Spring, 1950), pp. 43-49.

——. "Why Non-Aristotelian," A letter to the Editor, *Etc.,* IV (Spring, 1947), pp. 224-225.

Kossel, Clifford G. "Principles of St. Thomas' Distinction Between the *Esse* and *Ratio of Relation,*" Part I: Science, Semantics and Order, *The Modern Schoolman,* XXIV (1946-47), pp. 19-23.

LaBrant, Lou. "Words for Peace," *Education,* LXVIII (May, 1948), pp. 546-549.

Lachance, Louis. "The Philosophy of Language," *The Thomist,* IV (1942), pp. 547-588.

de Laguna, Grace. "Language and Reality," *Mind,* C (April, 1941), pp. 165-176.

Lee, Dorothy. "Lineal and Non-Lineal Codifications of Reality," *Etc.,* VIII (Autumn, 1950), pp. 13-26.

Lee, Irving J. "Evaluation: With and Without Words," *Etc.,* III (Spring, 1946), pp. 193-203.

——. "General Semantics," *Quarterly Journal of Speech,* XXXVIII (February, 1952), pp. 1-12.

——. "General Semantics, 1952," *Etc.,* IX (Winter, 1952), pp. 103-118.

——. "General Semantics and Public Speaking," *Quarterly Journal of Speech,* XXVI (December, 1940), pp. 594-601.

Lins, Mario. *"The Supports of the New General Semantics,"* Proceedings of the Eleventh International Congress of Philosophy, Brussels, August 20 to 26, 1953, pp. 115-120.

Lintz, Edward J. "The Unity in the Universe According to Alfred North Whitehead," *The Thomist,* VI (July and October, 1943), pp. 230-253.

Leary, William G. "Studies in Language and Culture in the Training of Foreign Service Personnel: The School of Languages and Linguistics of the United States Department of State," *Etc.,* IX (Spring, 1952), pp. 192-202.

Loomis, William F. "On Korzybski and the Teaching of Science (embryology)," *General Semantics Bulletin,* nos. 4-5 (1950-51), pp. 59-60.

Malinowski, Bronislaw. "The Problem of Meaning in Primitive Language," Supplement I in C. K. Ogden and I. A. Richards, *The Meaning of Meaning.* 2nd edition, revised. New York: Harcourt, Brace and Co., 1927, pp. 296-336.

Maloney, Martin. "How to Avoid an Idea," *Etc.,* XIII (Spring, 1956), pp. 214-224.

Martin, James S. "Why Am I Always the Bridesmaid?" *Etc.,* XIV (Autumn, 1956), pp. 47-50.

Maslow, Abraham H. "Toward A Humanistic Psychology," *Etc.,* XIV (Autumn, 1956), pp. 10-22.

Meiers, Ann Dix. "Avoiding the Dangers of Semantic Adolescence," *Etc.,* IX (Summer, 1952), pp. 273-277.

"Institute of General Semantics," *Mental Hygiene,* XIV (April, 1940), pp. 329-332.

Meyers, Russell. "The Nervous System and General Semantics: I. The Aim of General Semantics and the Method of Science," *Etc.,* V (Summer, 1948), pp. 231-243.

———. "The Nervous System and General Semantics: IV. The Fiction of the Thalamus as the Neural Center of the Emotions, *Etc.,* VII (Winter, 1950), pp. 104-127.

———. "Perceptual Response and the Neurology of Abstraction," *Etc.,* VI (Spring, 1949), pp. 169-196.

Michie, Sarah. "A New General Language Curriculum for the Eighth Grade," *Modern Language Journal,* XXII (February, 1938), pp. 342-347.

Murray, Elwood and Perdue, James. "General Semantics in an Interdisciplinary Educational Program: Plan for a Laboratory in the Integration of Knowledge," *Etc.,* XIV (Autumn, 1956), pp. 38-46.

Murray, Elwood. "Semantics of Rhetoric," *Quarterly Journal of Speech,* XXX (February, 1944), pp. 31-41.

———. "Silent Factors in the Classroom," *Education,* LXX (October, 1956), pp. 80-84.

McCarthy, Ephrem. "The Logical Empiricism of Alfred J. Ayer," *Philosophical Studies,* Maynooth, Ireland, II (1952), pp. 18-52; III (1953), pp. 40-66.

192   *Bibliography*

McCue, George S. "Salvation Through Semantics, or Sacred Cow₁ Is Not Sacred Cow₂," *Elizabethan Studies and Other Essays in Honor of George F. Reynolds* (University of Colorado Studies, Series B. Studies in the Humanities, II, No. 4. Boulder, Colo.: University of Colorado, 1945), pp. 38-44.

MacWilliam, J. A. "The Bond Between the Physics and Metaphysics of St. Thomas," *The Modern Schoolman*, XXII (1944-45), pp. 16-23.

McNicholl, A. J. "The Uneasiness of Science," The New Scholasticism, XXIV (January, 1950), pp. 57-68.

Nock, S. A. "Sound and Symbol," *Philosophical Science*, VIII (July, 1941), pp. 352-370.

North, Richard. "Semantics; the Science of Mutual Understanding," *Hibbert Journal*, XLV (April, 1947), pp. 227-233.

Northrop, F. S. C. "Mathematical Physics and Korzybski's Semantics," the Alfred Korzybski Memorial Lecture, *General Semantics Bulletin*, nos. 16-17 (1955), pp. 7-14.

Oesterle, John A. "The Problem of Meaning," *The Thomist*, VI (July, 1943), pp. 180-229.

———. "Another Approach to the Problem of Meaning," *The Thomist*, VII (April, 1944), pp. 233-263.

Osburn, W. J., Huntington, Muriel, Meeks, Viola. "The Language of Relativity as Related to Reading Readiness," *Journal of Educational Research*, XXXIX (April, 1946), pp. 583-601.

Osburn, J. Worth. "A Symposium on General Semantics in Industry at the 1953 Convention of the American Psychological Association," *General Semantics Bulletin*, nos. 12-13, 1953, pp. 69-71.

Osgood, C. E. "The Nature and the Measurement of Meaning, "*Psychological Bulletin*, XLIX (May, 1952), pp. 197-237.

Owens, J. "Our Knowledge of Nature," *Proceedings of the American Catholic Philosophical Association*, 1955, pp. 63-86.

Pap, A. "Semantic Analysis and Psycho-physical Dualism," *Mind*, LXI (April, 1952), pp. 209-221.

Paul, Sherman. "Whitehead, Langer and the Uniting of Fact and Value," *Etc.*, VI (Winter, 1949), pp. 103-107.

Philippe, M. D. "Abstraction, Addition, Separation dans la Philosophie d'Aristote," *Revue Thomiste*, XXXII (1948), pp. 461-479.

Rapoport, Anatol. "Aims and Tasks of Mathematical Biology," *Etc.*, VIII (Summer, 1951), pp. 254-269.

———. "Alfred Korzybski, 1879-1950," *Etc.*, VII (Spring, 1950), pp. 163-165.

———. "The Criterion of Predictability," *Etc.*, II (Spring, 1945), pp. 129-151.

———. "Dialectical Materialism and General Semantics," *Etc.*, VI (Winter, 1948), pp. 81-104.

———. "General Semantics and the Behavioral Sciences," *Etc.*, XIII (Autumn, 1955), pp. 46-50.

———. "How Relative Are Values?" *Etc.*, VIII (Spring, 1951), pp. 180-192.

————. "The Role of Symbols in Human Behavior," *Etc.,* XII (Spring, 1955), pp. 180-188.

————. "Semantic Aspects of Language and Mathematics," *Etc.,* III (Winter, 1946), pp. 106-115.

————: "Semantics: The Problem of Meaning," *American Philosophy.* Edited by Ralph Winn. New York: Philosophical Library, 1955, pp. 64-83.

————."Technological Models of the Nervous System," *Etc.,* XI (Summer, 1954), pp. 272-283.

————. "What Is Semantics?" *Etc.,* X (Autumn, 1952), pp. 12-24.

Read, Allen Walker. "An Account of the Word 'Semantics,'" *Word,* IV (August, 1948), pp. 78-97.

Reiser, Oliver. "Non-Aristotelian Systems and General Semantics," *General Semantics: Papers from the First American Congress for General Semantics.* Collected and Arranged by Hansell Baugh. New York: Arrow Editions, 1938, pp. 36-40.

Reinfeld, George. "Semantics and the English Teacher," *Clearing House,* XXVII (March, 1954), pp. 428-429.

Royall, Norman N., Jr. "Logical Positivism Revisited," *Etc.,* IX (Winter, 1952), pp. 139-147.

Sandmann, Manfred. "On Linguistic Explanation," *Modern Language Review,* XXXVI (April, 1941), pp. 195-212.

Schlauch, Margaret. "Mechanism and Historical Materialism in Semantic Studies," *Science and Society,* XI, 2 (1947), pp. 44-67.

————. "Semantics as Social Evasion," *Science and Society,* VI, 4 (1942), pp. 315-330.

Seegers, J. Conrad. "Semantic Basis for Reading," *Education,* LXVII (March, 1947), pp. 412-415.

Semmelmeyer, Madeleine. "The Application of General Semantics to a Program of Reading Readiness." *Supplementary Educational Monographs,* no. 51, University of Chicago Press, October, 1940.

————. "The Use of Extensional Methods in Dealing with Higher Order Abstractions in Reading," *Elementary School Journal,* L, 1 (1949), pp. 28-36.

Shoben, Joseph. "Sociology and General Semantics," *Sociology and Social Research,* XXXI (September, 1946), pp. 37-42.

Smith, Ed. C. Review of *The English Language Arts* prepared by The Commission on the English Curriculum of the National Council of Teachers of English, *Etc.,* XIV (Spring, 1957), pp. 227-232.

Smith, Nila Banton. "How Will the Semantic Emphasis Affect Reading Instruction?" *Education,* LXIX (May, 1949), pp. 556-561.

————. "Reading Readiness: Semantic Implications," *Elementary English,* XXVI (December, 1949), pp. 451-460.

Spriesterbach, C. "The Role of General Semantics in Counseling," *Education,* LXX (April, 1950), pp. 515-518.

Story, M. L. "Semantics and Democratic School Administration," *Educational Administration and Supervision,* XXXVIII (March, 1952), 155-159.

Society for General Semantics. Charter and By-Laws, adopted April, 1942, *Etc.,* IV (Spring, 1947), pp. 236-237.

"A Soviet Account of Semantics," Translated by Fenton Jameson in *Language, Meaning and Maturity,* Harper and Bros., 1954, pp. 347-349.

Strang, Ruth. "Many-Sided Aspects of Mental Health," *Mental Health in Modern Education,* Fifty-Fourth Yearbook of the National Society for the Study of Education, Part II. (Chicago: University of Chicago Press, 1955), pp. 46-49.

Thomas, Cleveland A. "Exploring Language in Senior English," *English Journal,* XLII (May, 1953), pp. 250-255.

Thompson, Loring M. "Meaning in Space," *Etc.,* VIII (Spring, 1951), pp. 193-201.

Thorndike, Edward L. "Psychology of Semantics," *American Journal of Psychology,* LIX (October, 1946), pp. 613-632.

———. "Science and Values," *Etc.,* I (Autumn, 1943), pp. 1-11.

"Always Either -or," *Time,* LIV (August 1, 1949), p. 51.

Todd, Edmund. Letter to the Editor, *Etc.,* XI (Spring, 1952), pp. 234-235.

Ushenko, A. P. "The Problem of Semantics," *Journal of Philosophy,* XXXVIII (December, 1941), p. 676.

Veatch, Henry. "Aristotelian and Mathematical Logic," *The Thomist,* XIII (1950), pp. 50-96.

———. "In Defense of the Syllogism," *The Modern Schoolman,* XXVII (March, 1950), pp. 184-202.

Vogt, William. "On Structure and Survival," The Alfred Korzybski Memorial Lecture, *General Semantics Bulletin,* nos. 10-11 (Autumn-Winter, 1952-53), pp. 7-16.

Wein, Hermann. "Towards Philosophical Anthropology?" *Etc.,* XI (Autumn, 1953), pp. 21-27.

Welby, Lady Viola. "Significs," *Encyclopedia Britannica.* 11th ed., Vol. XXV, p. 78.

Weiss, Thomas M. "Experimental Study Applying Non-Aristotelian Principles in Measurement of Adjustment and Non-Adjustment," *Science Education,* XL (October, 1956), pp. 312-316.

White, Leslie A. "The Symbol: The Origin and Basis of Human Behavior," *Philosophy of Science,* VII (October, 1940), pp. 451-463. Also in *Etc.,* I (Summer, 1943), pp. 229-237.

Whorf, Benjamin Lee. "The Relation of Habitual Thought and Behavior to Language," *Etc.,* I (Summer, 1943), pp. 197-215.

Whyte, Launcelot. "The New Mathematical Philosophy," *General Semantics Bulletin,* nos. 4-5 (1950-1951), pp. 44-47.

Winthrop, Henry. "The Problem of Multiple Psychological Language," *Psychological Review,* XLIX (May, 1942), pp. 251-271.

Yorke, Gertrude Cushing. "Preventive Group Counseling: A New Technique," *Education,* LXX (April, 1950), pp. 523-534.

Unpublished Materials

Harcourt, Brace and Co. Letter giving names and locations of colleges and universities using Hayakawa's and Wm. Leary's books, July 1, 1957.
Harper and Bros. Letter giving names and locations of colleges and universities using Lee's and Johnson's books, May 13, 1957.
Jewett, Arno. Talk given on July 5, 1957, at Duke University and on July 10, 1957, at Indiana University on current practices in language arts courses in state and local school systems.

A NOTE ABOUT THE AUTHOR

Margaret Mary Teresa Gorman, R.S.C.J., was born in Kingston, New York, in 1919, and was educated at Trinity College, Washington, D.C. (A.B. 1939, *magna cum laude*), Fordham University (M.A. 1952), and The Catholic University of America (Ph.D. 1958). She is now Chairman of the Department of Psychology, Newton College of the Sacred Heart, Newton, Mass. Research for her book, originally published by The Catholic University of America as *The Educational Implications of the Theory of Meaning and Symbolism of General Semantics*, was carried on at the Library of Congress, where she consulted "every available book on general semantics."